FOR HER GOOD ESTATE

THE NEW MIDDLE AGES

BONNIE WHEELER

Series Editor

The New Middle Ages presents transdisciplinary studies of medieval cultures. It includes both scholarly monographs and essay collections.

PUBLISHED BY ST. MARTIN'S PRESS:

Women in the Medieval Islamic World: Power, Patronage, and Piety
edited by Gavin R. G. Hambly

The Ethics of Nature in the Middle Ages: On Boccaccio's Poetaphysics
by Gregory B. Stone

Presence and Presentation: Women in the Chinese Literati Tradition
by Sherry J. Mou

The Lost Love Letters of Heloise and Abelard: Perceptions of Dialogue in Twelfth Century France
by Constant J. Mews

Understanding Scholastic Thought with Foucault
by Philipp W. Rosemann

For Her Good Estate: The Life of Elizabeth de Burgh
by Frances A. Underhill

Constructions of Widowhood and Virginity in the Middle Ages
edited by Cindy L. Carlson and Angela Jane Weisl

FOR HER GOOD ESTATE
THE LIFE OF ELIZABETH DE BURGH

Frances A. Underhill

St. Martin's Press
New York

#41090646

Library of Congress Cataloging-in-Publication Data
Underhill, Frances A. (Frances Ann), 1929-
  For her good estate : the life of Elizabeth de Burgh / by Frances
A. Underhill.
    p. cm.—(New Middle Ages)
  Includes bibliographical references and index.
  ISBN 0-312-21355-7
  1. De Burgh, Elizabeth, 1295–1360. 2. Great Britain—
History—14th century Biography. 3. Clare College (University of
Cambridge)—History. 4. Women—England—History—Middle Ages,
500–1500. 5. Women benefactors—Great Britain Biography.
6. Nobility—Great Britain Biography. I. Title. II. Series.
DA237.D4U53   1999
941.03'7092—dc21
[B]   99–23067
                                            CIP

Design by Letra Libre, Inc.

First edition: December 1999
10 9 8 7 6 5 4 3 2 1

For my husband, Richard

CONTENTS

SERIES EDITOR'S FOREWORD

The New Middle Ages contributes to medieval cultural studies through its scholarly monographs and essay collections. This series speaks in a contemporary idiom about specific but diverse practices, expressions, and ideologies in the Middle Ages; it aims especially to recuperate the histories of medieval women. *For Her Good Estate: The Life of Elizabeth de Burgh* by Frances A. Underhill, is the twelfth book in the series and the first biography of one of the most prominent Englishwomen of the fourteenth century. Elizabeth de Burgh's life, Underhill argues, is a model of "good lordship" as well as what we now might call deft "networking." This biography traces for us the avenues one woman of power negotiated during the course of a significant life. Underhill forcefully reminds us that deep female friendships were not invented in the modern era: Elizabeth is seen here not only embedded in her family and in the reverberations of personal and national politics, but also as a beloved friend in easy harmony with women and men from various walks of life. Among the other accomplishments of her long widowhood, Elizabeth de Burgh founded Clare College, Cambridge, and her ideas about education deepened with age. Elizabeth invested this foundation with lasting and influential institutional vitality as she moved "from her earlier utilitarian ends to a broader and more humane vision of education."

Bonnie Wheeler
Southern Methodist University

ACKNOWLEDGMENTS

Years ago at a Southeastern Medieval Association conference when I presented my first paper on Elizabeth de Burgh, the session chair, Judith Rice Rothschild, encouraged me to continue and expand the research. Her kind interest was followed by others, to whom I give my unreserved thanks.

The National Endowment for the Humanities and the Faculty Research Committee at the University of Richmond provided funding at critical junctures. I appreciate the wonderful resources of the London Public Record Office, but I am also grateful for the Inter-Library-Loan program, which allowed access to library treasures beyond my campus. The History Department arranged teaching schedules that opened time for research, and Boatwright Library and its staff provided a quiet carrel, reference help, and gracious support.

I have been heartened by the genuine interest of my students; I owe my book title to Katherine Clark who used it for her senior thesis on another medieval woman. My colleagues Kathleen Hewett-Smith and Barbara Sella read and made helpful comments on early drafts; W. Hamilton Bryson and James Gwin shared ideas that furthered my work. I was fortunate that my series editor, Bonnie Wheeler, found some merit in my original sprawling submission, and encouraged me throughout. I appreciate the knowledgeable and focused guidance of John Carmi Parsons for propelling the manuscript to book form. Many thanks to Rick Delaney, Brooke Goode, and Jen Simington of St. Martin's Press for their patience and kindly assistance.

My four children and their spouses—Alexandra and Will, Stefan and Mary Pat, Tim and Kristen, David and Joy—have been unfailingly supportive, besides offering cheerful hospitality as I used university libraries near their homes. Above all, I acknowledge and cherish my husband, Richard, for his constant encouragement and abiding faith.

CHAPTER 1

ELIZABETH'S LIFE: AN OVERVIEW

The individuals we remember from fourteenth-century England are kings, war leaders, a few churchmen, the more notorious royal favorites, and mystics. Few women crowd to the forefront of our recollections: perhaps Queen Isabella, the "she-wolf of France," for her public humiliation by Edward II and her adultery with Roger Mortimer, or Queen Philippa, for her cheerful disposition and persistent fecundity. More fourteenth-century women should be remembered, however, among them especially Elizabeth de Burgh, lady of Clare. Today Elizabeth's castles stand ruined, the foundations she endowed for friars and for perpetual prayers swept away by sixteenth-century changes in English ecclesiastical policy. She has, however, a living memorial at Cambridge University; there she founded Clare College, and more than six centuries after her foundation, students remember her in annual ceremonies.

Elizabeth de Burgh carried out a noblewoman's traditional domestic roles, and moved as well into more commanding roles in a last, long widowhood. In all her initiatives, she skillfully utilized the advantages of royal kinship, wealth, and connections, all needed in an environment uncongenial to female power and influence. Medieval women rarely functioned independently unless unfettered by ties to a male, for while noblewomen often served as pawns in the shifting alliances of the early fourteenth century, they were largely peripheral to the politics and warfare that dominated the period.[1] Law and custom coalesced to preserve total male dominance of the central features of English institutional life. Historians discussing the fourteenth century typically concentrate on the growth of parliament and England's wars with France and Scotland, genuinely masculine enterprises. Neither estates nor lineage qualified women for parliamentary summons, so they were excluded from the development of that important institution. Women paid war taxes on their properties, but were

spared the hazards of war as well as its profits. They were desirable specta-
tors in the chivalric spectacles that glorified military skills, but they played
passive roles, offering up approving choruses that required little talent or
ability. England produced no Joan of Arc, rallying her compatriots to deeds
of martial valor.

It was rather as wives, mothers, sisters, grandmothers, and guardians
that women of the magnate class functioned. Families planning marriages
for their sons naturally looked to women whose natal ties promised important political and social links and who would bring wealth to their
marriages; families loved daughters but had no qualms about consigning
them to marriages that promoted family interests, not personal preferences. As most noblewomen had some disposable income, merchants valued their custom and clerics appreciated them as potential benefactors. As
wives, they conventionally managed households, entertained visitors, provided comfortable retreats for their spouses, and assumed broader duties
in their husbands' absences. Prized for their biological role in childbear-
ing and for their nurture and care of the young, mothers usually directed
the early education of sons and daughters, relinquishing the boys, around
the age of seven, to male tutors, but continuing to school daughters for
later duties as wives and mothers.[2]

When a woman married, her husband assumed control of her property.
The king controlled the subsequent marriages of his tenant-in-chiefs' widows; even the homage due the king by a female tenant-in-chief was performed by her spouse. Men thus considered heiresses valuable marriage
partners, but even great heiresses were required to operate by indirection
when married, relying on husbands' affection and appreciation of their
judgment and contributions rather than power based on economic independence: if women brought wealth from one family to another, they had
no role in its administration. While women could receive testamentary bequests of personal property, male beneficiaries were preferred. Rules of
primogeniture favored the inheritance of intact family estates by the eldest
son; in the absence of male children, surviving sisters divided the inheritance into basically equal shares. But contemporary opinion deplored the
latter possibility, opening the way for more frequent use of entails to ex-
clude female inheritance.

If marriage was the normal state for adult noblewomen, a few did gain
legal and economic freedom through strategies that kept them unmarried
yet firmly in secular society. Free of male tutelage, women could control
vast economic assets, manage estates, employ staff, and build networks of
clients. They could not offer their retinues the joys or spoils of war but
could provide good lordship, enhancing personal power through fostering
promising contacts and attending to the needs of local gentry and lesser

nobility. Without husbands but with independent wealth, women could transcend restrictions imposed on their sex by law and custom and could contribute successfully to cultural, social, and charitable objectives. Elizabeth de Burgh was one such exceptional female, though before attaining independence as a widow she experienced a typical round of marriages. In early life, she was thus controlled by her brother, her uncle King Edward II, and her husbands, and so was peripheral to major events. After a vow of chastity in widowhood protected her from further marital adventures, she emerged as a shrewd administrator, a focus for family relationships, and a patroness courted by ecclesiastical fund-raisers.

Little is known of Elizabeth until she was nearly 30, however, because until then family or spousal associations subordinated her to men. She was born Elizabeth de Clare and customarily used her first husband's surname, but was called occasionally by her third spouse's surname. For the last 38 years of her life, she functioned in widowhood as an independent woman of the magnate class, albeit limited by her gender from opportunities open to men of that rank. K. B. McFarlane defined those opportunities: the Church, the law, service, trade, war, and possibly marriage, with royal service and the military highest in importance.[3] But these avenues for establishing position and enhancing wealth were entirely limited to men; others were likewise closed to noblewomen, or offered them the barest of opportunities. Yet Elizabeth de Burgh and some of her female friends flourished despite gender barriers. She chose alternative methods to advance herself: friendships, patronage of ecclesiastical and semi-clerical charities and foundations, exploitation of kinship ties and the practice of good lordship. Men could utilize such tactics too, but Elizabeth apparently did so more fully than male contemporaries, perhaps because she lacked alternatives. She inspired loyalty among her staff, many of whom served her for long periods, and she had a gift for cultivating friendships among the nobility; Duke Henry of Lancaster visited her often, and the Black Prince was a frequent visitor in her old age. Her dearest woman friend, Countess Mary de St Pol of Pembroke, shared Elizabeth's interests for some 40 years, and nearly as enduring were her associations with Queen Isabella and Joan of Bar, countess of Surrey.

As Elizabeth supported educational projects, it is not surprising to find leading intellectuals of the day among her visitors. Clerics visited often, perhaps to enjoy hospitality and good conversation, perhaps hopeful as well of personal gifts or professional advancement. As the king's cousin she had access to royal favors for herself, family, neighbors, and clients. She could not attend parliament, but sent her staff to lobby or present her petitions at its meetings, and used the law courts to amend her grievances. When the canons of Walsingham opposed her plans for a friary near their shrine, the lady never deferred to this masculine ecclesiastical opposition. Elizabeth cherished her personal independence, yet docilely accepted societal norms of early marriages for her daughters and granddaughters. She was no feminist as we understand the term today, but never doubted that women could count in her male-dominated world.

Studies of medieval men rarely note much interaction with women, either because the men were celibate clerics or because lay masculine routines centered on warfare or politics. A nobleman's wife might bring him estates and bear his sons, and privately she might advise him astutely, but her public roles rarely touched the heart of his activities. Even if women did attain the independence Elizabeth enjoyed, the medieval milieu was dominated by men. Untroubled by anti-male bias, Elizabeth evolved enduring friendships and economic associations with men, her foundations catered to a masculine clientele, and males dominated in her council and household. Men were thus important to Elizabeth, and some she loved; as custom demanded, she remembered and honored the husbands imposed on her. But women mattered to her in ways perhaps unfamiliar to her male contemporaries, or at least to their chroniclers. Her closest friends were women, especially several widows who shared her position in society. She sponsored female spiritual development and elected burial in a convent where she had shared the sisters' devotions. Elizabeth cherished her granddaughters; perhaps her male friends cherished theirs too, but no one mentioned that affection. Studying her life allows us to see her contemporaries, both male and female, but the emphasis will be on female relationships, in part to redress the imbalance, in part because daughters, granddaughters, sisters, and female friends are relevant to her story. These issues and people dear to Elizabeth's heart are the topics for the later chapters.

Birth to Early Widowhood

Historians studying the life of any individual are both led and limited by the surviving source materials. These are more abundant for Elizabeth than for any contemporary female, indeed most males. Because of her distinguished ancestry and her control of vast lands and rights, she appears frequently in the public documents of her time. A superb but incomplete series of her household accounts illustrates costs and spending while witnessing Elizabeth's alms-giving and legal initiatives, travel, and friendships. None of her letters survive, but her voice may be heard in her secret 1326 protest against royal injustices, in her testament, and in her foundation statutes for Clare College at Cambridge.

Members of the medieval elite knew the dates and places of their births, but found it less needful to record such facts than do modern people. Thus while Elizabeth de Clare was born a granddaughter of the reigning king of England, historians differ over the date and place of her birth. The date was almost certainly September 16, 1295, the place likely at or near Tewkesbury, a Clare stronghold on the English-Welsh border where Elizabeth's parents may then have been living because her grandfather, Edward I, had recently deprived her father of his Welsh lands.[4]

Elizabeth's parentage was illustrious on both sides. Her father, Earl Gilbert de Clare of Gloucester, belonged to a family who had come to England with William the Conqueror and had increased its lands and importance over the centuries. Gilbert came into his lands in England, Wales, and Ireland in 1263–64 and was "the single most powerful magnate in the realm" until his death in 1295. He was a colorful man, not only because of his bright red hair but because of his personal animosities and prompt martial responses to territorial infringements. Some English families with lands in the Welsh March, the area along the English-Welsh border, had slowly penetrated parts of Wales on their own initiative without significant royal backing, so their descendants claimed a freedom of action lacking in their English holdings. The "Red Earl" exploited his position as a Marcher lord to increase his holdings there, to quarrel with other Marcher families and to test the limits of Marcher independence from royal intervention. Gilbert defied the Crown on several occasions to defend Marcher privileges, but lessened his impact by wielding his great power without a well-developed focus.[5]

Elizabeth's mother was Joan "of Acre," born to King Edward I and Queen Eleanor of Castile while they were crusading in the Holy Land in 1272. On the leisurely journey back to England, the royal party stopped in Picardy to visit Queen Eleanor's mother, the widowed Queen Joan of Castile, countess of Ponthieu in her own right. When Edward and Eleanor went on to England, they left Joan with her grandmother for four years, so she was nearly seven when she first came to England. Edward was already planning to win continental allies through Joan's marriage. He had arranged for her to marry Hartman of Habsburg, king of the Romans, in 1279, but duties and problems delayed Hartman's journey to England for the ceremony. On his way to marry her at last, he was drowned in the Rhine.[6] Earl Gilbert's first marriage, to King Henry III's niece Alice de Lusignan, ended in annulment in 1285 after producing two daughters but not the spousal accord that sometimes resulted from marital association. He and Joan wed in April 1290 after seven years' negotiations. The final agreement between king and earl called for Gilbert to surrender all his estates to Edward, who granted them back to Gilbert and Joan to be held jointly. The lands would remain with the surviving spouse for life, and then pass to the heirs of their bodies; if they left no children, the estates would revert to the Crown. As the agreement deprived the daughters of Gilbert's first marriage of any hope of inheriting his lands, and as Gilbert, himself, essentially lost control of the devolution of his inheritance, his acceptance of the agreement is hard to fathom. Perhaps he was gambling on a lack of male issue to inherit Edward I's throne, thus opening the royal succession to Joan's children; perhaps Edward I hoped the marriage would tame this powerful earl. But the marriage was a royal victory, not a comital one.[7]

Joan and Gilbert both possessed a strong sense of independence. The earl continued his periodic defiance of the king after marriage; Joan has been described as "the most spirited and independent of all Edward I's children." The newlyweds manifested their lack of submissiveness to king and queen by leaving court to honeymoon at Tonbridge Castle. Her parents promptly confiscated her bridal finery as punishment, but the couple returned only at their pleasure. The quarrel ended and, at the family level, relations between the royal couple and the earl and countess appear to have been amicable. Still, the king did not hesitate to imprison Gilbert briefly in 1291–92, nor to seize his lands in 1295. The Clares settled in a fine establishment at Clerkenwell, but visited the earl's other manors and castles as well, traveling with over 200 attendants. Their first child, Gilbert, was born in May 1291 at Winchecombe near Tewkesbury, Eleanor in 1292 at the Clare fortress of Caerphilly in Glamorgan, Margaret probably in 1293, and Elizabeth in September 1295. The earl died at Monmouth in December 1295. His children cannot have known him well, but unfamiliarity with fathers was not unusual for noble offspring.[8]

The Red Earl died in his early 50s; his widow, Joan, was 23. Joan's worth had escalated, as the jointure arrangement at her marriage provided that the survivor of the Clare couple would hold Gilbert's vast estates; these were surrendered to her in January 1296 after she had performed the requisite homage. Edward I lost no time in trying again to forge continental ties through her marriage, even announcing her engagement to the count of Savoy. But Joan had moved more quickly and had already married a knight of her own choice, Ralph de Monthermer, who had served Earl Gilbert as a squire and remained in Joan's entourage after the earl died. She arranged for the king to knight Ralph before she secretly married him, probably in January 1297.[9] When Edward learned of the marriage, he confiscated Joan's lands and imprisoned Ralph in Bristol Castle. The king possessed the power to punish Joan and her new husband but could not abrogate the marriage, as the Church recognized that a valid marriage existed when both parties gave their free consent. To soften her father's stance, Joan sent her daughters to him before she pleaded her cause in person, with some success. She received back most of the confiscated lands, and Ralph was freed and granted the title earl of Gloucester and Hertford during his wife's lifetime.[10] Joan had evaded her father's rights as overlord to have a say in her marriage; legally she should have obtained his license for her second marriage, but obviously that license would have been denied. Dynastically, her union wasted the matrimonial potential of a king's daughter and brought nothing to her family or the Crown. Females exercised little political power in their own persons, but could serve as conduits for the transfer of wealth and power to males, and Monthermer's good fortune rested on his marriage to Joan.

Joan's son, Gilbert, was taken to court to be supervised by the king's second wife, Queen Margaret.[11] The move was perhaps punitive, but reflected normal practice: boys often left their families around age seven for education in other noble households. The royal household surely offered premier opportunities for social and political training for a young boy who would succeed to his father's earldoms. A surviving, undated account roll from Edward I's time shows Gilbert was attended by five squires, five valets, and 16 lesser servants, and was supplied with six greyhounds, ten running dogs and 13 horses.[12] In contrast, the records reveal little of his sisters, Eleanor, Margaret, and Elizabeth. They soon had several half-siblings: Mary, Joan, Thomas, and Edward de Monthermer.[13] Joan was assigned quarters in Windsor Castle and perhaps the girls stayed there, or traveled with her and their stepfather. Joan and Ralph spent time at Marlborough Castle, and Joan traveled north with Ralph during his service in the king's wars in Scotland, but her young daughters presumably did not accompany her.[14] It seems likely that the Clare sisters were educated at the convent at Amesbury in Wiltshire. This alien priory, a dependency of Fontevrault in France, had attracted English royal and noble women for some time. The sisters' aunt Mary was veiled there in 1291; Edward I's mother retired there in widowhood. Joan de Monthermer and Margaret de Clare's daughter would live at Amesbury; Elizabeth would retreat there at a major crisis in her life, and would remember the priory in her will.[15] As a place of retirement for royal ladies, such a wealthy, aristocratic convent possessed appropriate credentials to house the king's granddaughters, and its sisters could impart the education the nobility increasingly desired.

The Clares' mother, Joan, died in April 1307, aged 35, just as her children were entering the adult world through marriage. She was buried at the Augustinian friary at Clare in Suffolk, a family foundation. Miracles were said to occur at her tomb, especially the healing of toothache, back pain, and fever.[16] Ralph lost his title at Joan's death but still received royal favors, probably for a noteworthy war record and his association with the royal house. Ralph apparently retained the charm that had attracted Joan, for he contracted a second, secret marriage with Isabella de Valence, widow of John de Hastings and sister of Earl Aymer de Valence of Pembroke.[17] For men, marriage could mean upward mobility, but marriages to rich heiresses normally resulted from royal awards rather than secret weddings. Though medieval noblewomen were raised to expect arranged marriages, Ralph twice persuaded wealthy, high-born women to neglect the values of their class to marry him, even in the face of predictable royal displeasure and the prospect of heavy fines.

As marriage was often a defining element in a woman's life, the Clare sisters' marriages offer some relevant insights. If Joan's marriage to Monthermer raised issues of free choice in the sisters' minds, their first marriages were conventional: marriage contracts reflected family needs and aspirations or the desires of those who held wardships, not the indulgence of romantic attachments. Well-born girls expected nothing else. Eleanor de Clare married Hugh Despenser junior in the summer of 1306. Knighted in May of that year, Hugh came from a family that had served Edward I in various capacities, but was not among the great families in the realm. Edward I, however, owed Hugh's father large sums of money and bought young Hugh's marriage from Hugh senior for £2000, a huge sum for a young knight.[18] Then Edward chose his granddaughter Eleanor as young Hugh's bride. Her royal descent conferred prestige, but since she was not an heiress she brought Hugh no lands. Joan's holdings from the Clare marriage were all in jointure, preventing the loss of the lands but also limiting her ability to arrange her children's marriages, since wardship rights over them remained with her overlord, the king.[19] Though Hugh stood to inherit sizable properties in south and central England, the marriage seemed mediocre for a Clare daughter in 1306. But kings exploited their daughters' marriages for their own ends, and it was in character for Edward I to treat a granddaughter's marriage similarly. He did not share in marriage plans for his other Clare granddaughters, however, for he died on July 7, 1307, leaving his son, Edward II, to marry off his young nieces.

Margaret, the second sister, was soon married to Piers Gaveston. Edward I had banished Piers from England because he feared his influence on the heir to the throne, Prince Edward, whose wish to enrich his friend with the county of Ponthieu caused the old king great anxiety. Edward I was also fearful of his son's inordinate affection for Piers, possibly a homosexual attachment.[20] Edward II recalled Piers to England shortly after Edward I died; Piers and Margaret were married three days after the old king's October 1307 funeral. Some magnates criticized the marriage, not out of fear for Margaret's happiness but because a Clare daughter had been awarded to one who had risen too rapidly for their tastes. The marriage of the king's favorite to a girl of 14 may seem callous to modern sensibilities, but the *Vita Edwardi Secundi* says the king wanted "to strengthen Piers and surround him with friends."[21] And there were material rewards for Margaret: Piers was created earl of Cornwall, so she became a countess at marriage, and the king was generous with gifts.[22] As noted, the king enjoyed rights of wardship and marriage over the children of his tenants-in-chief. Still, Margaret's marriage to the king's favorite was possibly part of a deal with her brother Gilbert, who received seisin of the Clare estates shortly after her marriage though he was only 16. The fine for obtaining seisin was pardoned, and five months after the marriage Gilbert held the lands and titles of the earldoms of Gloucester and Hertford. Of course, Gilbert's early majority may not have concerned Piers or Margaret at all, but rather reflected the king's need for Gilbert's support. As baronial opposition to abuses in the royal administration had surfaced by January 1308, Edward II may have been eager to enlist Gilbert as an earl in his camp.[23] The *Vita's* reasoning is compelling: Gilbert the earl was a more valuable friend for Gaveston (and the king) than Gilbert the king's ward.

Elizabeth de Clare's marriage was entwined with that of her brother, Gilbert. He married Maud, daughter of Earl Richard de Burgh of Ulster; Elizabeth wed Maud's brother John, heir to the earldom. Gilbert had been granted the right "to marry whomsoever he will," and the double Ulster marriage suggests he also had the right to Elizabeth's marriage. The Irish connection may have been urged by Gilbert's Irish Clare cousins, recently established in Thomond.[24] In retrospect, he perhaps chose badly, as the heyday of Anglo-Norman power in Ireland was past, but this was more evident in 1318 than in 1308, and the earl of Ulster ranked first among the English lords of Ireland, with immense properties throughout the island and some estates in England, making the earldom "at least comparable with that of the house of Lancaster in England."[25] Gilbert was not alone in taking a Burgh bride: Robert Bruce of Scotland married a Burgh daughter in 1302, while other daughters married Irish earls. Elizabeth's wedding to John was celebrated at Waltham Abbey on September 30, 1308, her brother's either just before or just after that. The king probably attended, as he stayed at Waltham from September 28 to October 3.[26]

Still in their teens, all the Clare children now embarked on adulthood; childhood ended early for most noble offspring. They had lost their father when they were very young, their mother as they crossed the threshold into adult life, and their grandfather, Edward I, only a few months after that. The impact of these deaths on the Clare children's lives cannot be measured; their uncle's reign would be disastrous for three and a windfall for one.

The earl of Ulster generously granted his son and daughter-in-law jointly lands, profits, and rents in several areas.[27] Elizabeth could expect to become countess of Ulster; her prospects for a congenial and prestigious future seemed better than that of either of her sisters. Certainly she and

John possessed greater material resources than Eleanor and Hugh Despenser, but the vagaries of favoritism or death could play havoc with long-range expectations. Elizabeth stayed in England for a year before going to Ireland on October 15, 1309.[28] The chroniclers ignored her residence there except to note her son William's birth in 1312, a year before John de Burgh's premature death.[29] Probably in thanksgiving for her safe delivery, Elizabeth founded an Augustinian friary at Ballinrobe in Connacht, now county Mayo. While the house was endowed from lands given jointly to her and John de Burgh when they married, Elizabeth is credited with the foundation; probably John was already dead when the building program there began. The Clares had introduced this order into England some 60 years before, so Elizabeth's affiliation with the friars had a familial aspect lacking for her husband. Elizabeth had already shown an interest in pious works by donating wood and money to the new Franciscan church in London; with her brother and sisters she was counted a founder of that church.[30] Ballinrobe, however, marked her first independent foundation and the experience must have appealed to her. We know nothing of her ongoing concern for the friary, but Ballinrobe's foundation initiated her habit of pious initiatives into new regions, or in pursuit of purposes others of her class had neglected.

English claims to overlordship in Ireland dated from the twelfth century, but the English occupation was incomplete and haphazard. While successive kings sent royal governors to the island, their power was often overshadowed by the Anglo-Irish lords who were carving out large fees held from the king. These conquerors competed fiercely among themselves for power and land, and fought, or forged shifting alliances with, the native Irish chieftains.[31] When Earl Richard de Burgh came to Ireland to claim his earldom in 1286, he embarked on an expansionist policy in the west and north, which embroiled him with other Anglo-Irish lords and native Irish. Usually he triumphed and when his daughter-in-law Elizabeth arrived in Ireland in 1309, he was the greatest of the Anglo-Irish lords. Elizabeth's role, however, was merely that of spectator as the wife of the earl's eldest son. Typically for medieval heirs during their fathers' lives, John de Burgh's activities remain elusive. Poet and publicist celebrated the youthful deeds of William Marshal and the Black Prince, but such works are exceptional; writers usually ignored noble heirs-in-waiting.[32] As a matter of courtesy, Edward I and Edward II sent John de Burgh letters similar to those sent to his father. It has been suggested that John built Dunluce Castle in Antrim as a "caput" of his apanage, but Dunluce may date only from the late fourteenth or fifteenth century.[33] Though the chronicles said little of him, John must have been involved in clashes between native Irish and Anglo-Irish, or in persistent Anglo-Irish quarrels. His death at Galway on

June 18, 1313, perhaps resulted from such strife, but the laconic notices of the event leave it unclear whether he succumbed to illness, accident, or warfare.[34] He was 23, too young to leave a mark on his world without benefit of title or power.

Little in Elizabeth's background in England's settled conditions could have prepared her for the Irish experience, but her residence there afforded ample experience in practical politics and social understanding. As an onlooker, she learned of the violent strain in Irish politics. These years introduced her to the responsibilities of marriage, maternity, and the management of a noble household. Probably she maintained an independent household in widowhood, though perhaps in a residence belonging to the earl of Ulster, with whom her friendly relationship continued after John's death. Her first independent foray into religious foundation and patronage had taught her something of the planning and prosecution of building projects. Possibly by this time too, Elizabeth had organized a group of men into a council to direct her affairs, a very early example of this sort of household administration. She was astute enough to assess men who could serve her in legal or administrative capacities—men she later would employ to manage her Irish affairs.[35] Elizabeth would leave Ireland in 1316, never to return, but to the end of her life maintained her interest in the colony for the income it afforded her: her jointure lands there were an economic prop to her widowhood.[36]

Well provided for, she remained unmarried until another family tragedy associated with England's Scottish wars increased her economic attractiveness. Anglo-Scottish warfare stretched back many years. By 1314, the Scots had a strong leader in Robert Bruce, who unified most of Scotland under his banner, while Edward II lacked his father's enthusiasm for warfare in the north, perhaps because of disunity in England. Of Edward's humiliating defeats at the hands of the Scots, the most disastrous was Bannockburn in 1314. The many English nobles killed there included Elizabeth's brother, Gilbert. His loss was both a national and a family tragedy, for though he died at 24, his service to Crown and community had moderated much of the strife of Edward II's first years as king. Gilbert had served his uncle loyally, counseling moderation in the quarrels over Gaveston, the early demands of Edward's cousin Earl Thomas of Lancaster, and the barons' reforming experiments. With Gilbert's intelligent and responsible advice lost, baser men could influence and distort royal policy.[37]

Natural disaster coincided with political and military troubles to cause enormous suffering in Ireland and England. Excessive rains fell on both islands in 1314 and 1315. Crops could not ripen, nor new plantings be completed; food prices escalated and ultimately there was famine.[38] If the Anglo-Irish elite were insulated from their tenants' acute misery, they did

share in the problems caused by the May 1315 invasion of Ireland by
Robert Bruce's brother Edward, whose landing in Antrim exacerbated
quarrels among the Anglo-Irish lords. Some joined the Scots. The *Vita
Edwardi Secundi*'s author commented, "If the earl of Ulster is loyal their
plots need cause no alarm," suggesting some doubt as to the earl's fidelity.
Earl Richard had ties to Scotland: his daughter was Robert Bruce's wife,
a sister was the wife of the High Steward of Scotland, and many settlers
and mercenaries in Ulster came from Scotland. The real problem with
the earl's leadership against the invasion was his failure to unite the
Anglo-Irish forces. He regarded the attack (which focused first on Ulster) as a personal issue, not one demanding cooperation with other English lords and royal deputies in Ireland. When he did battle the Scots, his
army broke and fled.[39] Ireland was in turmoil for some time, for while
Bruce's occupation centered in the northeast (where the bulk of Elizabeth's more profitable jointure lands lay), his invasion devastated many
parts of the island.

As Gilbert de Clare left no surviving issue, his death at Bannockburn
dramatically entwined his three sisters in the grim politics of Edward II's
reign; his widow claimed to be pregnant, but bore no child. English inheritance customs dictated that in the absence of surviving offspring or
male siblings, Gilbert's estates must be divided among his three sisters. In
these circumstances, Edward II recalled Elizabeth from Ireland in the winter of 1316. Perhaps he acted out of avuncular concern, but his aim was to
exploit her matrimonial potential for his own ends. Her February voyage
to England was hazardous; Bruce's ships were at sea to damage English ves-
sels.[40] Edward settled Elizabeth in Bristol Castle, where she awaited his
pleasure. The parceling-out of Gilbert's estates would be a lengthy process,
but the prospect of controlling such a rich heritage would have excited
potential suitors. His sisters' stock therefore rose sharply in the marriage
market, but so did their vulnerability.

Since Eleanor de Clare married Hugh Despenser junior in 1306, he
had attended the king as a courtier, but the years between 1307 and 1314
give few hints of his later arrogance, greed, or boldness. He lived in somewhat straitened circumstances, helped along by Eleanor, one of Queen Isabella's ladies-in-waiting. His father, Hugh senior, granted Hugh junior a
few of his manors in 1310.[41] If Eleanor's position in 1314 seemed reasonably secure if not remarkably affluent, the lives of Margaret and Elizabeth illustrate the hazards of life for women of the fourteenth-century
English magnate class. Neither money nor power, title nor status, protected them from natural calamity, personal loss, or political violence. Edward II's infatuation with Margaret's husband, Gaveston, provoked deep
animosity among English earls and barons, less offended by what may

have been a homosexual attachment between the two than by Piers' foreign origins and rapid rise from the lower nobility. Royal patronage and grace flowed at Gaveston's beck and call, often in his own direction.[42] Noble demands for reforms prompted the king to banish Piers in 1308, and Margaret shared his exile in Ireland. His influence had not diminished. Edward II continued to show contempt for baronial hostility by granting favors and pardons at Gaveston's request, and heaping new grants on his banished friend.[43] Nonetheless, to end Gaveston's exile the king reconciled with his magnates and won approval of the pope and the French king, Philip IV, who had been offended by Edward's open preference for his favorite over his young queen, Philip's daughter, Isabella.

After Edward conceded redress of certain grievances to the reforming barons, Piers returned to England a month before the formal end of his exile. A year's absence seems to have intensified his hold over the king; renewed hostility from the earls resulted.[44] Most great nobles and barons, united by antipathy to Gaveston, pushed the king to agree in 1310 to the appointment of the Lords Ordainers to reform the realm, which meant in part reducing Piers' sway. The baronage's genuine grievances against the Crown dated from Edward I's later years. Claiming military necessity, royal officials frequently seized people's goods and were slow to pay at fair prices. The war against Scotland was pursued desultorily despite levies voted by parliament for its orderly prosecution. Magnates and barons believed Edward's ineffective government stemmed in large measure from Piers' evil counsel and the depletion of royal treasure on his behalf. The Ordainers were to restrain royal mismanagement by watching over the king's activities, something Edward never accepted in spirit, and rarely in fact. The Ordainers compiled a long list of charges against Gaveston. The most serious was that he had usurped royal power and dignity. As a result, he was again exiled in November 1311, but at Edward's order returned to England by Christmas 1311 and probably shared the holiday with the king. At York in January Margaret gave birth to Joan, her only surviving child by Gaveston. Margaret's churching ceremony of thanksgiving and purification was on February 20 at the Franciscan church there; Edward paid the minstrels who played at the celebrations.[45]

The Ordainers had meant Gaveston for permanent exile, so his early return to England increased their enmity toward him and Edward, who ignored reform efforts even on less personal issues. The archbishop of Canterbury excommunicated Piers; the earls of Lancaster, Pembroke, Hereford, Arundel, and Warwick swore an oath to capture him, with the actual arrest assigned to Pembroke and the earl of Warenne. Piers was taken, but the favorable terms granted him and Pembroke's negligence in guarding Piers irked Warwick, who stormed Piers' quarters and took him to his own castle. Ignoring Pembroke's pleas to respect his word of honor to Gaveston, Arundel, Lancaster, Hereford, and Warwick debated Piers' fate. The only real issue was the means of death for, in courtesy to Piers' brother-in-law, the earl of Gloucester, the earls hesitated to hang him as a thief or draw him as a traitor. After staging a trial to put a judicial gloss on what was essentially political murder, they beheaded Gaveston as a nobleman.[46]

The *Vita Edwardi Secundi* movingly described Edward's sorrow: "But I am certain the king grieved for Piers as a father grieves for his son. For the greater the love, the greater the sorrow. In David's lament for Jonathan, love is depicted which is said to have surpassed the love of women. Our king also spoke thus." As he died excommunicate, Piers' body lay unburied for two years before his lavish funeral in a Dominican house at Langley, provided by the king.[47] No chronicler recorded Margaret's reaction to Piers' death; fourteenth-century English culture did not celebrate widows' displays of ritualistic grief. Piers has been portrayed so unfavorably that it is easy to assume his widow felt only relief, though perhaps she felt chagrin and shame at his execution. Her family had disapproved of him: from 1311 her brother, Gilbert, had joined the opposition to Piers, if less fervently than other earls. Yet Piers had admirable qualities, and was perhaps as reasonable a husband as most medieval men. In material terms, Margaret could claim a third of the couple's property. The king assigned her dower by September 1312; later there were exchanges of lands, but Margaret was well provided for. By 1316 these grants were made contingent on her marrying with the king's license, for by then she, too, was a widowed heiress.[48]

Margaret may have lived in Oxford before Piers' burial. In 1314 she requested a license for the prior and convent of St Frideswide to acquire lands and rents in mortmain; as she was not previously associated with this priory, her intervention was perhaps prompted by the canons' hospitality in her early widowhood. Later she lived in the king's household, and went with him on a 1316 progress from London to York. There he and his suite stayed at the Franciscan priory, where Edward paid for Margaret's chamber renovations. Edward was solicitous, too, for Joan, Margaret's daughter by Piers. The girl lived in the convent at Amesbury, with an allowance from the Crown. Edward sought a marriage for her with Thomas, John Wake's son and heir, but Thomas instead incurred a 1000-mark fine for marrying another woman without royal permission. The king then agreed with Thomas de Multon, lord of Egremont, that the latter's son would marry Joan when both were "of reasonable age." The agreement was sealed by Multon's recognizance for £10,000, but Joan died at Amesbury early in 1325, before the marriage could take place.[49]

Wedded and Widowed Again

Elizabeth de Burgh returned in 1316 to an England wracked by natural and political calamities. Inclement weather prevented normal agricultural production and spread famine throughout much of Europe between 1315 and 1322. A murrain of sheep in 1315–16 compounded the desolation. The Scots raided northern England, burning homes and goods and attacking helpless defenders; substantial or continuing English protection was lacking. But while medieval governments, in general, lacked the ability to respond meaningfully to nationwide natural disasters, responsibility for failing to mobilize against the Scots belongs primarily to Edward II. As a prince, Edward had acquitted himself well in the field, but did not meet medieval expectations of regal martial ability or enthusiasm. He also lacked the resources to defend the realm successfully, in part because he had inherited massive debts from Edward I, in part because he squandered his wealth on personal favorites and expensive whims. Edward possessed good qualities, but his most evident virtue, loyalty to his friends, often worked against political stability. He was stubborn and in critical moments seems to have had no sense of measure. His whims, or those of his favorites, directed policy, and his private enmities intruded on affairs of state.

Within a year of her return to England, Elizabeth became a pawn in one of Edward's schemes to promote a favorite, but his plans were thwarted when Theobald de Verdon abducted her from Bristol on February 4, 1316, and married her without the king's license. It is less certain whether he did so without her consent. Theobald insisted that they had been engaged before Elizabeth left Ireland—not impossible, for he had served as justiciar there in 1313–15.[50] Abduction and clandestine marriage offered advantages to men greedy for an heiress's wealth, for normally the king pardoned the offense on payment of a fine; the practice became fairly common by the later Middle Ages. Many women were seized, raped, and married against their will, but it is unlikely that this happened to Elizabeth. A sham abduction and feigned opposition could conceal a woman's personal choice of spouse if she were party to the charade. Elizabeth might well have had her mother's second marriage in mind, and Theobald testified that she came to him freely; but as she was confined to Bristol Castle, abduction was needed to implement the plan.[51]

The king's practice of pardoning such offenses illustrates the problems of arranged second or third marriages for women in Elizabeth's position. Magna Carta, in theory, guaranteed that a widow whose marriage was in the king's gift could not be forced to marry against her will. The king's license was needed, however, if she wished to marry a man of her choice, and, since the king had prior plans for Elizabeth, her requests for such a license would have been denied or endlessly delayed.[52] The Church joined the issue by emphasizing the necessity of both parties' free consent for a valid union to exist. As neither the king nor Elizabeth raised the matter of her consent, it must be presumed that she agreed to the union and so met the Church's requirements of validity. Perhaps she genuinely desired marriage with Theobald or—implausibly—perhaps his courtship was sufficiently brutal to elicit her "free" consent. Theobald gambled, hoping to pacify the king through a fine; his timing was excellent as he had ties to Earl Thomas of Lancaster, in 1316 still prominent in the royal government. That the king's rancor limited a few of Verdon's liberties was a small price to pay for a share in the mighty Clare inheritance.[53]

Born of a family that came to England with William of Normandy, Theobald de Verdon was born in 1278 and was knighted by Edward I in 1298. His seat was at Alton Castle in Staffordshire, with manors in Warwick, Leicester, Buckingham, Gloucester, and Shropshire. In Ireland he held the lordship of half of Meath, and much of Louth—enough to place him just below the magnates in wealth and opportunity. Perhaps Theobald's connection with the Marches through his Gloucester and Shropshire lands favored his first marriage in 1302 to Maud, daughter of Edmund Mortimer of Wigmore; she bore him three daughters and died in 1312. Possibly sponsored by Thomas of Lancaster, Theobald was named justiciar of Ireland in 1313, but was recalled before Bruce's invasion. Little in his career distinguishes him from others of his class.[54]

Theobald's term as justiciar in Ireland was not especially noteworthy, but it presumably meant that he and Elizabeth were acquainted before they married. He went to Ireland as a recent widower; she was lately widowed. His Irish lands were situated near Burgh manors, moreover, and Verdon and Clare lands lay in close proximity in the eastern Welsh March. Prior acquaintance between them seems natural, indeed likely, but unprovable. Elizabeth perhaps wanted to leave Ireland and found Theobald a reasonable, even attractive, prospect to ensure a return to England. Her father-in-law, the earl of Ulster, may have found a Verdon match expedient too; it would cement an alliance with an important landlord at minimum cost to himself. That the earl's friendship with Elizabeth continued until his death adds weight to the idea that her new marriage received his blessing.

Theobald installed his new wife at Alton. She had left her son, William, in the tutelage of his Irish uncles, but she now acquired three young step-daughters—Joan, Elizabeth, and Margery. Later in life, she would maintain close ties with the younger sisters and their husbands; the eldest lived most of her married life in northern England, so her lack of contact with her stepmother must be attributed to distance. No details survive of Elizabeth's brief tenure as Lady Verdon before Theobald died on July 27, 1316, a probable victim of the typhoid epidemic that accompanied the 1316 famine. He was buried on September 19 at Croxden Abbey, a Cistercian house under his patronage.[55] In addition to his young daughters, he left Elizabeth, who was pregnant.

Royal bureaucracy responded swiftly at the deaths of tenants-in-chief, with little apparent concern for spouses' or children's feelings. In Theobald de Verdon's case, the Crown quickly gave the wardship of his English lands to Roger Damory and his Irish lands to two Verdon brothers during the heiresses' minority. The immediate disposition of his daughters is not clear. Their custody and marriages were in the king's hands, but Edward II never brought all his wards to live in his own household. In August 1316 he granted the eldest daughter's marriage to William Montague, a royal favorite; eventually the second daughter, Elizabeth, married Bartholomew de Burghersh. The rights to Margery's marriage were purchased by Roger Damory. Joan's life in the months just after her father's death provides a poignant example of the fate of such young heiresses. Born in August 1303, she was not yet 13 when Theobald died. The grant of her marriage to William Montague probably meant that shortly after her father's funeral she entered the Montague household or a convent, to await further developments. She married Montague's son and heir, John, in the royal chapel at Windsor in April 1317; he died the following August.[56] Within 13 months, Joan had lost her father, probably changed residences once or twice, married at 13 and was widowed at 14. By the next February she had married Thomas Furnivall. Medieval and modern sensibilities differ markedly, but one must wonder what traumas might have attached to such rapid shifts in status and relationships.

A Third Marriage and Its Aftermath

Even before Theobald de Verdon's funeral, Edward II began pressuring Elizabeth to preserve her "well-being and honor" by a third marriage.[57] Her circumstances hardly favored refusal. Wardship of Theobald's lands had been assigned to others, so she was expected to vacate the premises; her Irish lands from the Burgh marriage were menaced by the Bruce invasion; the Clare lands had not been partitioned. Her parents were dead, so there was no ancestral home to which she could flee. In the medieval tradition, one looked to the mother's brother for support, but in Elizabeth's case this was the king himself, who was making demands upon her. Elizabeth named attorneys to recover her dower in Ireland and England in October. Orders in December to deliver her dower from the Verdon lands may have eased her economic situation, but she was still a vulnerable woman facing a determined king.[58]

At some point between September 1316 and February 1317, Elizabeth retreated to Amesbury Priory in Wiltshire, where her aunt Mary was a nun. Amesbury's buildings have vanished; only the church remains. A lovely brook runs through a meadow on the grounds, screened off from the town. It must have been a peaceful place in which to await the birth of her child, but Edward pursued his heavy-handed tactics, bringing to Amesbury her prospective groom, Roger Damory. Probably he also sought to weaken her resistance by sending Queen Isabella to see her. As his sister, the nun Mary depended on Edward for allowances and gifts to satisfy her rather worldly tastes; she too may have urged marriage to Damory. Elizabeth's choices were limited. Edward had the right to approve her marriage partner and was bent on coupling her with Damory. Magna Carta protected a widow's right to refuse an unacceptable marriage, but if Elizabeth insisted on that protection she might jeopardize her share in the still-undivided Clare inheritance. Presumably she could have taken religious vows, but this course had disadvantages. As a nun, she would forego maternal duties and joys, and her share of the Clare lands would be assigned to her son in her place. Possibly within six weeks after she bore her Verdon daughter, Isabella, on March 21, 1317, Elizabeth bowed to Edward's wishes and married Roger Damory.[59]

Isabella de Verdon was baptized in the Amesbury church, the bishop of Salisbury officiating with Queen Isabella and the royal nun Mary as godmothers. Edward did not attend, but gave a silver-gilt cup worth £1 10s. to Mary's valet who informed him of the birth.[60] Elizabeth would not have attended the baptism; women waited until after their purification (or churching) to resume participation in divine service. The custom of churching was based on Jewish practice and Christian tradition, which looked with distaste on women's bodily functions and demanded that they undergo a purification ritual after childbirth, though official ecclesiastical language emphasized the rite's elements of thanksgiving for the mother's safe delivery. Churching was performed about 40 days after childbirth, in keeping with the model of the Blessed Virgin whose purification was celebrated as a major feast of the Church on February 2.

Elizabeth did, however, observe another popular religious practice by making a pilgrimage of thanksgiving in the late spring. She married sometime in the spring, but perhaps the journey, with pious overtones, was a convenient means of postponing daily life with Damory. The nun Lady Mary headed the party, which included Elizabeth and Isabella of Lancaster, daughter of Earl Thomas's brother, Henry; Isabella became a nun at Amesbury and may already have been professed at the time. The king paid the ladies' considerable expenses.[61] His sister Mary enjoyed forays outside her convent, either visiting court or making lengthy pilgrimages. Medieval nuns were supposed to stay within conventual grounds, but fourteenth-century discipline in the nunneries was lax, with trips to one's family or for pious purposes allowed fairly often; the royal nun Mary was given, or took, more freedom than other nuns. Perhaps by financing this journey, Edward rewarded Mary for any part she had in leading Elizabeth to marry Damory. Meanwhile, Elizabeth's sister Margaret married another courtier, Hugh Audley, on April 28. Margaret had no more options than Elizabeth, perhaps fewer since she had spent at least part of her widowhood in the king's household and at his expense. Yet the circumstances of her marriage seem less brutal and unfeeling than those of Elizabeth's, perhaps because Audley was seemingly a rather nicer fellow than Roger Damory. Elizabeth's third marriage was perhaps celebrated a few days after Margaret's, when the pilgrim party spent five days at Windsor with the king in early May. Edward II never had much affection for his niece Elizabeth, and her apparent willingness to circumvent his plans for her by marrying Verdon had only heightened his antagonism. He might have enjoyed watching her discomfiture at marrying Damory. The possibility of a Windsor wedding is enhanced by the fact that Elizabeth's churching should not have taken place before April 30. When the pilgrims recommenced their journey to Canterbury and St Albans, the number of horses increased markedly, only to decrease again when Elizabeth left the party some days later, suggesting that Damory had assured his new wife a suitable escort.

The 16 months after February 1316 were tumultuous for Elizabeth. She married twice, once to an alleged abductor and then to a man forced on her by the king. Her maternal role quickly grew to encompass three stepdaughters and a new daughter of her own. From Bristol she moved to Alton, then found tranquillity at Amesbury before her pilgrimage to Canterbury and St Albans. For the first time in her adult life, Elizabeth was drawn into the royal court's intrigues, its cajolery and threats, which brought about her eventual submission. After a month's pilgrimage, she left for another, scarcely less turbulent round of conjugal life with Roger Damory, whose ambition would eclipse Elizabeth in the predominantly masculine political world—at least as far as the documents allow us to observe. This typifies the problem of searching for information about married women in this period, for contemporary sources ignore female existence except when it impinged on male activities. Elizabeth was valuable to Damory for her estates as well as for her illustrious descent, connections, and social skills. Roger was ten or 15 years older than she, but she had experiences beyond his. She knew more of Irish and Welsh politics than he, and her contacts in those regions were familial and close. Roger's service with her brother, Gilbert, and with the king had undoubtedly taught him about comital and royal society, but one imagines that he looked to Elizabeth for continuing information and guidance. In one sense she was a spectator during this marriage, but her private roles had considerable import.

Marriage to Damory entailed downward mobility for Elizabeth, who perhaps consciously retained her first husband's surname during her later marriages to underscore an earlier, grander union. This is unsurprising, for an hierarchical view of world and society, reinforced by monarchy and Church, was ingrained in medieval thinking and behavior. The Burghs nearly matched the Clares in power; the Verdons lacked the Clares' wealth, but held significant lands in England, Wales, and Ireland. In contrast, the Damorys were of only local importance, though their position had been enhanced by service to the Crown in various capacities. Roger was not even the head of the family, but a younger brother. Early in his career he had served Gilbert de Clare, who gave Roger his first landholding, a life interest in the manor of Easton. He was knighted by Michaelmas 1306, when a document calls him a knight of Buckinghamshire. His older brother, Richard, had achieved some official standing by then, but while his offices and grants put him in a position to further his family's fortune, none was of premier rank. At Bannockburn, Roger's bravery attracted Edward II's notice. Thereafter, his increasing favor with the king rapidly brought tangible rewards from royal gifts and patronage. He moved into a vacuum left by Gaveston's death, certainly in terms of his growing wealth and perhaps in terms of his personal relationship with Edward II.[62]

Edward II's reign was dominated by constitutional and military issues, but his kingship's dynamic was sparked by his personal attachments to various men, unrestrained by any sense of measure. The obvious examples are Piers Gaveston, early in the reign, and later Hugh Despenser junior. Between 1315 and about 1319, however, other men jostled for favor, and Roger Damory prevailed over such competitors as Hugh Audley and William Montague. Just as Edward II's loyalty to Gaveston elicited calls for reform and the emergence of the Lords Ordainers, so his affection for Damory stalled accommodation with his mightiest lord, Earl Thomas of Lancaster. The magnates' grievances against Gaveston had centered on his control of royal patronage and on the belief that the king should seek counsel, in traditional fashion, from the earls and barons and not upstart courtiers. After 1315, the favors Edward heaped on Damory, Audley, Montague, and the Despensers rekindled old hostilities. Through their marriages in 1317 with the Clare sisters, the greatest gifts at Edward II's disposal, Damory and Audley received vast landholdings and associated rights; their resources could thereafter support their political influence. The division of the Clare lands accelerated in 1317, after Edward took Despenser's, Audley's, and Damory's homage. Earl Gilbert's widow's claims to be pregnant were now discounted after some two years.[63] Garbled information from various inquisitions on the inheritance had delayed the award of the sisters' purparties or shares, but these had now been settled. Late in 1317 the bulk of the Clare castles and manors, apart from the widow's dower, were distributed to the sisters' husbands. Under English law, co-heiresses shared more or less equally, and there was an attempt to give each sister some land in England, Wales, and Ireland. But the largest share went to Hugh Despenser since, as the eldest sister's husband, he had first choice and naturally opted for the richest lands.[64]

Damory's entry into Elizabeth's share of the Clare lands illustrates well the importance of currying royal favor. In January 1317 Edward had granted him 200 marks yearly from the Exchequer until lands or rents to that amount were otherwise provided him. Elizabeth's Clare purparty added Clare Castle and manors in Suffolk, manors and boroughs centered on Cranborne in Dorset, forest land and an iron mine in Kent, and manors and rights in Essex, Norfolk, Cambridge, Hertfordshire, Somerset, and Huntingdon. In Wales, her Clares' lands included the lordship of Usk and Caerleon with castles and manors, and in Ireland, one-third of the Kilkenny lands. In addition, Roger controlled her jointure lands from her first marriage and her Verdon dower lands, giving him lands and rights in Leicester, Warwick, Buckingham, Wiltshire, and Ireland. He held the remaining Verdon lands in wardship until Theobald's daughters came of age.[65] Subsequently the king heaped more riches on the Damorys. Hallaton manor came to Roger in February 1317 "for his good service against the Scots at Stryvelin and also on account of his marriage with the said Elizabeth." Sandhall manor in Yorkshire was granted on the same terms, as was Vauxhall. Even this list may not reflect all Roger's assets.[66]

In a few years Roger had cultivated the king's friendship with all its attendant rewards, had married into one of England's premier houses, and amassed a fortune in lands and rents. These events inevitably irritated many of the king's traditional counselors, the earls and barons, especially Edward's cousin, Earl Thomas of Lancaster, who since 1310 had upheld the reforming Ordinances more assiduously than other earls. Thomas was a complex man, variously called a fourteenth-century leader of English constitutionalism, a popular saint, and a man lacking in political instincts or timely leadership. He insisted on the need to reform government and to curb royal excess; at the same time, he achieved his objectives through petty legalism, enjoyed causing the king minor annoyances, and showed a petulance that did little to advance his aims. By 1316 Thomas commanded more land, wealth, and retainers than anyone but the king, but resented the flow of patronage away from himself and his followers and despised those who did receive royal largesse. Thus Damory became a prime target of Thomas's hostility after 1316.[67]

Lancaster must have chafed at Damory's influence with Edward, for the king heeded the earl only reluctantly, and Thomas had failed to direct Edward's policies effectively during his period of dominance between 1314 and 1316. Probably, too, Lancaster was disgruntled by the marriages of his cousins Margaret and Elizabeth de Clare, who were better suited as consorts for magnates' sons than for upstarts like Audley and Damory. The earl of Surrey had abducted Thomas's wife; Thomas also blamed Damory and others for this disruption of his domestic life. Lancaster believed the act was plotted at a February 1317 council held at Clarendon, where the court party dominated.[68] Lancaster seems to have been more than usually angered by Damory's hold on the Verdon lands and on the two youngest Verdon daughters' marriage rights. In short, Thomas had general and specific grievances against Roger, though his hostility was certainly sufficient to encompass the whole group of courtiers.

Damory may have been catapulted into the magnate ranks by his control of his wife's lands, but she had no control over that process or over most others in his life. Her public role in these years was limited. Many of the king's grants were to her and Roger jointly, but Elizabeth probably had little influence with her uncle. He had awarded her sister Margaret 2000 marks yearly before she wed Audley,[69] and showered Eleanor Despenser with gifts later in the reign. Elizabeth received no such signs of affection, probably because of Edward's pique at the Verdon marriage. Two entries on the Patent rolls in these years do record something of her methods at this time. She requested nothing for herself, but sought grants on behalf of others. Robert de Scales thus received exemption for life from court offices and administrative duties, and "in consideration of his good service to Elizabeth de Burgo"; John de Horsele was given a bailiwick in Shropshire during the king's pleasure.[70] Such acts were not unusual; intervention for favors bound ties of loyalty more tightly. They demonstrate Elizabeth's knowledge of how her world operated, and strengthened personal ties without reference to her husband.

In 1317 and 1318 important men were increasingly distrustful of Damory. He, Audley, Montague, and the Despensers swore to a series of recognizances binding each to the others for £6000. The recognizances' purpose is unclear: to reinforce unanimity among them, or to inhibit emerging distrust within the group. Later Elizabeth and Audley would claim the recognizances were forced, but by then both hoped to be pardoned the debts that had fallen to the Crown.[71] In November 1317, Damory made another indenture with the earl of Pembroke and Bartholomew de Badlesmere, who were not courtier-favorites. They have been called "capable and experienced counselors," and certainly served Edward II loyally and responsibly, with greater concern for the interests of the realm than for personal gain. Some historians have seen the November 1317 indenture as initiating a "Middle Party," positioned between Lancaster and the king. A more compelling argument sees Pembroke and Badlesmere hoping to curb Damory's irresponsibility. By this indenture Damory promised to amend his ways, to give counsel to the king on the advice of Pembroke and Badlesmere, and to try to limit the king's gifts over £20, a clause potentially damaging to himself. He further agreed to work with Pembroke and Badlesmere to persuade the king to do nothing prejudicial to the realm. Pembroke and Badlesmere limited themselves to defending Damory against all men save the king. Clearly, they feared Damory might further damage the peace of the realm. To seal the indenture, Damory swore on the Host and pledged £10,000 as surety for his promises. No one has offered a plausible explanation for Damory's willingness or need to enter into this indenture; in November 1317 he seemed firmly entrenched in royal favor.[72] Perhaps he feared a return to court by the earl of Lancaster, armed with more reform demands. By accusing Lancaster of treason, Damory had already impeded attempts to reconcile the king and the earl, which was necessary for tranquillity in the kingdom and for effective defense of the north against the Scots.[73] Naturally, Damory's interests ran counter to reconciling earl and king, for Lancaster stood firm on limiting the reckless flow of royal patronage on which Damory's fortune was built.

Lancaster had seized Knaresborough Castle, where Damory was keeper, and Alton Castle in the Verdon lands, in Damory's ward. Despite these assaults on his favorite, the king needed to end Lancaster's mighty isolation and to enlist his support for resistance to the ever more menacing Scottish raids. A tentative agreement at Leicester in April 1318 offered the earl major concessions: Edward accepted the Ordinances, agreed to the removal of his favorites and to an inquiry into royal grants of lands. Edward formally agreed to the program in June 1318, though the Despensers, Montague, and Damory tried to weaken his resolve, especially when he ordered on June 9 that royal gifts be reclaimed by the Crown. This radical order probably led some of the favorites, including Damory, to seek accommodation with Lancaster, promising him safe conduct to the king while admitting their role in prolonging the royal cousins' estrangement. In the course of negotiations in July, the earl softened his stance on several issues, but was adamant that Montague and Damory be dismissed before he met with the king. He demanded they leave court and make amends to him. The *Vita Edwardi Secundi*'s author noted the earl's victory in August: "Roger D'Amory and the rest, except Hugh Despenser and the Earl

Warenne, humbly presenting themselves before the earl, were received into his grace."[74] This took place at the time of the accord known as the Treaty of Leake, which settled outstanding differences between king and earl and provided for regular magnate counsel for the king. Conflict was briefly averted, only to resume in 1319 and 1320.

Elizabeth and Roger entertained the king at Clare from March 23 to at least March 27, 1318. While Edward and Roger discussed political issues, Elizabeth was concerned with the indulgence sermons for her mother, Joan of Acre. Bishop Thomas Cobham preached the sermons at Clare friary and left a lasting impression on Elizabeth, for she remembered him in her statutes for Clare College 41 years later. She had other joys: a child was expected in May. In addition, Roger, in March 1317, had purchased for £200 the marriage rights of her daughter Isabella and her step-daughter Margery.[75] But in the summer of 1318, Damory left the court temporarily. His departure was not a punishment, but this must have been a tense period in his life, for a review of past royal grants was scheduled for the York parliament that autumn. In the end, Edward, with parliament's assent, confirmed Roger and Elizabeth in possession of Sandhall, Vauxhall, and Hallaton. Free warren was granted them; Roger again began to give information to the king, though less often than in 1316–17.[76] No one seems to have meant to punish Damory for past excesses, but nor was there the former royal enthusiasm for him; the reformers' new royal chamberlain, Hugh Despenser junior, was rapidly displacing Damory in Edward's affections.

By November 1318 and into 1320, Damory lent large sums of money to various people: £400 to a knight named Simon Warde, 100 marks to William Marny, £2420 to several other men. Some were ordinary loans; others disguised sales of lands. Warde, for example, had granted Roger the reversion of lands in Escrick and Kirkby Underknolle in Yorkshire, and the £400 loan represented the cost of the sale. Roger tried to expand his lands through other purchases, notably the manor of Kennington in Surrey.[77] Despite cessation of the king's grants, Damory's cash flow supported a luxurious way of life, witnessed by extant Clare accounts from 1319. The earliest of these, badly mutilated, covers a few days around midsummer, without location; Elizabeth is not mentioned. The second covers four months from late September 1319 to January 1320, with reference to earlier expenses.[78] The rolls clearly indicate that the household was the lord's; Elizabeth is referred to once or twice as "the lady," and her whereabouts are rarely stated. The accounts note payment for typical needs of a noble household: furs, spices, red sealing wax, parchment. A goldsmith, Robert de Ludlow, furnished works in silver for the lord; Italian merchants were paid over £250 for earlier purchases. There were mundane expenses as Roger and Elizabeth pursued legal actions. In the winter of 1319 they were pleading against her widowed sister-in-law, Maud de Burgh, over land. Their London attorney, John de Cornhulle, received payments, as did his narrator, Gregory atte Shire. An attorney at the Bench, William de Coleshulle, was paid a 20-mark annual retainer, and Sir Thomas de Breynford, a London attorney, received four barrels of sturgeon. No accounts survive between January and October 1320, and the public records offer few insights into Damory's activities at this time. The king had planned a trip to France in February 1320, but instead wandered about southeast England, visiting Roger and Elizabeth at Kennington on April 21–22. Damory had had letters of protection for the French journey and probably joined the king's meanderings before he accompanied Edward and a host of dignitaries to France between June 19 and July 22, when Edward did homage to the French king for his Gascon lands.[79] Elizabeth perhaps went too, but this is conjecture, as she almost totally disappears from surviving documents during her Damory marriage. In those five years she had her daughters to nurture, and her son, William, had joined her by 1317; contemporary chroniclers ignored any role she may have taken in Damory's career in the turbulent years between 1320 and 1322.

The most critical sequence of circumstances for the Damorys at this time, indeed for the whole realm, was Hugh Despenser junior's ascendancy in the king's confidence and counsels. Hugh always utilized his father's support to advance his career and relied on the influence of his wife, a favored royal niece who undoubtedly promoted his affairs whenever possible. But he was also independently, often recklessly, self-seeking. He chafed at the slow division of the Clare estates and at the long wait for the disavowal of Gilbert's widow's pregnancy, and in May 1315 his grasping nature and impetuosity surfaced when he seized Tonbridge Castle from the widowed countess. Arrogant, desperate, or stupid, the attempt failed but did not alienate Hugh from the king, though he had to wait two years more for his wife's share of the inheritance. Hugh's rashness emerged again in 1316 when he killed Llywelyn Bren, a Welsh rebel in his custody.[80]

When the Clare lands were at last divided in 1317, Hugh seized the chance to expand his share of them outside the law. Before Audley could take possession of his wife's lands in Gwynllwg, Despenser offered the men of the area liberal terms in return for their oaths of allegiance to him. The king made unsuccessful non-military attempts to dislodge Despenser; Audley eventually agreed to exchange the lands for English manors worth considerably less.[81] Despenser had begun to stake a claim to all the Clare lands in Wales, an audacious plan that ignored Audley's and Damory's rights. Despenser then pursued his plan with characteristic ferocity and greed; by 1320 he had also supplanted Audley and Damory in Edward's favor. In this endeavor he differed from them crucially: he alone held an official position near the king, for the reformers had made him royal chamberlain in 1318. In contrast, Damory and Audley attended Edward only at his pleasure. They gave him information, witnessed charters, fought his wars, and participated in his council meetings, but they lacked a formal status that did not depend on his whims. Despenser's office, in contrast, gave him continual access to Edward, and Hugh cleverly transformed access into royal infatuation. By the fall of 1320 Edward was ready to back Hugh's schemes, even at the cost of alienating magnates and barons, who now had trouble getting past his careful guard over the king. Damory's last gift from Edward, a respite of fines, came in the fall of 1320, perhaps only as a sop to detach Roger from growing aristocratic hostility to Edward's intrusion in Wales at Hugh's behest.[82]

Marcher lords cherished traditional liberties that minimized royal interference in their affairs, a legal tradition dear to Marcher pride. The same sensitivity to diminution of these rights that had animated Elizabeth's father, the Red Earl, inspired the Marchers in 1320–22 when the issue centered on the lordship of Gower. As this complex case would later figure in Despenser's moves against Elizabeth, some detail is needed here. The Gower story began when William de Braose settled the reversion to Gower on his daughter Alina and his son-in-law John Mowbray, stipulating that should the Mowbrays die childless, the reversion would belong to the earl of Hereford. But Braose had money woes, so later he ignored this settlement and obtained a royal license for the Mowbrays to all his estates except Gower, which he then offered for sale. Hugh Despenser junior hoped to purchase it, for it would add substantially to his Welsh holdings, but with the backing of Hereford and other Marcher lords, Mowbray seized Gower. Despenser appealed to the king, claiming that no royal license had been issued as the law required. Hugh urged Edward to seize Gower, an action the Marchers believed contravened ancient custom. Hugh then accused the Marchers of treason, setting the scene for armed challenge. The Vita *Edwardi Secundi's* author explains the widespread antipathy to Hugh:

> . . . John de Mowbray for the land of Gower, in which Hugh Despenser had tried to supplant him; Hugh D'Audley for the castle which he had withheld; the Earl of Hereford for the wrong done to his son; Roger Clifford for the disherison of his mother, procured by Hugh to his damage; Roger Damory, co-heir of the Earl of Gloucester, could have no affection for his deadly rival. The two Mortimers were hostile because he proposed to despoil the one, and had promised to avenge the death of his grandfather upon each of them. . . . [83]

From October 1320 to March 1321, the Damory household was scattered and peripatetic, but always near London.[84] The roll is dated from Kingston in October, though horses were stabled at Byfleet and Kennington; in December the account was kept at Kennington, and in February from Byfleet. Though the king did not visit the Damorys at this time, Queen Isabella and her retinue stayed with them in October and November. Isabella's visits reflect continuing royal friendship, for Roger was still close enough to Edward II to be allowed to hunt in royal forests at Hampton and Clarendon in early January 1321. It is tempting to speculate that Damory did not commit to the anti-Despenser faction until relatively late. Unlike the other Marchers named in the *Vita Edwardi Secundi,* Damory had no specific grievance against Despenser, only a general, familial, rivalry;[85] unlike Audley, he had no Marcher background save through his wife, nor any visible associations with Mowbray, Clifford, or Hereford. The winter of 1320–21 may have been a time for Roger to assess his standing with the king against Despenser's rivalry. His position depended on royal largesse; it must have been difficult for him to oppose the source of his fortune, but Damory the favorite gradually became Damory the foe. From March 1321 until his death a year later, Roger was a major leader of the opposition to Despenser and Edward, which escalated into open revolt early in 1322.

By March 1321, the king knew of Lancaster's plan to aid the Marchers and had left for Wales with Despenser and an army.[86] There was a flurry of activity as the king and his favorite hastily strengthened their fortifications in the Marches, and the opposition mustered its forces. The barons insisted that Despenser leave the king and be delivered to Lancaster's custody, a demand that must have chilled Edward if he thought of Gaveston's fate. Edward called for a conference with the barons at Gloucester; they refused because of Despenser's presence, and threatened to renounce their fealty to the king. The stalemate ended when the Marchers began a systematic devastation of Hugh's lands in May 1321, taking "vengeance upon Hugh of their own authority for default of justice."[87] Audley assumed, or was assigned, possession of Newport Castle, once part of his wife's inheritance. Damory took Caerphilly and other Despenser holdings in Glamorgan; his allies gave him custody of the town of Cardiff. The Marchers seized Despenser's Welsh lands and ravaged whatever goods could not be taken away; some of Hugh's English lands were seized as well.[88] Even so, their aim of ending his ascendancy over the king was not achieved.

Lancaster had promised to aid the Marchers, but provided little. The Marchers still looked to him for leadership, however, and met him at Sherburn in June. Despite the earlier enmity between Damory and Lancaster, Roger attended the meetings. The objective at Sherburn was to unite the

Northerners, the Marchers, and the earl's retainers, and to appeal to other disgruntled elements in society by drawing up a list of charges against the Despensers for presentation at a future parliament. The complaints were formally presented to the king at London on August 1. The author of the *Vita Edwardi Secundi* summarized neatly: "Hugh was accused of being too greedy and thus unsuitable to be with the king; he was accused of evil council; of conspiracy and falsehood; of being a destroyer of the people, a disinheritor of the crown, an enemy of the king and kingdom." The assembled prelates and nobles agreed, and Edward reluctantly accepted the necessity of the Despensers' exile, though in his heart he determined that this was only a temporary expedient. In August the elder Hugh went to France, but the younger embarked on a career of piracy in the Channel— a "sea-monster" as the *Vita*'s author put it.[89] After the Despensers' departure, the barons should have released to the king the property they had seized. On August 16 and again on September 9 and 25, Damory and Audley were told to deliver Hugh's Welsh lands to the king. Damory replied that he had been given possession by the magnates and men of the area, and while he was ready to give the king the issues of the land, the threat of war prevented his delivering the castles and manors.[90] Audley claimed he held only estates that were part of his wife's share of the Clare inheritance. The reluctance of Damory and Audley suggests that Despenser had no monopoly on greed.

Once Hugh's exile had been achieved, the baronial leaders were pardoned for their actions between March and August 1321. Their followers were then pardoned on their testimony; 89 of Damory's followers, for example, were pardoned at his testimony on August 20.[91] But, by the fall of 1321, Edward was acting with renewed vigor against his enemies, usually known today as the Contrariants. In November, he ordered Damory's lands confiscated: Clare Castle and its honor as well as his lands in Essex, Hertford, and Suffolk. Damory's Irish lands, goods, and chattels were also to be taken into the king's hand, and his Welsh castles given to the king's appointed keeper.[92] In the next months Edward sought to eliminate all Damory's resources. His ship at Weymouth was seized, a horse he had sent to Anglesey Priory was to be delivered to the king, and Edward sought to arrest London merchants who sold crossbows and other arms to Roger. In early December, Edward ordered his sheriffs to arrest Damory and other leaders. In fact, Damory and his fellows may have flirted with treason at this time. Lancaster had gathered various opposition factions at Doncaster in early December. With his allies and the Marchers, the earl reiterated grievances in a petition drawn up there, and there is evidence that Lancaster was maneuvering the group into alliance with the Scots. He claimed that Hereford, Damory, Audley, Clifford, and others subscribed to a plan for Scottish assistance. If true, the episode suggests either that the barons were mesmerized by Lancaster's mystique, or fearful for the outcome of their enterprise.[93]

After a December assembly of prelates declared the Despensers' exile illegal, the king revoked it and hastened to his army at Cirencester. In the ensuing military action, Damory took Worcester after Edward retired northward; Damory was also accused of burning Bridgnorth. Initially frustrated, Edward scored a major victory by late January, when the Mortimers and several other key figures submitted with their retinues.[94] The Mortimers' surrender opened the way into Wales, but Edward soon moved north. Lancaster had besieged the royal castle of Tickhill in January, giving the king cause to move against his detested cousin. The Marchers were more timely in coming to the earl's aid than he had been in joining them; perhaps they despaired of any other course. A remnant of the Marchers hurried north to defend Lancaster's castles, Damory, Audley, and the earl of Hereford among them. Lancaster had won few northerners to his cause; the revolt was over within weeks. Roger Damory was captured at Lancaster's castle of Tutbury on March 11, 1322, already mortally wounded. The day before Roger's death, Edward and a group of loyal magnates and barons declared him and other Contrariants guilty of treason. Traitors could expect to be drawn and quartered: dragged behind a horse to the scaffold, hanged but cut down alive, disemboweled, and hacked to pieces that usually were displayed publicly. Edward respited this punishment because he had loved Roger well in the past, but the charges against him remained, which meant that his heirs were permanently disinherited.[95]

Damory's character is difficult to assess. He must have possessed qualities that made him a leader in the Marcher struggle, presumably resourcefulness, bravery, and generosity in sharing Despenser spoils. But nothing suggests his vision extended beyond personal gain. J. R. S. Phillips, foremost present-day authority on Edward II's reign, calls Roger "malignant," "irresponsible and dangerous." The *Vita Edwardi Secundi*'s author noted that many found him ungrateful for the royal favors that transformed his life. If his arson and looting in Wales and Gloucestershire in 1321 manifest a taste for gratuitous crime, he was probably no more violent than his peers. If he forced peaceful people from their holdings, he was never the Despensers' equal in that regard.[96] Still, little in Damory's career commends him. The impression is of a grasping, reckless mediocrity with a petty crook's mentality, not a master criminal's audacity.

Neither public documents nor the Clare accounts offer insights into Damory as husband or father. Self-interest, however, would have impressed on him Elizabeth's importance to his career, and probably he treated her well. Roger was likely astute enough to realize that her connections gave him easy access to important families. Her godmother, for example, had been her aunt, Edward II's sister Countess Elizabeth of Hereford, a bond with the Bohuns Damory could not equal. In these turbulent years, her children and her family lands mattered enormously to Elizabeth, and Damory supported her in both areas. He ensured that she raised her daughter Isabella de Verdon, and perhaps welcomed her son, William de Burgh, in the household after 1317; cordial relations with a future earl would enhance Damory's standing while satisfying Elizabeth's maternal feelings. Roger certainly would have responded as well to Despenser moves against Elizabeth's Welsh lands, and probably she urged him to do so. Support for such an hypothesis, however, comes only from her alms schedule after Roger's death. Each year, she generously distributed food to the poor on St Gregory's day (March 12), the anniversary of Roger's death. She may have felt Damory needed all the prayers he could garner, but it is tempting to see this as an acknowledgment that she encouraged his resistance to the king and the Despensers.

When Roger headed north to join Lancaster's forces, he left his wife, the children, and their household undefended. A few days before he died, Elizabeth was arrested at Usk. She and her children were confined at Barking Abbey, east of London, where the abbess was ordered to keep her within the walls.[97] Arrest and confinement were only a prelude to a host of problems Elizabeth would face in the four and a half years of Despenser triumph that were to follow. From another vantage point, however, these difficult years mark Elizabeth's emergence as an individual rather than a nearly invisible daughter, sister, or wife. The royal army crushed Lancaster's forces at the battle of Boroughbridge on March 16, 1322; the revolt ended with the barons and magnates who had opposed the king either captured or dead. Many who hoped for mercy or clemency instead faced Edward's vengeance. He executed Lancastrians, Northerners, and Marchers, often using their own lordships as the venue in order to terrorize neighbors and followers. Even the Marchers who had surrendered in January were kept in prison for long periods; wives and children were collected and imprisoned as well. Royal capriciousness, not even-handed justice, pervaded the atmosphere after Boroughbridge.[98]

Family loyalties were divided in 1321 and 1322. Roger Damory, for example, had led the opposition, while his brother adhered to the king. Across England, old friendships and family alliances were shattered, increasing the stress for those who lived in a world that had been based on family interests and loyalties. The defeated opposition fell into several categories. Damory had been judged a traitor, so his estates could be confiscated by the king. Hugh Audley escaped hanging only through the pleas of his wife, Margaret. Those who had surrendered early, as well as others of lesser rank and some special cases, were imprisoned with no immediate chance of freedom, though some magnates' followers could hope to pay their way back to normality. After 1322, recognizances thus figured more largely than the traditional ties to the Crown, as Edward forced survivors of the revolt to use this device to acknowledge huge fines to him. Failure to pay on schedule meant confiscation of property, giving the king a sustained weapon even against the nominally pardoned.[99] Widows whose husbands were executed should have had protection from full confiscation of family property, for their dower rights and inheritances were in theory guaranteed by law, and Edward at times did respect such rights.[100] But the world of the upper stratum of society was poisoned with fear and mistrust. Edward and the Despensers were now unhindered by even nominal opposition. Vast confiscations of property and the threat of further seizures shattered the economic security and political will of people throughout England. The judicial machinery used legal forms to mask the perversion of justice. Survivors were terrorized by an unprecedented number of executions, often by hanging, drawing, and quartering.[101] The agenda of the remnants of the opposition and their families rested on survival, on reacquiring economic bases, avoiding the king's or the Despensers' greed, and reestablishing relationships among peers.

Public records document dislocations and confiscations. Elizabeth provided a more personal account of the Despenser years in a secret memorandum dictated in May 1326.[102] Her purpose in recording her grievances will be discussed later; her recollections of the injustices and malevolent measures taken against her in 1322–1323 fit here chronologically. Nothing in the official documents contradicts her testimony. Elizabeth relates that she was captured at Usk before Roger's death, of which she learned at Barking. Her children shared her confinement; their safety and future determined her actions at every turn. The king held her lands and Roger's, but she could hope for restoration of her inheritance and dower, perhaps even the lands she and Roger had held jointly. Edward dangled such an offer before her, provided she complied with a scheme to enrich Despenser (though of course the demand was not couched in those terms). Issues arising from the tenure of Gower had ignited the Marchers' revolt, and in the summer of 1322 the lordship was in Edward's hands. In July, he presented Gower to Hugh and Eleanor Despenser, with its castles, towns, manors, and tenements.[103] He then demanded that Elizabeth exchange Gower with the Despensers for her more valuable lands centered on Usk. She asserted that Edward promised not only to restore her Clare heritage, her dower, and the lands held jointly with Roger, but also to provide her with other lands to make up for Gower's lesser value. However, a helpless prisoner frightened for her children, herself, and her inheritance, she had no choice but to agree to Edward's demands.[104] On July 10, she received license to give Usk to the Despensers; they were given a similar license to enfeoff her of Gower. After the exchange, Edward gave Elizabeth her inheritance and dower but only one manor of her jointure lands, and nothing to cover her losses from the Usk-Gower transfer. Equally nastily, Despenser ordered his men to strip Gower for "our profit" before the exchange and received a royal grant of the "corn, hay, grass, cattle and goods" at Usk. But the exchange won Elizabeth and her children their freedom, and after November 2, when Edward ordered the keepers of her lands to deliver them to her, she should have been able to begin rebuilding her life and estates.[105]

Edward invited Elizabeth to the Christmas festivities at York that year. According to her memorandum, she hoped he would release her jointure lands and remember his earlier promises. Instead, he tried to force demands on her including the quitclaim of Usk and its associated holdings. Her refusal led to her counselors' arrest and her flight from York. Edward seized all her lands in January, threatening that unless she submitted, "she will hold nothing of him."[106] Again she had no recourse, and finally complied because of her passionate attachment to her inheritance. Her reluctant acquiescence does not diminish her bravery in facing Edward's anger. She had done so at Amesbury while pregnant in 1317, and now did so again as a traitor's vulnerable young widow whom the king could consign at will to another marriage. She stood especially alone in 1322–23, when many friends and relatives were imprisoned or dead, her supporters few in number. As most of her old staff was taken into the king's service or was seeking more favorable prospects, Elizabeth also faced the need to recruit new householders and retainers. The few exceptions included Robert de Scales and John de Horsele, for whom she had obtained favors in 1317. Robert de Cheddeworth, constable at Clare in 1319, still served her, having represented her when she sought her Verdon dower in England and Ireland in 1316; his brother Thomas, a clerk, was her most trusted associate from at least 1323 to his death 25 years later.[107] Such men showed courage and loyalty by staying with the lady. Service with a prime Despenser victim offered little hope of reward or even a safe career.

Indeed, as Elizabeth faced property losses and royal reluctance to restore her estates, Hugh Despenser was showered with gifts; Edward pardoned all debts and arrears the Despensers owed the Exchequer because of the losses they had suffered. The largesse Hugh junior enjoyed dwarfed Gaveston's riches. Natalie Fryde estimates that Hugh amassed lands valued at over £3000 and goods worth above £1800—about 44 percent of his total wealth.[108] He soon surpassed the last earl of Gloucester in his Welsh holdings and net worth. Hugh's greed knew no limits, and in 1324 he promoted an essentially fraudulent plan to deprive Elizabeth of Gower. At Hugh's instigation, William de Braose brought a writ of novel disseisin against her to recover Gower. Given judicial cooperation with Despenser, Braose recovered Gower and gave it to Hugh Despenser senior, who presented the lands to his son.[109] Elizabeth petitioned parliaments for redress, but no grace or justice was forthcoming. She showed great courage in presenting her petitions; because father and son controlled judges and other officials, most injured parties waited until the Despensers were dead to seek redress. As the *Vita Edwardi Secundi* put it: "The harshness of the king has today increased so much that no one however great or wise dares to cross his will. Thus parliaments, colloquies and councils decide nothing these days. For the nobles of the realm, terrified by threats and penalties inflicted on others, let the king's will have free play."[110]

As the king collected, or tried to collect, his defeated opponents' debts, rebels' widows faced obstacles and delays in obtaining dower, often stingily apportioned when assigned at all. Most rebels' properties were forfeited; the king exploited them in businesslike fashion to increase his treasure or to reward his supporters. So Edward disposed of Roger Damory's former properties, including some he and Elizabeth had held in jointure: the king's cousin the earl of Richmond received Caythorpe and Robert de Insula Roger's London houses and rents, the elder Despenser got Kennington and Vauxhall, and Damory's lands in Yorkshire were parceled out too. The king presented priests to churches in Elizabeth's or Roger's gift: Hallaton, St Cross in Sudbury, Brettenham and Bishamwell. Repayment of Roger's debts enriched Edward, not Damory's heirs. In 1324 Elizabeth still had not entered Hallaton, the one jointure manor the king allowed her; claiming he was unsure of her rights, the keeper refused to admit her.[111]

In no respect was Elizabeth singled out for especially harsh treatment. She was treated shabbily, but suffered less than her sister Margaret in her person and her material situation.[112] The sisters' dilemma was especially poignant, as their husbands—especially the junior Despenser—pursued policies bound to damage the other sisters' interests. Some strains must have accompanied Hugh's spoliation of his sisters-in-law's lands but there are no indications in this period about the sisters' relationships with each other. Nor do we know if Eleanor encouraged Hugh's actions or tried to shield her sisters. Margaret's husband, Hugh Audley, was imprisoned from 1322 until 1326. The king limited any hint of fresh rebellion from the defeated opposition by inquiring into their old debts and those of their ancestors, and Audley seems to have been among those so pursued. The Audley estates were confiscated, the Welsh and Gloucestershire lands soon gravitating to Despenser control. In May 1322, Margaret was confined to Sempringham Priory with a maid and two yeomen; the king later allowed

her 5s. daily for her expenses. Her daughter Joan Gaveston died at Amesbury early in 1325, while Margaret was still at Sempringham.[113] Forced
separations or shared imprisonments illustrate the domestic tragedies of the
late years of Edward II's reign.

The eldest Clare sister, Eleanor Despenser, came to enjoy great wealth.
The king sent her expensive gifts and visited her often. She had borne
Hugh junior several children during their nearly 20 years of marriage, and
for his part Hugh led an active sex life both at home and at court, where
he may have been Edward's sexual partner. Indeed, a foreign chronicler asserted that Edward and his niece had an incestuous relationship, though no
English chronicler so much as hinted at the possibility.[114] Even if no such
ménage à trois was unfolding under her nose, Queen Isabella was developing an unshakable aversion to Eleanor, who had long been among her
ladies-in-waiting. This hostility perhaps dated from 1321 when Isabella
openly supported the Despensers' exile; it must have intensified by 1324,
when Eleanor began to act as a watchdog over the queen. This state of affairs evolved as Edward's rights in Gascony entangled him in a brief war
with France. He was alarmed at a French war following closely on yet another defeat at the hands of the Scots. English dependencies of French religious houses near the coast were evacuated, French aliens in England
were detained, and Isabella, French by birth, became an object of suspicion
and diplomatic maneuver. Her lands were taken into Edward's hands in
1324, though she was provided with funds for her maintenance. Isabella's
support of those crushed by Edward's victory of 1322, coupled with the
emergence of his new male favorite, must have led her to despise the Despensers. In this context, Eleanor began to act as a spy in Isabella's household,[115] but this lasted only until the spring of 1325 when Edward decided
to send Isabella to Paris to mediate the problems between himself and her
brother Charles IV. Eleanor Despenser stayed in England.

Meanwhile, the junior Despenser continued to expand his holdings in
Wales through intrigue and violence. In 1324 Edward gave him Talgarth
and Blaenllyfni Castle, forfeited by Roger Mortimer of Chirk. Elizabeth
Comyn surrendered her castle and manor of Goodrich under duress; as she
resided with the elder Despenser, she could easily be badgered into acquiescence, especially by threats of lifelong imprisonment and possible injury.
Elizabeth Comyn's co-heir to the late earl of Pembroke, Laurence Hastings, was in Hugh Despenser's ward by the king's gift; Hugh engineered an
unfair division of the estates favoring Hastings, who could then marry a
Despenser daughter. The earl's widow, Mary de St Pol, was thus cheated of
her dower in Pembroke, and claimed that the king and Despenser had deprived her of goods and chattels worth more than £20,000 in order to
force her to relinquish her late husband's bills, still unpaid by the Crown.[116]

Little in the Marches escaped Despenser's grasp; he did extend his property interests outside Wales, but nowhere near the same scale. The Despensers' hold on Edward, and his ability to function without baronial constraint, seemed firmly in place in 1324. The king's internal command of the realm faced no obvious threat, but the regime was based on fear rather than affection or even respect. In 1324 he feared leaving England unprotected to fight with his army in Gascony, and parliament failed to vote him funds. Hatred of the Despensers smoldered under the surface, for they had connived against small landholders as well as magnates. Hugh junior even excited the common people's ill-will; a rare, semi-comic moment in these years was a plot to kill him by sticking pins into his wax likeness. Potentially more dangerous to Edward were the many bishops who denied him full support because of past slights or substantial losses he had inflicted on them.[117]

Conditions must have seemed bleak in England in 1324, with little hope of improvement. No leader was visible who might coalesce the scattered bases of opposition. Yet rescue from the Despensers' tyranny was to be effected in the autumn of 1326 by a most unlikely agent—Queen Isabella. When she went to negotiate in France in 1325, her brother received her warmly, and negotiations proceeded smoothly. The English position was weak, given their losses in Gascony and the French king's position as overlord. Charles pressed for formal homage from Edward II, an obligation the latter postponed. If the *Vita Edwardi Secundi* is accurate, Edward was afraid to leave England, or at least the Despensers feared for their own security should the king leave them exposed to the hatred of the English. England was beset by lawlessness, but neither a total breakdown of order nor a serious threat of revolt seemed imminent.[118] A sense of insecurity perhaps blinded Edward and Hugh junior, who made a critical blunder in the summer of 1325. The king ordered his wife to return to England after a treaty between the two kings was sealed. Isabella stalled, showing no inclination to return to a situation where she was humiliated by the loss of her lands, the imprisonment of members of her household, and by the constant presence in her personal life of Hugh junior or his wife. Her attitude could have embarrassed Edward but, by herself, Isabella posed no threat. The supreme folly Edward and Hugh committed was to give her control of the 12-year-old Prince Edward. The king was unwilling to go to France for the homage required for Gascony. Finally he agreed to send his son to perform it, a plan to which the French king agreed after Edward II invested the prince with the title to the disputed territories. Young Edward arrived in France in September 1325 and did homage to his uncle. Isabella now had the heir to the throne securely at her side; they were beyond Despenser's grasp and could negotiate a return to England on her terms.[119] In Paris, the queen soon became the center of a group of disaffected English barons and clerics. Resident in France or among Isabella's entourage, their loyalty to their king had been broken by antagonism to Despenser or defeat in the 1322 revolt. In Paris, Isabella took a lover from this group: Roger Mortimer, a Marcher lord whose surrender to the king early in the 1322 revolt had opened a breach in the baronial defenses. Initially imprisoned in the Tower of London, Mortimer had escaped by drugging his guardian and had fled to France.

Chroniclers variously assign the initiative for invading England to the barons, Mortimer, or Isabella. Certainly she helped to procure funds for the plan, exchanging the dowry from her son's betrothal to Philippa of Hainaut for the military assistance of Philippa's father, Count William II.[120] By early spring in 1326, England was bracing for an assault from abroad. The king ordered coastal defenses strengthened and warned John Sturmy, admiral of the fleet guarding the eastern coast, of potential attacks. Castles were to be fortified and constables were to increase their vigilance to prevent prisoners from escaping. He was well advised to shore up his defenses, as some were refusing the call to arms by mid-September.[121] Edward failed to rally the English, who despised Despenser and had a rich assortment of grievances against years of misrule. Unlike his father and his son, Edward II never mastered the art of propaganda or the political acumen to build enduring loyalty. Conversely, and despite her French background, Isabella had won English sympathies by petitioning the king for leniency or pardons on behalf of people of non-noble rank, and interceding for monastic houses and individual clerics. Her political reputation rested on her 15 years of mediation between Edward and the baronial opposition. Hostility to the Despensers enhanced sympathy for Isabella, who was often seen as an injured wife. Several bishops supported her, either because she had worked for their promotion or because they were alienated from the regime. Genuine affection for her, and antagonism to the Despensers' politics and malpractices, permeated English attitudes in 1326.[122]

Naturally, however, Edward and the Despensers were not without allies; they had tamed the judiciary and firmly controlled the offices of state. Surprisingly, though, the regime failed to appoint sheriffs devoted to its interests, revealing a strange indifference to, or lack of understanding of, the importance of reliable local personnel.[123] Beyond that, Edward lacked the ability to stir men to brave deeds, perhaps because of his own unimpressive record in warfare and chivalric sport. He had defeated his opponents in 1322, but neglected thereafter to pacify or unify the realm, adopting instead harsh retaliatory measures that subdued his critics but evoked resentment, not respect. As would become glaringly evident in his followers' rapid defections to Isabella's banner when she landed in England, he had calamitously misjudged the depth of commitment to himself and his cause.

Among many others, Elizabeth de Burgh was ready to welcome deliverance at Isabella's hands. Little is known of her life from 1323 to 1326. She petitioned parliaments for the restoration of her lands, with no success; she appointed attorneys to see to her interests in Ireland. The king did appoint judicial commissions to inquire into the theft of her goods, unlawful hunting and fishing in her parks and fisheries, and assaults on her servants. The Gower-Usk exchange and Gower's loss surely cut into Elizabeth's income, but if she suffered financially from 1322 to 1327 she was not a pauper. She controlled many of her estates after 1323, though she was not compensated for their earlier plundering by royal officials. Her extensive Clare, dower, and jointure lands in Ireland provided healthy revenues. She had sufficient cash to lend £500 to a Gloucestershire man in 1324. In the lay subsidies taken in 1327 and 1332, representing moveables previously amassed, she was the highest taxpayer in several vills in Suffolk and Dorset.[124]

Elizabeth had lost her Welsh holdings, but regained most of her other possessions and was spared the full impact of Despenser's greed. Her sister Eleanor Despenser may have tried to soften Hugh's treatment of Elizabeth, though their sister Margaret remained incarcerated all through the Despenser years. Efforts by Queen Isabella to protect her friends would have been frustrated by 1325, if not before. Two other factors seem more critical to Elizabeth's relatively benign treatment. Edward II recalled his affection for Roger Damory at the latter's trial, and perhaps that memory made him contain Despenser's ambitions against Roger's widow. More important, few other Despenser victims had such powerful friends as Elizabeth's former father-in-law, the earl of Ulster, with whom she remained on close terms. Earl Richard had failed to defend Ireland against the Bruces, but still represented the best hope for royal interests there. The earl's continuing key role in Irish politics must have been what saved Elizabeth from the harshness meted out to other noblewomen. In her memorandum, she obliquely acknowledged that Hugh's cruelty against her was decreasing by 1325, though she impugned his motives. Probably she reoccupied some of her Welsh properties by renting them from Hugh, for her 1329–30 accounts note payment of £170 to Eleanor Despenser "for the preceding four years."[125]

Elizabeth's household accounts for the years of Despenser's ascendancy are unfortunately lost. She was, however, most likely living at Clare Castle in Suffolk during this period. Here she faced the problems of reestablishing a household, securing loyal counselors, and weaving a network of local relationships with neighbors. In this process she encountered some obstacles, for Despenser's tactics had touched some of those close to Elizabeth. In February 1326, for example, four knights acknowledged a debt of £200 to Hugh; a year later, after Edward II's deposition, a memorandum was attached to this recognizance noting that it was made to provide Hugh "security to have the body of Robert de Cheddeworth before him at a certain day. . . ." This man had served as constable at Clare, and also as Elizabeth's attorney. The town of Sudbury, where she held the manor, mills, and leet court, was forced into a huge recognizance to Despenser, later acknowledged to have been forced upon the townspeople.[126]

It was at Clare in May 1326 that Elizabeth dictated her secret indictment of the Despensers and her royal uncle, in her usual Anglo-Norman. The document's thrust is hostile to the junior Despenser, slightly less so against the king who had acquiesced in Hugh's fraudulent schemes. Elizabeth recounted with passion and indignation the injustices suffered at the hands of her uncle and brother-in-law, and also with a firm understanding of the legalistic maneuvers used against her. Her description of the fear she felt for herself, her lands, and her children arouses compassion, both when she was confined at Barking and when she was isolated from her counselors at York in 1322. By 1326, she knew Hugh junior was worried about his ill-gotten gains at her expense; he was offering compensation. Perhaps a note of hauteur surfaced as Elizabeth dismissed this overture as a ploy to deceive the people. She was truly eloquent as she hoped for a time "when grace was dispensed more openly and the law of the land better maintained and common to all."[127]

Publication of this document probably would have resulted in another confiscation of her estates, even a charge of treason. By concealing it, Elizabeth showed her awareness that she was gambling with her inheritance and her children's safety, an uncharacteristic risk she would have taken only with some reasonable chance of success. The timing of her protest thus suggests that she had foreknowledge of Isabella's projected invasion, which was anticipated long before it occurred in September 1326. Probably Elizabeth's hopes rested on news from Isabella or her companions. The likely sources were two noblewomen with the queen in France, countesses who with Isabella and Elizabeth remained a quartet of intimate friends to the ends of their days. Joan of Bar, countess of Surrey, was Elizabeth's cousin, another granddaughter of Edward I, and sufficiently prominent in Isabella's company that Edward II wrote her under his personal seal(*secretum sigullum*) about the course of events. Mary de St Pol, dowager countess of Pembroke, was Elizabeth's dearest friend, a fellow-victim of Despenser greed.[128] As the correspondents were women, letters among them would have seemed harmless to English authorities guarding the ports. (This assumes that port authorities were not always apprised of the king's personal correspondence).

Isabella sailed from Holland with an army of Hainauters, avoided contact with the English fleet, and landed unopposed in Suffolk. Most of Edward's defenders soon defected to her. While Elizabeth had anticipated Isabella's landing, she did not join her military operation across England. Though the date of Elizabeth's first contact with the queen is uncertain—the lady's 1326 roll begins on September 29, several days after Isabella landed—the queen's new or newly-revealed supporters soon appeared at Clare. These included Sir John Sturmy, the admiral who had so conveniently missed the queen's ships. Elizabeth equipped one man at a cost of £8 and sent him to join the queen's army, though others serving her were equipped and sent to Isabella on "the lady's secret business," Robert de Cheddeworth among them. The lady's response to the invasion was primarily personal. She wrote often to Isabella, the first time in late September. Couriers and messengers had problems locating addressees, who might be moving about rapidly; a messenger on horseback sent to the queen late in her campaign took 11 days for the round trip from Clare, probably because he had only a vague indication of "the Gloucester region" as his destination. The account that records Elizabeth's letters to Isabella also furnishes an insight into the circulation of news, such as when Elizabeth sent a servant to Cheddeworth in mid-October to report news from the queen's court.[129]

Isabella's army moved west in pursuit of Edward and the Despensers, capturing the elder Hugh and executing him at Bristol. Hugh junior and Edward fled into Wales, hoping to rally support. None materialized, and after Edward's English supporters melted away in October the fugitives wandered around Wales until they were captured in November. Edward was taken first to Monmouth Castle and then Kenilworth. Vengeance was reserved for Hugh junior, who was hanged and drawn as a traitor. The parts of his body were sent to various towns for display. In 1330 Edward III allowed "Hugh's friends" to remove his bones from London, Bristol, York, Carlisle, and Dover; his widow honorably buried them at Tewkesbury among her ancestors.[130] But hatred of Hugh junior did not end with his death; hostility could be vented on political rivals' wives and daughters as well. Eleanor was sent to the Tower of London, where the Crown paid her "reasonable" expenses. Her daughter Isabella, married to the earl of Arundel's son, was spared her sisters' enclosure; Margaret, Eleanor, and Joan were sent to convents at Whatton and Sempringham to be "veiled without delay, to remain for ever under the order and regular habit of that house . . . to be professed in the same as speedily as possible." It was no humiliation to be sent to a convent and veiled a nun. Edward I consigned the daughters of Welsh princes Llewelyn and David to English convents; Edward II sent Roger Mortimer's daughters to convents, though they were not veiled. The aim must have been to prevent the Despenser daughters' marriages being used to reestablish their family, or any potential husbands from claiming Despenser estates.[131] Hugh Despenser III, son of Hugh junior and Eleanor, held out in Caerphilly Castle for six months and, even after a pardon, he was imprisoned for four years.[132]

Prince Edward was declared keeper of the realm in late October 1326, but some device other than the fiction that Edward II was abroad was needed if Isabella was to remain in power. She convened a parliament at Westminster in January 1327; grievances against Edward II were encouraged by clever propaganda and fiery sermons by Isabella's episcopal supporters. The parliament deposed Edward II, a popular act of dubious legitimacy, which he only reluctantly accepted. Proclaimed king on January 25, Prince Edward was crowned on February 1. Edward III immediately proclaimed the king's peace, ordering all sheriffs, the wardens of the Cinque Ports, the bishop of Durham, the justices of Chester, North and South Wales and Ireland, the mayors and bailiffs of Winchester, York, and Canterbury, and "Elizabeth de Burgo's bailiffs of Sudbury" to proclaim the news.[133] Though the coronation legitimized the new conditions, the 14-year-old king was a titular ruler; Isabella was the dominant royal figure, but beset with critical problems. She had invaded England with a short-term agenda of crushing the Despensers and regaining her rightful place as queen. The achievement of her aims complicated her political and personal situations. Her lover, Roger Mortimer, was greedy for power. Within a year, he recovered his Welsh lands, was granted confiscated Welsh properties, was appointed to the powerful position of justice of Wales, and was later created earl of March. Few found him as amiable as did Isabella; their adultery, coupled with her own acquisitiveness, lost her popular affection. Just as Edward II was criticized for heaping wealth on favorites, so Isabella was blamed more for her own greed and Mortimer's than for her adultery.[134] Roger's ambition alienated Isabella's supporters including Henry, the new earl of Lancaster, who was edged out of his association with the young king. Isabella surely saw that as her son matured, his legitimate right to rule must impinge on Mortimer's ambitions.

Meanwhile, the deposed king proved embarrassing in captivity. Imprisoned in Berkeley Castle after April 1327, he was a dangerous focal point for discontent. He had few supporters, but even these were able to engineer two escape attempts. The former king was murdered at Berkeley Castle in September 1327. The murderers' methods of achieving their mission, and even the certainty of Edward's death, have fascinated chroniclers and historians ever since.[135] Isabella held a splendid funeral for her late husband in Gloucester Abbey on December 20, 1327; among the nobles present was the deceased's niece Elizabeth de Burgh. She left her daughters in the care of Lady Hastings and traveled from East Anglia to Gloucester for the ceremony. On the day of his father's funeral, Edward III ordered his escheator not to distrain Elizabeth as "the king has taken her homage," and it might have been on this occasion that she formally did homage to the new king, though it was late for such recognition.[136]

The end of Edward II's reign and the Despensers' fall had ended any immediate threats to Elizabeth's prosperity, but her problems, like those of any aristocratic widow, were complex and persistent. In 1327–1328, both foreign and domestic strife touched her through her children rather than her estates. The Scots renewed warfare and defeated the English, who lacked the resources for successful military action. Responsibility for the war's outcome lay with Isabella and Mortimer, but Edward III had to accept humiliatingly unfavorable terms with the Scots. The treaty was to be confirmed by the marriage of his sister Joan to Robert Bruce's son David. The elder Bruce had often intervened in Irish affairs, and was the uncle by marriage of Elizabeth's son, William de Burgh, now about to take over his legacy as earl of Ulster. The treaty also threatened many English nobles, for it renounced their claims to Scottish territories without hope of compensation. These nobles joined with others, troubled by Mortimer's political ascendancy, in a brief clash known as the rebellion of Earl Henry of Lancaster.[137] This rebellion was more political than military; it failed to shake the positions of Isabella and Mortimer, and soon ended with a royal victory. It marked the end of Lancastrian support for Isabella and reinforced her reliance on Mortimer, who now paraded his power more shamelessly and tactlessly.

The Lancastrian rebellion placed Elizabeth de Burgh in an awkward position, for a solid network of relations existed between herself and Earl Henry of Lancaster. Her son, William de Burgh had just married the earl's daughter Matilda, and the earl supported William's early inheritance of the lands of his grandfather, the earl of Ulster. William and the earl's son, Henry of Grosmont, were close friends and fellow tourneyers. Elizabeth's daughter, Isabella de Verdon, was married to Henry Ferrers, a prominent Lancastrian supporter during the earl's brief rebellion, and Margery de Verdon, Elizabeth's youngest stepdaughter, was married to William le Blount, one of Earl Henry's attorneys.[138] None of these connections appear to have strained Elizabeth's friendship with Queen Isabella. The two women shared spiritual affinity; the queen was godmother to Elizabeth's daughter Isabella de Verdon, and the queen controlled her goddaughter's marriage since it had belonged to Roger Damory, whose wardships were forfeit to the Crown in 1322. The queen had visited Elizabeth during her Damory marriage; their contacts were probably more frequent than the fragmentary Clare accounts suggest. In 1318 Isabella had supported the court party, which included Damory. She and Elizabeth had lost property, chattels, and status through Despenser's agency, so they were linked by common enmity as well as sympathy. Most important, Isabella's triumph had led quickly to the restoration of Elizabeth's Welsh lands around Usk.[139]

Elizabeth's friendship with Isabella could expedite financial as well as political matters. Despite recovery of her Welsh lands, Elizabeth's finances were still tangled after the Despenser years. The Crown claimed several thousand pounds in Roger Damory's debts, and fines against Roger were demanded from his widow.[140] Elizabeth naturally wished to improve her finances, especially with the extra expenses incurred in 1327–28 for her son's knighting and Irish enterprises. She needed as well to cultivate relations with Roger Mortimer, whose ascendancy in the Marches could threaten her as much as Despenser's had. Mortimer and Verdon lands were, moreover, closely intertwined in Louth and Meath in Ireland, where Elizabeth had dower rights and her daughter Isabella had an inheritance. Elizabeth's Irish attorney could not hope to challenge Mortimer, so cordiality with the queen's lover had to prevail.

Elizabeth was caught between the royal and Lancastrian camps with their different objectives, but for once her sex was advantageous: as a woman, she was not expected to field an army, participate in parliament, or serve as a royal advisor. Apparently she did not dwell on the various demands on her allegiance, but pressed hard to gain specific objectives. First, her children's future demanded her attention, and particularly that of her son, William de Burgh, heir to the earldom of Ulster after Earl Richard died in July 1326. Ulster had never fully recovered from the Bruce invasion, and declined further after the old earl's death. Elizabeth followed the situation closely to safeguard her own interests as well as her son's; in August 1326 she sent letters to the Irish magnates. Soon thereafter, she sent a trusted confidant, Thomas de Cheddeworth, to assess the situation. He reported that the decline could be halted if young William were knighted and sent to Ireland with military support. The knighting itself, proper equipment, gifts to bestow when taking homage, and preparations for the expedition were expensive, so the lady collected an aid to knight her son. It was a rather old-fashioned practice rapidly falling into desuetude, but remained legal; it netted a bit over £800, more than half William's expenses.[141]

The situation of Elizabeth's daughters changed too, for both were married in 1327 or 1328, though initially they remained with their mother.[142] Elizabeth's freedom to negotiate unions was minimal as both marriages belonged to the Crown, but she did collect an aid for her elder daughter's marriage in 1327–28. Married to Henry Ferrers, Isabella de Verdon had inherited substantial lands from her father. Elizabeth probably requested a

royal commission to reextend the Verdon lands, as the earlier division may
have slighted Isabella. The commission began work in February 1328, but
final disposition of the estates took some years.[143] Elizabeth Damory was
a less attractive partner; almost all her inheritance was in jointure lands her
mother held for life. Elizabeth supplied her a 500-mark dower, and she
married John Bardolf in 1327. As his father was alive, John Bardolf's holdings were minimal, so the young couple remained partly dependent on
Elizabeth, and as Elizabeth Damory's material future depended on the disposition of Roger's lands, tenacity in pursuing Damory claims was required. The marriage cost the lady more than the dower, as she promised
an annual pension to the groom's father, Thomas Bardolf, about the time
of the marriage. But Thomas did prove a useful contact. The fines levied
on Elizabeth by duress at Despenser's instigation in 1322 should have been
canceled by 1327.[144] Details remained to be settled in 1329, however, for
Thomas Bardolf joined in a commission to investigate the fines. Another
miscarriage of justice from the old regime was the demand that Elizabeth
pay all her brother's debts; in 1327 they were apportioned among all the
Clare sisters. Meanwhile, recovery of the Welsh estates and her jointure
lands greatly improved Elizabeth's finances.[145]

As Elizabeth reordered her life, Edward III was growing uncomfortable
with the regime of his mother, Isabella, and her lover. That the couple
made no attempt to conceal the liaison must have mortified the maturing
Edward; power and responsibility were denied him. Mortimer's arrogant
execution of the king's uncle Earl Edmund of Kent, on false charges of
treason in May 1330, must have been particularly repulsive to Edward. Between March and October 1330 Edward and his retainer William Montague,[146] plotted to overthrow Isabella and Mortimer. Their chance came
at a meeting of the Great Council at Nottingham in October. Edward's
followers covertly entered Nottingham Castle and seized Mortimer, who
was soon executed for treason. The way was open for Edward to rule as
well as reign. Isabella retired from public life but was not punished.

The coup of October 1330 opened a new era in English history. The
kingdom's problems did not evaporate, but a more settled atmosphere
spread across the land. Edward extended forgiveness to a host of people
who could have been labeled enemies, but were instead welcomed into his
service. Greed persisted, but never on the scale of Edward II's reign or
Queen Isabella's interlude. In a sense, Edward linked acquisitiveness with
his military designs, offering warriors both booty and glory. He, himself,
became the model for chivalric deeds and values, a genuinely popular
monarch for most of his long reign. Edward III would fall short of great-
ness as a monarch, but at least offered a measure of domestic tranquillity,
which had been lacking for several decades.

The Long, Last Widowhood

By 1330, then, Elizabeth's life encompassed two elements that remained constant until her death in 1360: a regime that generally treated her with honor and deference, and her position as a wealthy widow. For a four-teenth-century woman, widowhood provided the only real route to independence and liberation from male control. One contemporary female viewed widowhood with some enthusiasm: "Oh good lord, how is it that widows have a greater reward than married folk? How much better and more comfortable an estate we widows have than we had in marriage. . . ." This optimistic view depended on sufficient material assets, and Elizabeth had these: her Verdon dower, jointure lands from the Burgh and Damory unions, and her Clare holdings ensured an income that raised her financially even above some earls. Widowhood did not diminish her properties and meant that she, not a spouse, managed her assets. The sentimentality and romance often associated with modern marriage had not permeated medieval sensibilities, though it was beginning to be seen in literature. Elizabeth may have had cordial and affectionate relationships in her marriages, but her husbands' deaths probably failed to touch her in a deep, emotional sense. Remaining a widow seemed important to her, but a fourth, forced marriage remained possible. At some point before 1340, she solved the problem by taking a vow of chastity, which ensured a perpetual widowhood. The vow represented no anti-male bias, but was rather a safety measure for her person and her enjoyment of the Clare inheritance. The vow of chastity offered by the Church aimed to protect a female who chose a life of sexual abstinence, preferred by clerics, while remaining in the secular world. The vow was solemnly sworn before a bishop or archbishop, who gave the woman a plain ring and a simple outfit of russet cloth symbolizing retirement from worldly entanglements.[147] (Elizabeth wore russet gowns on occasion, but never dressed solely in this penitential costume). The Church hoped to promote an ascetic ideal, but the ceremony could be used for protection against the threat of an unwanted union. Though she was pious, Elizabeth's primary purpose in taking her vow was to insure her own independence.

If her early years had been adventurous, her later life was a time of achievement requiring diligence, thoughtfulness, and political astuteness. After 1327, Elizabeth faced critical issues that demanded her energetic intervention. Her children were all married but maternal concerns persisted, especially for her son, William. Troubles in Ireland continued after his arrival, exacerbated perhaps by his youth and inexperience. He needed to impose order on his inheritance, to contend with native Irish ambitions, to discipline his cousins, especially in Connacht, and to resolve Anglo-Irish quarrels.[148] Presumably Elizabeth worked for his interests behind the scenes. In August 1330, she entertained King Edward III at Caythorpe, and undoubtedly argued for royal support of her son. William visited Edward in the spring of 1331, when Edward appointed him his deputy in Ireland, and again that November. On trips to England, William visited his mother as well as the court.[149] In 1332, the king summoned his nobles, who were absentee Irish landholders, to prepare to join him on a Michaelmas expedition to Ireland, but the army never sailed because the Scots renewed hostilities in northern England. One chronicler suggested the earl of Ulster planned to join the king at Berwick with an Irish contingent, but this expedition never materialized. William was murdered in Ireland by his own men on June 6, 1333. Contemporaries ascribed the act to revenge by William's cousin Jill, whose brother had starved to death in the earl's prison, or Scottish sympathizers reluctant to move against their allies. A contemporary chronicler, Friar Clyn, wrote that William had a fine, natural ability and character and loved peace. Modern assessments of him differ. Orpen labels the murder a tragedy, noting that William's statesmanlike qualities overrode his kinsmen's aims when he saw these to be wrong. In contrast, Robin Frame sees his behavior toward tenants and kin as abrasive and apt to provoke vengeful feelings.[150]

After William's death his mother acted swiftly regarding lands he would have inherited from her. In October 1333, four months after the murder, Elizabeth secured a royal license to devise a large portion of her Clare properties by use. The use allowed a person to enfeoff trusted associates with properties which they then regranted to the original holder for life, after which the lands reverted to persons named, who might not be the lawful heirs. Land could not be conveyed by will in this period, but the use evaded that prohibition and allowed the choice of one's beneficiaries.[151] The license granted Elizabeth named her trusted clerk Thomas de Cheddeworth and her squire Henry de Colyngham as the enfeofees for "the castles and manors of Usk and Kaerlion and the manors of Liswyry, Little Tynterne, New Grange, Little Lantrissan, Trillek, Troye, Lancom and Woundy and of the manor of Berdefeld, co. Essex," as well as advowsons and religious patronage rights in Wales. By these actions, nearly the whole of her Welsh lands and Bardfield manor would pass at her death to her daughter Isabella and her son-in-law Henry Ferrers. A second use in 1337 diverted the castle of Tregrug to the Ferrers.[152] Clare Castle and its manor, the Dorset estates centered on Cranborne, scattered Clare holdings and various courts, advowsons, knights' fees, and other rights would descend to her granddaughter Elizabeth de Burgh. Young Elizabeth could also expect her father's Ulster inheritance, including some manors in England, as well as her grandmother's Clare lands in Kilkenny.

Only the bare documents remain, but we can speculate on Elizabeth's motives. She knew her granddaughter would not lack for land, though some of the Irish lands were currently worthless through war damage and native Irish denial of access to collect profits.[153] The lady still managed to take profits from her Irish lands, however, and assumed that with good management, her granddaughter could too. Elizabeth must have wanted a more affluent life for her daughter Isabella and for Henry; diverting part of her Clare lands to them would achieve this without unduly depriving her granddaughter. Edward III concurred because of his kinship to the lady and for Henry's devoted service. Personal affection played a role too, as a few years later Henry received a royal grant "in consideration of his service in continually dwelling by his [Edward's] side."[154] Edward's assent to the license for the use cost him little, pleased an important cousin, and benefited a trusted official, but in the end, Elizabeth's tactic failed because of Ferrer's early death and Edward's desire to enrich his own son. By 1341, he saw the lady's granddaughter Elizabeth as a choice bride for his second son, Lionel of Antwerp. She was eight and he was three when their betrothal was celebrated at Dunstable. Grandmother Elizabeth found occasion to visit Wales in 1341–42, thereby missing the engagement festivities.[155] Perhaps this was merely an example of her normal pattern of avoiding visits to court or perhaps it mirrored concern over long-term royal objectives for the Clare lands.

Elizabeth's daughter Elizabeth Damory, wed to John Bardolf, was the least wealthy of her children. John Bardolf's ties to the lady were seemingly affectionate, but she likely saw that his chances at a major national role were slight. Probably she had decided that Henry Ferrers was a likelier candidate to take over part of the Clare heritage. As the nobility normally accepted some inequality amongst their children's inheritances, Elizabeth thus made no effort to enrich the Bardolfs, but she did surrender Kennington and Vauxhall, in Surrey, to the Crown in exchange for Ilketshall and Clopton in Suffolk, to be held by the lady in her lifetime and the Bardolfs after her death.[156] In modern terms this would be a windfall for the Crown: lands in the London suburbs for rural estates. The medieval situation differed and probably had benefits for the lady in administrative coherence and immediate profitability. The Bardolfs, with their East Anglian orientation, would appreciate the same advantage.

Elizabeth had recovered lands lost after the Contrariant's defeat, and now turned to recovering Edward II's debts to Damory. A promising exchange took place in 1331 when the king granted a banker, Anthony Pessagno, various payments and future issues of revenue in Aquitaine and Cornwall to pay Edward II's old debts; Pessagno assigned £1,500 of the moneys to Elizabeth to discharge an old debt owed Damory. She promptly used the money to purchase the wardship of Laurence Hastings, an heir of Aymer de Valence, earl of Pembroke. The wardship included the castles and towns of Pembroke and Tenby, Castle Martin, and various appurtenances. The heir was aged about 11 years; the grant promised recompense if Elizabeth failed to gain the whole span of Laurence's minority. This issue surfaced in 1339 when the king granted early custody to Laurence, an order superseded on Elizabeth's petition as "it seemed that Elizabeth could not be amoved from that custody against her will before Laurence has come of age." As the ward had been held by Hugh Despenser junior, Elizabeth may have wanted to stress the new conditions, or possibly Elizabeth planned to let Mary de St Pol enjoy her title in the heart of Pembroke by giving her a residence close to her own at Usk. This is surmise, as nothing in her accounts shows income or much staff activity in the Pembroke lands.[157] Elizabeth must have allowed personal ends to intrude on financial ones in seeking the Hastings' wardship and tenaciously retaining it when the king decided to invest the heir a bit early.

Elizabeth persisted in recouping as much as possible from the past. In June 1334, Edward III pardoned £12,000 Roger Damory had pledged in recognizances to the Despensers, and which had subsequently escheated to the Crown. As late as 1338, she petitioned Edward about a gold and silver vessel pledged by Roger to the Bardi merchant society, but which Edward II had taken for his own use. The lady sought restitution from the Crown, and Edward III agreed to pay her its stated value, £141 14s. 4d. Elizabeth labored for 18 years to expunge Roger's debts, and in 1337 persuaded the king to grant her a lifetime respite so the debts would not be collected until after her death. A happier solution prevailed when, in 1340, Edward notified her that she was quit of all debts relating to Damory. Other financial problems lingered from earlier years. She was being distrained for moneys from part of her Clare purparty that she claimed never to have received; the Clare sisters were being distrained over their father's debts to Edward I. As late as 1343, the Dublin exchequer was singling out Elizabeth's Clare lands in Ireland and charging her the whole sum of debts on lands from her brother, Gilbert, that had been divided among the sisters. Elizabeth sought a remedy from the king; he ordered the Irish exchequer to investigate her claims and proceed to a fair apportionment.[158] Elizabeth's ties with the king eased her financial burdens in Ireland over many years as she received royal grants allowing her to schedule partial payments over long periods rather than meeting her obligations promptly. The key to Elizabeth's favorable treatment was her relationship to the king. The documents identify her as "the king's kinswoman" or even note that he was "wishing to shew favour to his said kinswoman."[159]

Not all Elizabeth's financial and legal problems were rooted in the past. Dorset was a case in point. Her ports, Portland and Weymouth, were vulnerable when a French invasion seemed imminent at the outset of the Hundred Years' War. After some meddling by royal commissioners of array, Elizabeth preferred "to provide for the safe custody of the island [Portland] herself." To avoid complications, she requested an exemplification of her possessions and rights in Portland and Weymouth and other liberties and lands in Dorset held by and acknowledged as her father's in 1280. The timing of the exemplification suggests it was related to a case where her cause needed bolstering. Edward III thought Elizabeth's men had seized two French ships in Weymouth, and wanted their wool and other goods forfeit. The ships apparently were English, for in 1342 she faced the owner's suit for restitution—and a king who wanted full disclosure. Perhaps she hoped the exemplification might support her position. She had the foresight in 1335 to pay for a license to grant lands in Dorset to Nicholas Pyk, who now served on the royal commission; in 1343 he received a squire's livery from her.[160] Another threat to the lady's Dorset property occurred when one Laurence Aynel procured a writ of novel disseisin against her, claiming 2500 acres of heath. At issue was whether the land lay in Dorset or Southampton. Elizabeth argued for the former, presumably as she had servants and friends in key positions in that shire. The king ordered the boundaries perambulated, but the outcome is uncertain.[161]

The Portland-Weymouth episode shows Elizabeth at the edge of legality. She stepped over it in 1340, when she evaded collectors of a parliamentary grant of 20,000 sacks of wool, claiming the wool kept at Caythorpe was hers, when in fact it had been stored there to escape collection.[162] Resistance to the wool-collectors was widespread, but as a widow who often looked to the king for favors, Elizabeth misread the situation. Once at war with France, Edward III thirsted to live out his chivalric ambitions; instead, in 1339–1340, financial constraint led to inaction and humiliating truces. The commons may have misunderstood his craving for glory but Elizabeth, nurtured in a noble atmosphere, had few excuses for seemingly misjudging the king's passion. Alienating him over a few sacks of wool seems rather foolish. Several of her friends were prominent in his war councils: Bishop Burghersh, the earl of Northampton, young Henry of Lancaster (now earl of Derby), and her favorite son-in-law, Henry Ferrers. Elizabeth had close associations with these men, but her normally sharp political instincts somehow failed her. Perhaps she was lulled into complacency by other friends, men who bore the brunt of Edward's wrath on his sudden return to England in November 1340. He dismissed Nicholas de la Beche, her old Damory associate; John de St Pol, keeper of the rolls and on Elizabeth's livery list in 1343, was imprisoned; John de Stonor and John de Shardelowe, royal justices Elizabeth liveried, were arrested.[163] Perhaps she had hoped to rely on these men to avoid penalties for tax evasion. No penalties are in fact recorded for her, as Edward III did not hold grudges like his father; by 1343 she reappeared in royal documents as his kinswoman.

Elizabeth acquired land, rents, and facilities in Standon in 1332 but, unlike many nobles, rarely expanded her lands. She took an active interest in her estates, however, granting a charter to Sudbury and petitioning the Crown for liberties for Usk and Caerleon. She looked to the king for commissions of oyer and terminer to remedy assaults on her men or theft on her estates. These commissions tried a single case from indictment to judgment; one commissioner usually was a judge from the central courts, but local worthies often participated. Proceedings took place locally and offered plaintiffs swift remedy, especially against criminal trespasses. Such commissions were appointed for a range of Elizabeth's suits: carrying off goods from lands in Suffolk, Norfolk, Essex, and Hertford, theft of trees in Gloucester, trespasses in Kent. She also brought action against men who seized cattle she had taken as fines in Caythorpe, troubled her Friday market there, poached her game, and assaulted her servants.[164]

In most of these cases, Elizabeth was able to place as judges men who wore her livery or served on her council. Some belonged to her household, a broad term covering the elite of her staff, her corps of servants, resident clerics, and occasional family members. She achieved coherence in this disparate group by an annual award of livery, which identified each person with the lady. Most nobles supplied householders and associates with elaborate outfits yearly. Elizabeth presented her great livery in the Christmas season after months of planning, shopping, and cloth preparation. Her extant livery list for 1343 names over 250 men and women who received livery suitable to their household status and relationship to her.[165] Livery served several purposes. The simplest was providing clothing for retainers; like other nobles, Elizabeth advertised her prestige and good lordship by dispensing clothing and furs. Donors also had the emotional satisfaction of bestowing gifts, but, as there was no reciprocity, livery promoted recipients' ties of dependency. Livery thus reminded donor and recipient of their relationship in a manner offering rewards to each.

Other secular routines are less obvious. Gift-giving and tips were customary for the nobility. Elizabeth gave gifts to noble friends, offered lavish hospitality to guests, and routinely tipped others' servants who brought her letters or gifts. She rewarded her servants for special performance, perhaps a small sum of money or new shoes. By making the decisions her staff implemented, she played a key role in managing these activities. She dictated many of the constant letters from the Clare household to friends, neighbors, and merchants. Presiding at meals, she set the tone of daily life. Like many of her peers, Elizabeth renovated her residences, especially Clare and Bardfield; accounts from the early 1340s abound in the cost of nails, laths, tiles, lime, locks, and gutters. Her chamber, that of her daughter, and the rooms of several of her staff were altered and work done on the gatehouse and outbuildings. She hired both general workers and first-rate craftsmen, four of whom are noted as architects. Clearly Elizabeth was a busy woman, but she found time for leisure: she read or was read to, played games, went hawking, and enjoyed music.[166] The household's devotional routine persisted year after year, as the Church calendar alternated penitential periods with festal occasions. More strictly than some clerical establishments, Elizabeth's household served no meat on Wednesdays, Fridays, or Saturdays.[167] She and her household observed Lenten abstinence, fasting on Good Friday, and vigils before certain feast days. While the whole Christian community observed great feasts such as Christmas and Easter, the many other feasts gave heads of households a choice in observing those most precious in their lives. Elizabeth, for example, showed a lasting preference for the Purification of the Virgin and the Feast of Corpus Christi. Some of these feasts are noted in her accounts; others are inferred from added luxury dishes. Beyond the routine of feast and fast, her pious acts included feeding the poor, an activity that escalated in her last decade.

Elizabeth spent most years at Clare or Bardfield in East Anglia. Before 1348 she typically went to Clare in late January, to Anglesey Priory for Lent and Easter, and back to Clare or Bardfield for summers and autumns.[168] In 1338, 1341, and 1348 (and perhaps other undocumented years) she visited her Welsh estates around Usk.[169] After 1353 she spent long periods at a house she built by the Minoress Convent at Aldgate in London. She rarely went to her Dorset lands, to the Verdon lands in the Midlands, or the Damory lands in the Northeast. At least 20 times between 1328 and 1347 she visited Anglesey, a small, Augustinian priory near Cambridge.[170] The Clares had long been the house's patrons, but the lady preferred it for more than familial reasons. Her friend Mary de St Pol often resided nearby at Anstey or Fotheringhay, or at Denny and Waterbeach, Minoress houses Mary patronized, and in the 1330s Anglesey was convenient for business concerning her collegiate foundation at Cambridge University. The convent was more than a handy *pied-à-terre,* however; she built a house and outbuildings for herself there, and founded a chantry honoring the Blessed Virgin.

In the 1330s and 1340s Elizabeth was generous to several religious houses, but she dithered over the recipients of four advowsons for which she had mortmain licenses: Litlington and Duxford(Duxworth) in Cambridge, Gransden in Huntingdon, and Bricham in Norfolk. She did not activate the licenses as soon as she obtained them, but repeatedly changed her mind about their disposition. Litlington was destined for the prior and convent of Ely in 1333, but was diverted in 1336 for the benefit of University Hall, later Clare College, at Cambridge University. The dean and chapter of St Paul's in London expected the Bricham advowson in 1333; in 1336 the lady gave it to the prior and convent of Ely. St Paul's seemed to recoup its loss when she obtained license to grant them the Gransden advowson in 1336, but by 1343 the Minoresses at Denny seemed more deserving. The sisters at Denny lost out in turn when Clare College got the Gransden advowson in 1346, the year Elizabeth purchased the Duxford advowson to add to her college's endowment.[171] Others changed the beneficiaries of their mortmain licenses, but the frequency of Elizabeth's move may have outdone them. She must have weighed the benefits each recipient could provide, deciding in the end that Clare College would receive three of the four advowsons. (As well as the advowsons, she bestowed the right to appropriate the churches, which gave recipients an annual income.) Resources for grand benefactions were less plentiful than in earlier periods, so donors throughout England exercised caution in their largesse. Yet they felt keenly a need to garner prayers for their souls, and Elizabeth planned for that need. In 1337 she received a royal grant allowing her executors "free administration of her jewels and other goods, to dispose of these for the saving of her soul and as her will shall direct."[172]

Elizabeth's Franciscan sympathies are indicated by her foundation at Walsingham, for which she received mortmain license in February 1347. Papal approval, requested by King Edward and Queen Philippa, came in October 1347; the friars were in residence by July 1348, when a license to acquire another small piece of land was issued, with a further license in May 1351.[173] The friars' early occupation was possible as Elizabeth perhaps began construction before the mortmain license was issued. Two prominent builders' names appear often in her accounts between October 1346 and January 1348: Master John atte Grene and Master John Ramsey, master masons known for work on Norwich cathedral's cloisters and Ely Cathedral's octagon. Her choice of Grene and Ramsey was perhaps assisted by the goldsmith Alan of Walsingham, sacrist and later prior of Ely, often credited with the fourteenth-century building program there; Elizabeth maintained cordial relations with Alan and his predecessor, John of Crauden. That Grene saw her at least three times in the months before she visited Walsingham, and Ramsey at least nine, implies she kept a good deal of control over the project. With friends and servants, she made the celebratory trip to Walsingham in June 1347.[174]

The sum of Elizabeth's good works by the end of 1347 was imposing. She had founded chantries, rescued Cambridge's ailing University Hall, and had begun its transformation into the more robust Clare Hall. She had

made financial gifts to several convents, and her Franciscan foundation was
a reality. She would have been justified in having feelings of achievement
and high hopes for the future. Such hopes faltered, however, with the coming of the Black Death to England in the summer of 1348. Elizabeth journeyed to Wales that spring with part of her household. Summer resembled
a homecoming, as friends arrived to welcome her. The bishop of Llandaff,
always appreciative of her hospitality, came on June 9. Later that month
Lady Berkeley, Lady Bluet, and Lady Monthermer spent several days,
quickly followed by Hugh Despenser III, to be joined by Gilbert Despenser, a member of the lady's *familia*. The company of friends pleased
Elizabeth, who spent time in Llantrisant before receiving Hugh, Gilbert,
and the Ladies Berkeley and Zouche at Tregrug.[175] During the summer
she moved among her Welsh estates at Usk, Trelleck, Tregrug and Tintern,
with friends visiting at each house. The Despensers must have enjoyed
their aunt for they kept returning, as Lady Monthermer did at least once.
The countess of Devon and Sir John Mowbray found Elizabeth at Tintern,
while Ralph Stafford (young Margaret Audley's husband) saw her at Trelleck. The summer of 1348 seems to have been a time of convivial inter-
change, with perhaps a bit of business transacted now and then.

News of the plague must have reached Elizabeth in late summer, for her
officials usually kept her well-informed. Her economic interests were directly involved, for the plague entered England at her port city of Weymouth. The contagion reached London in late September, and Bristol
soon after. Though by midwinter death rates were already high in Gloucestershire, Wales across the Severn was mostly spared until March 1349.[176]
There had been epidemics earlier in the fourteenth century, but familiar-
ity with widespread death does not immunize against fears in later epidemics. Little in the Clare accounts, however, suggests major deviations
from normal activity between fall 1348 and summer 1349. The pace of social life ebbed, though friends still visited. The countess of Pembroke visited Usk for three days in October 1348; she and Elizabeth often enjoyed
each other's company in the early autumn, and the Black Death did not
deter them. In October the lady honored the abbot of Evesham with a
feast, with herons and egrets. As his house suffered heavy mortality, he
could have given eyewitness accounts of the plague's ravages.[177] Bishop
John Paschal of Llandaff visited in December and March, but the only important noble visitor between October 1348 and April 1349 was the lady's
neighbor, Lord Mortimer, who spent two days at Usk in April.

The household maintained a normal round of feast and fast. Holidays
were celebrated with meals of swan, bittern, egret, and heron in addition
to game. Consumption of herons reached exceptional levels, with 53
served between October and July. The householders who normally

hunted game for pleasure or for the table still went to Trelleck with coursing dogs and greyhounds in the winter of 1348–49. As a great household
continually needed food and supplies, the lady's servants traveled to market towns and made purchases like those of pre-plague years, but now
with the added burden of finding new markets.[178] Consumption rates remained normal. The pantry baked 24 times between June 6 and September 29 in 1349, at least 1120 loaves each time; ale was brewed 12 times in
the same period, with the smallest batch being 880 gallons. Rushes to
strew on the castle floor and decorated dishes for festive meals continued
to be available. Carpenters and coopers were hired in for repair jobs at
Usk, and men came to clean the latrines. Woodsmen chopped trees at
Wellok for transport to Usk, and boys could be found to guard the beef
larder throughout the period.[179] Overall, Elizabeth's responses to the
plague combined caution and continuity. She apparently stayed within the
castle walls, but welcomed the few clerical and noble guests who ventured
to call; the lists of food consumed show festive signs amid the horrors of
widespread mortality. She sent her servants to disease-ravaged areas and
undoubtedly had contact with them when they returned, for she would
have lost the aura of good lordship if she had isolated herself from her dependents. Elizabeth may be faulted for risking servants to obtain such luxuries as Vernach wine and spices in London, but other mundane buying
trips were needed to supply the household. Perhaps she followed her routines fatalistically, assuming God would pursue His plans without reference to her actions or desires.

The accounts reveal no plague deaths among household or tenantry,
either in Wales or elsewhere on the Clare estates. The household rolls'
purpose was to record financial details, not personnel changes; servants'
deaths were noted only when Elizabeth paid for masses for their souls,
costs normally covered by her privy purse, the accounts of which seldom
have survived.[180] The rolls note only two illnesses in 1348–49. John
Havering, probably a marshalsea page, was sick in January, but appears
again in the 1349–50 rolls. William atte Stour, a groom at the Usk marshalsea reported sick in March 1349; as he disappears thereafter, he was
perhaps a plague victim.[181] Grain storage areas were prime habitats for
rats, so marshalsea personnel likely ran a high risk of infection. In general,
the 1348–49 plague tended to strike lightly at the nobility and wealthier
citizens, but Elizabeth's friends and family were not insulated from death.
Three of her summer 1348 guests were dead by spring 1349: Ladies Bluet
and Monthermer and the lady's nephew, Hugh Despenser III, who died
in February 1349. Her daughter Isabella Ferrers also died that year in East
Anglia. Post mortem inquisitions do not state a cause of death, however,
so these deaths may only have been coincidental with the pestilence. The

months of seclusion at Usk were over by July 1349, when Elizabeth moved to Tregrug for a week. Sisters of the Usk convent visited later that month, and noble visitors began their social çalls. Lady Despenser visited in July, August, and September, Lord and Lady Stafford twice each in August, and the earl of Salisbury in September. The lady and Mary de St Pol shared four days in September at Usk and Tregrug. Edward III hunted at Trelleck on September 12; Elizabeth sent him bread, wine, and a selection of salmon, pike, bream, and eels.[182]

The household arranged Elizabeth's trip to Hereford in October 1349. She left Usk on October 19, going by stages to Troy, Munkeaton, and Bolingchep (or Bolingchop), where she stayed four days at a manor of the dean and chapter of Hereford Cathedral.[183] The lady entertained the king and the Prince of Wales on October 25 and departed the next day for Usk, arriving on October 29. The king had hunted at her Trelleck manor in September, but she had not gone that short distance to see him then; a month later, she entertained him near Hereford at great cost. The accounts suggest no reason for the trip, but it probably related to her Ferrers grandchildren. A few days earlier the king and council granted William Ferrers some of his inheritance, though he was a minor; his sister Elizabeth de Atthele first appeared in the lady's household that month, and the other Ferrers sister, Philippa Beauchamp, joined her by May 1351.[184] With both their parents dead, Elizabeth was naturally concerned for her grandchildren's futures, and with reason. The original use to benefit the Ferrers assumed that the affected properties would descend to their heirs: "with remainder to Henry de Ferariis and Isabella his wife, in fee tail and if they die without heir to the right heirs of the said Elizabeth." William Ferrers was the heir and, if he died without heirs of his body, his sisters would become the heiresses. The lady's trip to see the king may well have centered on hopes the use might continue in the Ferrers' favor. Her attorneys had drawn the use correctly, and she had obtained the requisite royal license. Legally she had no worries but, as Elizabeth astutely realized, her diversion of these estates diminished the potential properties of the king's son Lionel. There is no record that the uses were cancelled, but certainly William Ferrers never inherited the lady's Welsh lands; her granddaughter Elizabeth de Burgh and Lionel of Antwerp received all her Clare estates. Perhaps the issue was settled when the lady met Edward III in October 1349. She lost, as her 1355 will tacitly acknowledged.[185]

Elizabeth had been at Usk for nearly two years; she never returned after 1350. The place evoked grim memories of the plague, but Elizabeth was growing older as well. The progresses of former years may have been daunting, but her last trip from the Welsh borderlands to Clare Castle had a touch of grandeur. Household officers planned ahead; advance men pre-

pared chambers and collected provisions wherever she would stay. Churchmen and friends provided wagons, horses, and grooms, almost as if vying
for her favor. Some came from Tewkesbury and Evesham; London's bishop
and Ely's prior sent grooms and horses to Tewkesbury. Others came from
houses at Walsingham, Dereham, and Clare, and the earl of Hereford contributed horses and grooms. The marshalsea began feeding up to 53 oxen
five days before the journey; probably because of their slow gait, they were
sent ahead of the main party. Most seem to have been used to get material to Tewkesbury where men, carts, and animals assembled. The marshalsea
paid 23 grooms' wages on April 6; a week later, there were 67, and 18
pages. The household had to coordinate men, animals, and carts, as well as
pack residents' belongings and gear to be taken to Clare. The staff was further burdened on April 10, when Mary de St Pol came to bid Elizabeth
good-bye.[186]

Elizabeth left Usk on April 12, 1350, after John Gough and Henry
Dene had arrived from Clare with more horses. She reached Troy that
night, then Ross, and later crossed the Severn to Tewkesbury. The ferry-
ing cost 12s., but people, animals, and baggage had to be moved. Other
servants with provisions converged on the town: cattle driven up from
Usk and a barrel of salmon brought by oxcart. Abbot Thomas Legh of
Tewkesbury[187] transported goods from Troy; the lady paid the cost. She
was at Tewkesbury from April 15 to 19. The abbey had been linked to the
Clares for two centuries and many relatives rested there: father, brother,
Despenser and Zouche brothers-in-law, her nephew Hugh Despenser III.
Her sister Eleanor had assumed the major patron's role at Tewkesbury, but
Elizabeth's sense of her natal ties made her at home there too. She gave a
feast on Sunday, April 18, with game, swans, and herons, perhaps to honor
the family dead also remembered in abbey church's glorious stained-glass
windows.[188]

On Monday, Elizabeth traveled to Stanway, Chipping Norton, and
Bletchingdon. Roger Damory had held the last manor by grant from his
brother Richard, who recovered it at Roger's death; Elizabeth held it by
knight's service in 1350.[189] She had never been attached to the place, but
it was convenient to her route. Her train now included 134 horses, 28
hackneys, and 22 oxen, and supplying such a large retinue was a major consideration. Her servants could rely more confidently on manorial officials
to gather provisions than on availability at local markets. Elizabeth thus
transported from place to place supplies unlikely to be readily available en
route. Wine routinely came from previously purchased stock, though
bulkier ale was bought locally each day. The herons she brought with her
must have been a sight, lumbering along in cages on the carts; Elizabeth
served them up, and swans too, when she gave at least two more parties on

the way. Facilities at her own estates were used; a crew had been sent ahead to bake at Bletchingdon. From there, she moved to Bicester and Buckingham, giving a feast at one of those places. Bicester had ties to two of her husbands. Verdon had held a nearby manor at Hethe, inherited by Isabella Ferrers and her son, William. The Damorys had close links to Bicester Priory, where many of them were buried.[190] Either link could have roused Elizabeth's interest in 1350; certainly she was concerned for her late daughter's estates. On April 23 she was at Woburn, where an oven was rented to bake and the abbot provided carts and men to take food to her next destination, Chicksands, a desperately poor Gilbertine house of canons and nuns. Elizabeth's benefactions had never included this order, but the prior had visited Elizabeth often. She at least offered the house a respite from financial woes by giving a feast.[191]

As she neared Clare, Elizabeth renewed contact with friends and staff. Her former receiver Robert de Stalyngton was rector at Litlington near Cambridge, where he had studied; he could inform the lady of conditions at Clare Hall and the university, which the plague had struck heavily. John de Lenne, a former wardrobe keeper, had a house in Radwinter, the last stop before Clare. Anne de Lexeden, once a household damsel, was as an anchoress in a house near to John's; Elizabeth would have solicited her prayers for the dead and the living. The plague had ravaged East Anglia more than any other area in England. The devastation was only now ending in the spring of 1350, with about half the population dead.[192] Elizabeth knew of the mortality from Clare servants who had come to Wales, but Stalyngton and Lenne could provide details. Carts from Stoke priory helped bring the last of the baggage to Clare. The trip had required ingenuity, the help of lay and ecclesiastical friends, provisions from unfamiliar markets, and endless patience and good will. On April 28, the lady was safely back in her castle, welcomed by the loyal retainers who had remained there during her stay in Wales.

Elizabeth de Burgh lived for ten and a half years after she returned from Wales. Some activities remained constant in her last decade, but the plague years and advancing age had affected her. Contacts with friends and family never diminished and, in some cases, seemed to escalate. Her first guests in May 1350 arrived just six days after she reached Clare; her last extant household roll, from the summer of 1359, shows her still extending hospitality.[193] Social interaction was important for many reasons, from the conduct of business affairs to the joys of companionship. Thus she created a pleasant milieu in which her Ferrers granddaughters could mingle with royal and noble contemporaries. Philippa de Beauchamp could expect to be the countess of Warwick, her sister, Elizabeth, countess of Athol; enjoying the company of the Prince of Wales, Lionel of Antwerp and his wife,

John of Gaunt, and other nobles gave the sisters access to eminent life allies and helped them develop social skills the nobility prized.

Elizabeth usually entertained at Clare and Bardfield, but in 1352 she hired an architect to plan and supervise construction of a London house and paid rent to the London Minoresses for the building site. The dwelling took about a year to build. The accounts show payments of just under £145, plus £1 3s. 4d. in gifts to the architect, Richard Felsted, with whom ties reached back to 1326 when she gave him a gift of 100s. Thereafter, she consulted with him several times and probably had employed him on projects in Clare, Anglesey, and perhaps Cambridge and Walsingham. Felsted had been Edward II's Master of the Works at Hanley Castle and worked for Henry of Lancaster at Kenilworth Castle. As no contract survived for Elizabeth's London house, it is impossible to tell if her payments to Felsted included materials, labor, or supervisory expenses. She paid him six times more than he received for the two-story tavern he built in London, where materials and masonry work were not included; probably, then, her London house was substantial.[194] She stopped in London in April 1353, en route to Canterbury and on her return. Her first long London stay is recorded in 1354.[195] No accounts are extant after Michaelmas 1359 but, for the years between 1354 and 1359 where documents survive a new pattern emerged: the lady spent three or four months in London, with the rest of the year divided between Clare and Bardfield. She traveled from London to East Anglia in October 1354 and back to London in July 1355, repeating that pattern in October 1355 and July 1356. In 1358 and 1359 she left for London in May, returning to East Anglia in September 1358 and in August in 1359.[196]

When Elizabeth resided in London, her staff used the London markets for specialized products, but many commodities were brought from Clare or Bardfield. Standon served as a holding depot for poultry, fish, and meat from these manors and other East Anglian suppliers. When the London house required additional meats, a servant drove animals from Standon to the city.[197] The men of the poultry office continued to use some of the old eastern markets, but also purchased closer to London, in Barking, Royston, and St Neots. Ale was shipped in by water, unloaded by the Thames and carted the short distance to the house, at the cost of a few pennies per shipment. The original brewing site is never mentioned, but may have been nearby, for several entries note the brewing of small amounts of ale in London, averaging about one-quarter the normal production of a brewing day on the East Anglian estates.[198] The pantry staff baked in London at a rate approximately one-third of the East Anglian baking days. Probably the staff rented local baking and brewing premises, or perhaps used the Minoress' facilities. Because of space limitations, economy, or to preserve the quiet appropriate to monastic precincts, horses, chariots, and wagons boarded in Tottenham. The marshalsea accounts for feeding and shoeing horses, and repairing household gear, indicate her officials often traveled to London. The Minories house served as a spiritual retreat, but one tempered by the lady's interest in her estates and by her hospitality to men of affairs, friends, and family.

Elizabeth's social life continued in London, but the new house served another purpose. In the post-plague years, her spiritual interests embraced a deeper participation in female religious exercises, and her sojourns in London allowed her to share the Minoresses' religious life.[199] If these retreats represent a growing interests in the life of the spirit, other short trips suggest a sentimental attachment to the East Anglian countryside and an enjoyment of its delights. Between 1351 and 1359 she often visited Hundon near Clare, and nearby Birdbrook and Stoke by Clare. Familiar places, but now she settled in for a few days, perhaps because extended travel was becoming wearisome; on trips to and from London, there were increasingly long pauses as she lingered at North Weald. *Familia* and staff hunted frequently at Hundon, and perhaps the lady still savored the chase too, remembering to send game to friends including the nuns of Denny and Campsey Ash.[200]

Elizabeth remained active in business and legal matters. She served as trustee in two enfeoffments to use by David de Strabolgi, husband of one of her Ferrers granddaughters.[201] She vigorously pursued rights and complaints through the judicial system. John Wyberd faced outlawry until he agreed to render accounts of his term as her receiver; two men surrendered themselves at Fleet prison to answer her charges of trespass in Lincoln and a 50 mark debt. The last extant rolls of her household record purchases of numerous writs against those who had violated her trust or her notion of her rights.[202] She could be arrogant and tenacious in legal dealings. A servant was placed in stocks by angry villagers while on the lady's business. She fined for his freedom and complained to the king who named an oyer and terminer commission to explore the issue. Elizabeth defended Stephen Bonde from her Cranborne estate, who had killed a man; the king accepted the act as self-defense and pardoned him.[203] Thus she demonstrated loyalty to subordinates, animosity to those infringing on her privileges, and willing recourse to the legal and gracious remedies open to her by law and by her relationship to the king. Here Elizabeth showed an unrelenting, high-handed, and stubborn side—not qualities that characterize her whole persona, but ones that balance her acts of piety, amity, and nurture. Fourteenth-century society applauded the latter, but understood the need for severity too.

Elizabeth responded as ever to family and friends, but death was reducing their ranks. A favorite young friend, Hugh Despenser III's widow, Elizabeth, was buried at Tewkesbury in June 1359; Elizabeth sent her official Robert Fleming to the funeral. Her friend Queen Isabella was failing rapidly in 1358, and died at Hertford on August 22. Elizabeth returned to East Anglia before Isabella's November burial in the choir of the London Franciscan church, where Fleming again represented the lady. She sent David Cursoris for details of Isabella's alabaster tomb, with Edward II's heart in the effigy's breast and images of archangels at the corners.[204] Such interest in the queen's tomb suggests Elizabeth was contemplating her own memorial in 1358. She may have been ill by the spring of 1359, when Master Simon de Bredon joined her *familia* in London. A Gloucester man educated at Oxford, Bredon had attended Queen Joan of Scotland in a medical capacity in 1358. His 14 scientific and mathematical works included a text on diagnosis and prediction of the course of disease; contemporaries thought well of his work,[205] and his experience as a physician could have recommended him to Elizabeth. If she were indeed ill in 1359, the statutes she delivered to Clare Hall that March suggest her mental faculties were unimpaired.[206] She had anticipated her death when she dictated a testament in 1355. Medieval people often delayed preparing wills until shortly before they died, but she was likely aware that few of her peers lived much past 60, her age in 1355. Since she enjoyed controlling situations whenever possible, she may also have wanted to be sure she would be the one to ordain the dispersal of her goods and chattels. In her last decade, the lady had set her stamp on Clare Hall, deepened her spiritual life, and enhanced her charitable activities; but, as her last account ends at Michaelmas 1359, we have no record of her final year. She died on November 4, 1360, probably at her beloved Clare or Bardfield, surrounded by her staff and clerics who would form the cortege that carried her body to the London Minories, where she had chosen to be buried. There, among those she had loved and with whom she had interacted in life, her body would rest for all eternity.[207]

CHAPTER 2

HER GOOD ESTATE

Elizabeth could live in a grand manner, pursue pious aims, and consort with royal and noble friends because her wealth allowed her those choices. Landed estates formed the core of her wealth, bringing her rents and produce for consumption or sale; judicial profits, advowsons, feudal incidents, gifts, and sales of household surpluses supplemented her income. The household accounts never reflect the totality of annual profits, rarely including non-manorial income. Still, the sums mentioned, of between £2,000 and £3,000 a year, put her among the wealthiest persons of her day, comparable to a modern-day multimillionaire. Her annual income in the 1330s and 1340s exceeded that of Westminster Abbey, but not the earl of Lancaster's income of over £6,000.[1]

Resources

Her Clare purparty provided over £2,000 in properties, augmented when her sister-in-law's dower portion was parceled out. These, plus properties from her three marriages, made her an important landholder in parts of Ireland, eastern and southern Wales, East Anglia, Dorset, and the Midlands, with a few manors elsewhere. Elizabeth followed the noble practice of dividing her English and Welsh holdings into bailiwicks, manageable groupings of manors with some geographic coherence. Her English bailiwicks centered on East Anglia, Dorset, and the Midlands; Usk was the administrative center of her Welsh lands. As long as Ireland was relatively peaceful, she maintained separate agents for Kilkenny and her northern and western jointure lands, but as hostilities grew, a single agent assumed responsibility.

The Clare bailiwick, made up of East Anglian holdings, was important for family sentiment and her two residences there, though it was not her most profitable bailiwick.[2] Elizabeth held the castle and town of Clare, with its market, annual Wentford fair, and various rents. Town courts extracted fines from tithing groups, for infractions of the bread and ale assizes and for encroachments on her pasture and ponds. She kept the courts under her official's control, but alternatively leased the market or profited directly from stall rents and entry fines.[3] The lady profited when Clare experienced a modest burst of economic activity in the 1330s and early 1340s, perhaps without her encouragement, but she did patronize its businesses: renting a pig shed, hiring local smiths, and making purchases in the town.[4] When the French threatened the coast, Elizabeth depended on Clare townsmen for some military requirements. As she was landlord, patron, dispenser of justice and charity, her relationship with the town was friendly but complex.

Erbury, Clare's manor, was the home farm, producing many supplies required by the household. Besides arable land for grain, Erbury had pasture for sheep and cattle, meadows, water mills, and cherry, pear, and apple orchards.[5] All the East Anglian manors operated in a rational fashion; most grew grain or animals for consumption in the lady's household, returned moneys from commodity sales and often produced specialized items. For example, Bardfield and Hundon woodlands supplied cooking and heating fuels and manufactured charcoal.[6] Standon manor had good pasturage so the lady's horses boarded there often; it also served as a collection depot for supplies gathered in East Anglia for her use in London.[7] The Southwold bailiff supplied herring and money to cover that coastal manor's obligations. Walsingham officials occasionally bought fish for Elizabeth's household, but its primary receipts came from rents, courts, a fair, a market, and grain production. Elsewhere in the Clare bailiwick, Elizabeth held a collection of courts and rents in Essex, Norfolk, and Suffolk.[8]

In the 1330s, Elizabeth acquired Ilketshall in exchange for Kennington and Vauxhall, but she exploited it directly for only a few years before renting it to John de Lenne. She later rented Hawkedon, a manor five miles from Clare. Her sergeants reported in from Freckenham by 1344–45, but the accounts are silent on how she acquired the manor, which became her prime source for rabbits. Horses were boarded at Stebbing in 1339–40 and her men made wine there the next year, although the manor belonged to the Ferrers. The lady rented Tonbridgehall from the prior of Tonbridge for over 20 years, maintaining a chase in the forest where both *familia* and her professional hunters took game, and using its wood for London fuel needs.[9]

Courts, markets, and mills were important on Elizabeth's Sudbury manor, though some were leased to townsmen. The lady always exhibited a keen interest in mill construction, because mills brought in sizable monetary returns. She commissioned an advanced design appreciated by the abbot of Glastonbury, who asked Elizabeth to allow his carpenter "to copy her horse-mill," though the model he admired was probably in Wales rather than Sudbury. A different sort of commercial enterprise operated in the Southfrith, Kent ironworks, which produced iron blooms for sale. Sometimes her officials operated the works and other times it was leased out; she did expend money on capital improvements on several occasions.[10] Otherwise, the lady exhibited willingness to tap commercial enterprises: mills, fairs, markets, and ironworks.

While Elizabeth took a personal interest in her eastern holdings, buying from her neighbors, visiting her manors, and dispensing alms to the needy, that intimate interaction was missing in her Dorset manors, which she exploited rather impersonally. The accounts mention only one visit to Dorset on her 1341 journey to Wales. Manors in the Dorset bailiwick produced grains, animals, and wool, which were sold for her profit; a shipment of fish might originate there, but the more typical commodity for personal use was game. Her huntsmen, with coursing dogs and greyhounds, often hunted there, salting and packing the game for consumption at Clare or Bardfield. While the lady supported her own staff, she accepted the proceeds from the Dorset bailiwick with minimal response to local people. Dorset was a "cash cow," interesting primarily for its production of funds and supplies.[11]

English dower lands from Theobald de Verdon and Damory jointure lands formed a small bailiwick centered on Brandon. Its officials delivered their renders at Clare or alternatively sent in money, making the bailiwick more integrated into household production than the Dorset estates. Elizabeth demonstrated no personal concern for these manors, although Caythorpe was the most profitable of all her manors because of its production of fine wool. Brandon manor supplied some pigs, but more often stabled horses or boarded dogs. By 1355 she rented Brandon and Newbold manors to her Verdon stepdaughters, after which Lutterworth became the bailiwick's administrative center. Farnham sent in herons and wood and provided rabbits before Elizabeth acquired a more convenient source. Hallaton had a Clare official in 1339 and 1340, but in the latter year, the Bardolfs gave a life-grant in the manor to Nicholas Damory, perhaps Elizabeth's most trusted lay official. How the Bardolfs gained possession is not clear; the transaction cost Elizabeth about £40 to £50 a year. In the 1350s, Bletchingdon was rented to her Zouche nephew, William (a Glastonbury monk), and later to Nicholas Poer.[12] The Brandon bailiwick's manors were in different shires; none were Clare family lands. The manors represented economic assets, but lacked the emotional tie Elizabeth had with her natal family estates (Ilketshall and Clopton were the only non-Clare lands integrated into one of the old Clare bailiwicks).

The Usk bailiwick centered in the lowlands of eastern Wales, roughly between the Wye and Clwyd rivers on the east and west, the Bristol channel and the lordship of Monmouth on the south and north. Usk, the most profitable of Elizabeth's bailiwicks, supplied nearly 38 percent of her landed income and over half her court profits. Most of the manors followed English customs, although Elizabeth had Welsh tenants in the bedelries of Trelleck, Usk, Llefnydd, and Edelegan.[13] The lordship was well supplied with forests, useful for fuel, wood products, and game, while rents and court profits came from the towns of Usk, Caerleon, and Trelleck.[14] The bailiwick supplied basic household needs when she visited the Marches and dispatched specialized products to East Anglia. For example, cattle drives from Usk to East Anglia were fairly routine. Once six boys with 74 cattle ferried across the Wye, bought pasturage en route, and arrived at Bardfield 11 days later. More experienced drovers brought 109 cattle across in 1335–36. Salmon, sparrowhawks, and russet cloth were often sent to the lady from Wales. Hunting was declining in Wales during the fourteenth century because the forest produced more saleable commodities, but Elizabeth routinely sent huntsmen to take game at Trelleck, which they prepared for shipment to her East Anglian residences.[15] All across Wales in the fourteenth century, Marcher income was falling. Elizabeth responded by shifting some arable from grain to sheep raising, exploiting fisheries, and selling wood and charcoal. Rents and judicial profits continued as stable sources of income. Even with falling revenues, her Marcher lands brought in considerable cash, often conveyed to Clare.[16] Elizabeth grieved over the loss of these lands in 1323, in part from family pride, but also because of the major loss of profits.

The lady sent officials from her council to check on operations in each bailiwick. Manorial accounts were scrutinized to insure that bailiffs, provosts, and sergeants were honestly and efficiently managing their responsibilities.[17] These men needed to be knowledgeable agriculturalists, managers of villein labor, collectors of rents from free tenantry, and astute sellers on the local market. Presumably they were literate enough to read instructions, although their own accounting might be by tally. They accommodated officials or hunting parties sent to their manor, deducting those expenses from their renders. In return, these manorial officials received annual fees and livery robes appropriate to their offices. Elizabeth rewarded a few with money gifts and she remembered many with legacies. As a group, these men were her most talented professionals outside the top staff of her central administration.

Like many English nobles, Elizabeth was an absentee landlord in Ireland, but she differed from them in maintaining an active interest in the island. She never returned to Ireland after 1316, so she depended on officials to manage the estates and send in profits, which contributed 10 to 15 percent of her yearly income.[18] Elizabeth understood the importance of cultivating the gratitude of the Kilkenny seneschal: Arnold le Poer and his son Eustace joined William de Burgh's retinue when he was knighted and probably accompanied him to his earldom in 1328, demonstrating Elizabeth's power of patronage. The Poers responded by preserving a good income from Kilkenny. Other officials proved less satisfactory and by 1357 Kilkenny ceased to be a profitable venue: renewed warfare by native Irish disturbed revenue collection and plague mortality emptied her acres. The rapid decline of Kilkenny's economic returns surprised absentee English, both noble and royal. Elizabeth suffered a real loss, for in 1348–49 her Kilkenny income was £128.[19]

Until at least 1337 her dower lands in Louth and Meath were leased to her brother-in-law Nicholas de Verdon, but by 1350–51, the lady's officials were reporting on income there, though the holdings mentioned are only a partial listing of her dower properties.[20] Just as in Kilkenny, gross receipts were divided among staff maintenance, royal dues, local expenses, and moneys delivered to Elizabeth. Her five-month marriage to Theobald netted her income for about 40 years. Elizabeth extracted money from her Burgh jointure properties in Ulster and Connacht for an even longer period, with rents, tolls, and judicial profits forming the core of Ulster receipts, along with 11 mills. Fisheries on the River Bann brought in comfortable profit, mainly from boat leases. Robin Frame suggests Elizabeth realized decent Ulster returns because four manors there were coastal towns, allowing her to tap port and fishing revenues. Her officials also pursued small sources of income: the occasional sale of a beached porpoise or a cow received as heriot. As late 1350–51 Elizabeth's officials sent her fine Irish horses, but later concentrated on delivering cash because of increasing difficulty in transporting goods. Her men labored under tough conditions since money needed to be collected from manorial stewards in several regions, delivered to the Irish receiver who then arranged for escort and boat hire for the sea voyage to England. Once there, the escort rode across England to deliver the money to Elizabeth's English receiver.[21]

Elizabeth kept herself informed about Irish conditions. She engaged attorneys (who often acted as her Irish receivers) to represent her interests in Ireland, expecting they would report back to her. Hugh de Burgh, keeper of her wardrobe from 1326 to 1332, later served as baron and chief baron of the Irish exchequer and was one of her Irish attorneys. When her daughter-in-law Matilda went to Ireland with her new husband, Ralph Ufford, Elizabeth probably received detailed information from them directly or through the earl of Suffolk, Ralph's brother. John Morice, former seneschal of Kilkenny, visited the lady in 1347, after his appointment as chancellor of Ireland. She entertained Thomas Rokeby in 1356, just before his second stint as Irish justiciar; the bishop of Connor wrote Elizabeth with descriptions of the devastation occurring in the land.[22] Elizabeth's awareness of Irish conditions contributed to her successes in that land.

Although royal income from Ireland declined precipitously after 1333, Elizabeth realized profits because many Burghs paid their rental obligations to her more readily than to Countess Matilda of Ulster, or to Lionel of Antwerp and his wife, Countess Elizabeth. Elizabeth had lived among the Burghs, had produced the earldom's heir and titular family head, and had founded an Augustinian friary at Ballinrobe.[23] The Burgh kin included many unruly and murderous types, but some of the family must have accepted the lady of Clare. It was a remarkable achievement for the lady to collect rents in distant Connacht without benefit of a military presence or significant coercive powers.

Besides profits accruing from the manorial system, the lady realized some income from her position in the feudal hierarchy. Most of her own lands were held of the king in-chief; her ancestors had subinfeudated some of the properties to others, who thereby incurred military and financial obligations to their immediate overlord. While the overlords' military demands diminished by the fourteenth century, responsibility for feudal aids persisted, and it was from these and from the honor courts that profits accumulated. Elizabeth exploited the remnants of feudalism by collecting an aid for her son's knighting and for the marriage of her oldest daughter in 1327, but these were one-time payments. Wardships, marriage rights, and relief payments due when an heir came of age and received seisin of the inheritance, provided recurring sources of income, but not always for the immediate overlord. The Crown developed the concept of prerogative wardship which meant that the king commanded all wardships and marriage rights of minors whose legacy included property held in-chief of the king. Consequently, income potential from subinfeudated land depended on chance rather than any coherent arrangement. By the fourteenth century, non-judicial feudal income for all, save the king, had diminished considerably. Elizabeth received some profit from feudal incidents, although the household accounts are rarely informative about this source of income. A woman paid her 66s. 8d. for the marriage rights of her two daughters, the size of payment suggesting a feudal rather than a servile relationship. A few household accounts document income from relief payments made by heirs to allow entry into lands held from her by knights' service.[24] Wardship could convey control over both the lands and the person of minor heirs, although either could be separately administered or sold. Probably Elizabeth garnered some profits from the wardship of lands of deceased tenants whose holdings fell outside royal claims to prerogative wardship.

Her household included a number of children, but the accounts never clarify their status as wards or children staying with her for education, experience, and the opportunity to mingle with leading noble families.

Elizabeth held patronage rights and advowsons of a number of churches. Advowsons provided an alternative source of income for clerical staff members, thus decreasing wage outlays necessary to retain their services; also recipients might feel gratitude, useful in a broader political context. Using advowsons for these purposes and for pious benefactions allowed Elizabeth to keep her landed estates intact. She directed household servants to practice some frugality, which brought in small sums of money. Margery Mareschal, one of her ladies, sold household wastes and "kitchen issues" (probably surpluses), while the marshalsea collected old wheels and rabbit pelts to sell. Cider surpluses from the orchards of Clare or Bardfield were sent to market.[25]

Throughout her widowhood, the lady practiced astute exploitation of resources, utilizing her personal knowledge of conditions and employing competent and trusted officials to administer her prescribed directions. Elizabeth economized where her prestige would not be diminished and spent grandly to promote respect, without falling into careless improvidence. Her financial aptitude allowed her to live well and enjoy her good estate.

The financial center of Elizabeth's various enterprises was Clare Castle, her primary residence and one that bore her natal family name. She valued all her properties for their income-producing capabilities; Clare symbolized the sacrifices made to protect her heritage. The castle, itself, spoke of her family's long tenure, from its eleventh-century beginnings through the additions of her ancestors. The stone keep was sited on a mound 53 feet high with two walled baileys to the east, separated by a fosse or ditch. Access to the grounds was through imposing gates: Nethergate, Redgate, Dernegate. Beyond was the castle moat, where Elizabeth kept her swans. Defensive towers protected the inner bailey and the castle: Auditorstower, Maidenstower, Constabletower, and Oxfordtower. Lesser servants had houses scattered around the baileys, where kitchens, larder, saucery, brewing houses, stables, and storage areas were also located. Huntsmen and dogs, dovecote and fishpond jostled for space with vineyards, orchards, and gardens.[26] Her home at Bardfield had no castle, but rather a house, which Elizabeth improved and enlarged, including installation of a bathing facility or stew. Her officials often hunted in Bardfield park with its seven and a half acre meadow mowed each winter for the "sustenance of the deer," who often appeared on holiday menus. Bardfield offered a pleasant retreat, large enough for entertaining, but less hectic than Clare Castle.[27]

Although Elizabeth resided in Wales less frequently than East Anglia, she improved domestic structures at Usk castle: a two-story hall, single-story chapel, bathing facilities. There were baking and brewing houses, garden, stables, granary, storage sheds, and a park. The small castle never challenged the grandeur of Caerphilly (her sister Eleanor's great Welsh castle), but sufficed for an administrative center and entertaining. Elizabeth created an environment in Wales similar to East Anglia except she visited Welsh outlying manors more frequently, staying at Tregrug Castle, Tintern manor where she made extensive renovations, Caerleon Castle, Lancombe manor, Llantrisant, and Troy.[28] The more extensive visitation in Wales may have been her antidote to the problem of absentee lordship. By showing herself throughout the bailiwick, she renewed ties with dependents and displayed the ceremonial trappings of wealth and power. Historian R. R. Davies asserts that because of the intensely personal bonds between a Marcher lord and his men, good lordship suffered when a woman held the land. The argument is not totally convincing in Elizabeth's case, in part because of the proximity of her lands to England and its practices, in part because she provided rewards of patronage to dependents. However, her visits to outlying manors show an awareness of local opinion and a program to counter any pockets of wavering loyalty. She employed local men, both Welsh and English, as staff and at least one man with a Welsh background, Philip ap Jevan, joined her central administration. Local gentry benefited from her patronage, but dependent peasantry did not. Although Elizabeth may not have exploited her human resources as ruthlessly as Hugh Despenser had during his tenure over Usk, her constant aim was to profit from the land and people. She made minimal charitable gestures in Wales, such as feeding the poor on fixed days, but little else that helped the local peasants.[29] Elizabeth found a devoted friend in the bishop of Llandaff and she was patron of the Usk nuns, but made no pious foundations in the Marches.

Domestic Arrangements

In each of her residences, staff concentrated on creating an environment where the lady could live "nobly." Elizabeth judged the success of household enterprises as they contributed to her honor and well-being, to the comfort of family and guests, and to the contentment of the scores of servants who shared her home and table.[30] Elizabeth's household organization conformed to noble practice, with departments devoted to providing food, drink, transport, housekeeping, and financial oversight. There was some hierarchical ordering among departments, with the poultry subsidiary to the kitchen, for instance. This arrangement resulted from the sensibilities of presiding officers and their need to account to the auditors; ordinary servants might have their services charged to the kitchen one day and the poultry another without any real shift in the nature of their duties.[31] Departmental tasks centered on the consumption needs of the lady and her household, which often led to production activities as well.

The pantry milled flour and baked bread on a flexible schedule, but usually new loaves were produced twice each week (with amounts ranging as high as 2,360 loaves for a baking day), necessary because the household staff received board as part of their wages. Presumably the bakers used several grades of flour, furnishing finer white loaves for the lady's table and less elegant fare for household grooms and paupers. Besides baking for the table, the pantry supplied the marshalsea with horse bread, usually made from legumes and probably processed with a pea rotator rather than a mill. Elizabeth's hunting dogs received a ration made from rye. The baking routine at Usk and Bardfield resembled that of Clare; when she visited Anglesey, a baking crew went early to anticipate her needs. On pilgrimages or long trips, the bakers rented ovens and purchased flour locally as it was too bulky to transport easily. Bakers (and brewers) faced a perennial problem in keeping grain supplies free of vermin. They hired rat-catchers; one was paid for killing 18 rats at Clare Castle.[32] Elizabeth's bakers spent years in her service: Robert de Shirewood from 1326 to 1349; William Pistor from 1331 to 1349; John de Rishton (or Rushton) from 1334 to at least 1358. Besides supervising bakery pages, these men kept records of output for the auditors' scrutiny. The pantry baked pastries as well as bread. Stephen de Paris, a waferer, appeared in 1326, a year when wafers were made with almonds, rice, and sugar. Sugar, currants, figs, raisins, almonds, and various spices were charged to the hall and chamber accounts, but were available for making the fancy dishes Elizabeth enjoyed.[33]

The buttery produced, purchased, and served the mealtime beverages, usually ale or occasionally cider, with wine for more exalted persons. Much of the ale was brewed at Clare, Bardfield, or Usk, with purchases supplementing the stock. Elizabeth's buyers often received a discount when they purchased in large quantities, a practice called buying with "advantage" (*avantagium*). The seller added extra gallons to the amount the purchaser had negotiated to buy, thereby discounting the transaction. In 1328–29 the household purchased 21,086 gallons of ale to supplement the 27,328 gallons brewed on the premises. The maltsters and brewers made at least two grades of ale, the better based on barley and the cheaper from drage, a barley and oat mixture. The resulting beverage was fairly robust, with about 58 gallons brewed from a quarter (a grain measure of eight bushels) of malt.[34] Alemakers faced a more demanding challenge than bakers, for they made malt and then brewed the ale, saving the dregs, which were sent to the larder for stock feed. Ale was stored in wooden barrels for drawing the daily rations, amounting to a gallon per person in most noble households. Household brewing occurred every four or five days, adjusted for seasonal needs, with normal runs about 900 gallons. When Elizabeth went to Anglesey her brewery staff preceded her to produce the requisite supplies at her brew house there; on longer trips ale was purchased locally. While brewers often had long careers in the household, malt-makers often came from outside; the five or six women who helped on various malting jobs were casual laborers hired for short periods.[35]

While ale production was local, wine generally came from abroad. Wine-buying occurred each year as medieval barrels could not be sealed tightly, resulting in wines that soured rather quickly, so consumers appreciated the new wine which arrived in English ports in late autumn. The Clare clerk noted in 1330 that new wine was first served on December 9.[36] Most English wine imports originated in Gascony, but Elizabeth also enjoyed Rhine wine and sweet wines from the eastern Mediterranean. The lady patronized several wine merchants, some in London and others in Ipswich, Colchester, and Bristol. She often bought on credit, adding "God's penny" to the transaction, which set up a sales contract. This example from 1350 illustrates a credit purchase and the complexities of medieval wine-buying. A boy arrived from Ipswich announcing the arrival of new Rhenish wine in October. The household wine-buyer, John de Southam, traveled to Ipswich and Harwich to inspect the cargo, purchasing two pipes of the wine for £14 9s.1d., the penny indicating a credit contract sale. The merchant appreciated the lady's custom for he added 48 gallons in "augmentations," necessitating the purchase of seven jars called "cruskyns." Carts traveled to Ipswich to transport the wine to Clare. The purchase price failed to reflect true cost, for the messenger boy received a tip, the cruskyns cost 6d., John's wages and carting costs needed to be paid. On another occasion hired men guarded the wine until carts arrived.[37] Southam served Elizabeth for at least 23 years. He and his wife, Agnes, jointly received a generous legacy in Elizabeth's will: four silver pots, a silver cup, an alabaster goblet decorated with silver gilt, a silver basin, and the coat, surcoat, and purple mantle from the lady's fifth best costume. Roger de Medfeld was Elizabeth's butler in 1330; Reginald le Ewer and Nicholas le Ewer presumably served at table.[38] The silver cups and mugs and the expensive silver, alabaster, and jasper goblets bequeathed in her will suggest the wine was served in elegant fashion. Elizabeth often chose to give wine as a gift and received wine from others in return. The nobility considered wine, game, choice meats and fish, hunting dogs, and horses to be proper items for exchange with their peers.

The buttery sometimes added sugar or spices to Gascon wine; clarey (a kind of wine based on Malaga raisins and flowering sage) was made at least once. Grapes were harvested for wine-making some years at Woodham Ferrers, but most local grape production probably was used for verjuice.

Milk appears in the accounts, but not in sufficient quantities to suggest it was a common beverage. Cider appeared irregularly and in small amounts, while perry, a fermented pear beverage, is mentioned once as orchard surplus rather than a mealtime drink.[39]

The kitchen department served the remainder of the menu, depending on other departments for supply. Nearby manors often paid part of their renders in stock, driving in the cattle, sheep, and pigs that formed the basis for flesh-day meals. Forcing animals to walk was more efficient and cheaper than carting carcasses and also gave flexibility to the kitchen. The larder tended and guarded the animals until the kitchen called for them, salted some carcasses, and processed less desirable animal parts.[40] Beef, pork, and mutton appeared regularly on Sundays, Mondays, Tuesdays, and Thursdays, with the cost charged to the kitchen; lamb and veal were eaten less often. Young goats were prized delicacies, received as gifts and considered appropriate for holiday fare.

The poultry supplied small animals such as rabbits and piglets as well as fowl. The accounts never mention care of domestic fowl, though pullets, hens, capons, and geese from stock were served often. The clerks tallied meat products originating on Elizabeth's manors, because they represented manorial obligations; costs of items produced in the household usually were ignored, as indicated by the absence of debits for care of chickens and geese. The Clare swannery fed oats to its swans, but most of their cost showed in the tally for Erbury manor.[41] Rabbits were sent in from Freckenham for most of the period. Professional and noble hunters rarely took rabbits as game because few existed in the wild; neither were rabbits fully domesticated. Nobles hoped for royal permission to have a free warren, where rabbits could be available for the holder of the warren while being protected from animal predators and human poachers. Freckenham had a warren, ideally placed on Breckland soils congenial to rabbit colonies. Rabbits were still expensive in the fourteenth century and were considered something of a luxury, perhaps more for their skins than their meat.[42]

Supplying fish for fasting days created more problems for the kitchen than ordering up meat carcasses from the larder. Southwold manor made its render in herrings each year, but not in sufficient quantities to meet the demand for several hundred herring for each of the three, weekly fasting days. Other manors occasionally sent along fish, especially salmon from the Usk region and lampreys from the Severn. Elizabeth received a lamprey rent from the Gloucester area and purchased lampreys from Nantes.[43] Clare, Bardfield, and Usk had some facilities for fishing and holding fish from nearby rivers or ponds. Staff fishermen commonly used nets rather than fish lines, because nets enhanced the chance of keeping fish alive in fishponds or troughs until needed; river eels were stored in submerged fish traps.[44] Holding fish alive until cooking offered an alternative to smoked or salted varieties. Elizabeth preferred salmon to all other fish, but unless she was in Wales, salmon (and lampreys) reached the kitchen in smoked, baked, or pickled form. The kitchen accounted for eels by sticks of 25; Elizabeth wanted fat ones for the Blessed Virgin's Purification. Pike was often called the royal fish, perhaps because it normally weighed over 30 pounds. The kitchen served it occasionally when there were no guests, but featured it when the king visited in May 1340. Sturgeon, another "royal" fish, was on the menu for Prince Edward and John of Gaunt.[45] Other freshwater fish in the accounts include trout, perch, bream, roach, and minnows.

More fish came from the sea, purchased at Yarmouth, Ipswich, or Lynn. Herring, either red smoked or salted white, dominated in quantity. Stockfish was another ubiquitous dish, though servants required extra wages for beating it into workable condition for cooking. Perhaps most stockfish originated in Norway, but "Icelandic" fish were specifically mentioned once.[46] Cod and mackerel were commonplace at the lady's table, but occasionally she indulged in the more exotic porpoise and whale (or grampus). Congers were purchased often, along with sole, cropling, ling, shad, John Dory, sea bass, mullets, and turbot.[47] The kitchen supplemented fish with smaller amounts of seafood: shrimp, whelks, and crabs. Elizabeth liked oysters, and the staff managed to find them even during the plague. Oysters and crabs were quite inexpensive, but added variety to counteract the endless herrings. Fish purchased in London or at the Stourbridge fair were already processed; fish bought in ports required some effort before transport. For example, after completing a whale purchase, the household buyer bought canvas for wrapping and salt for preservation. The routine for herring buying was similar, with barrels and salt purchased at port.[48] Household buyers needed expertise in selecting merchandise and skill in preservation techniques.

Medieval nobles appreciated game animals and birds illustrative of their hunting prowess. Celebratory occasions called for venison, desired for the prestige it gave to hostess or host, and Elizabeth's table was amply provided at holiday feasts. Since venison epitomized "living nobly," it was never purchased but came from endeavors of the household or as gifts. She may not have hunted herself, rather depending on her ranking officials or her professional huntsmen. Before Christmas, Epiphany, Corpus Christi, and other holidays, a few favorites—Robert Mareschal, Nicholas Damory, or Henry Dene—went hunting in one of the deer parks at Bardfield, Hundon, or Trelleck to supply the requisite venison, often accompanied by the lady's professional hunters. To insure a continuing supply, professionals hunted at Tonbridge, Cranborne, and Trelleck. On a typical trip, John Venator, two pages, two boys, seven greyhounds, and 18 coursing dogs went to Tonbridge to hunt in July 1351. The dogs' litter cost 12*d.;* the greyhounds' expense was 1*d.* a day for two; 1*d.* a day covered the cost of three coursing dogs. On this trip only part of Elizabeth's pack hunted; on another expedition 31 coursing dogs and eight greyhounds participated. Hunters used large amounts of salt to preserve the venison.[49] Occasionally the professional hunters pursued foxes, considered vermin, and pests who disturbed sheep-flocks and domestic birds.[50]

Falconers cared for an assortment of falcons, lanners, goshawks, tercels, and sparrowhawks used for hunting. Hawks were trained to hunt herons and bitterns in the period, but Elizabeth's supply was netted or trapped. She received shipments of live birds from Usk, Tonbridge, Southfrith, and Farnham, transported to East Anglia in cages. In the 1350–51 inventory, 77 herons were sent in from Wales and Tonbridge, and 19 bitterns and 12 herons were received as gifts.[51] Wild birds were as important as game so the poultry bought wild birds to supplement those normally hunted. Purchase may have been cheaper than sending out falconers, for in 1350 two partridges cost only 6*d.* and a plover 2*d. ob.* That same year teals (*cercells*), beketts, woodcocks, pheasants, and curlews appeared on the lady's table. Perhaps she even enjoyed birds baked in a pie, for larks seem a staple dietary item in the fall of 1350. In other years the household purchased spoonbills, fieldfare, and finches; peacocks were received as gifts. When Elizabeth celebrated a holiday or entertained important guests, she often ordered swans, whose presence on the menu almost defined a festive dinner. During the 1350 Christmas season, the poultry provided two swans a day for December 25, 26, and 30, with two more for Epiphany.[52]

Modern writers criticize medieval menus for their lack of vegetables. In Elizabeth's case, garden products rarely show on daily food lists and never appear in stock inventories. Since household products tended to be ignored, the absence of vegetables may be an accounting omission rather than a dietary one. The kitchen made a few vegetable purchases, including skirrewittus, a winter root vegetable related to salsify; peas and beans were cooked into soup. The larder possessed an onion chest for the frequent purchases of that vegetable.[53] Clare accounts do little to amend the impression of limited vegetable fare in medieval diets. However, Elizabeth indulged in fruit throughout the year, with some from the orchards at Clare and Bardfield. She ate apples, pears, and cherries in season and switched to dried fruits in other months, even sampling pomegranates. London merchants imported dried fruits from abroad, perhaps the rationale for their inclusion in the spice account. One year Elizabeth bought 62 pounds of dates, 4 pounds of Damascene prunes, and over 200 pounds of figs and raisins; in another year she added raisins from Tamil, currants and figs from

Malaga.[54] These fruits originated in Spain or the Mediterranean region; her spices came from even greater distances.

The medieval world lacked technology to bring in fresh products from faraway lands, but less fragile items were available in larger English markets for well-to-do customers. For example, in 1344–45 Elizabeth bought 343½ pounds of spices from Bartholomew Thomasyn and John Hammond. The cost of a pound of some spices was high: mace at 9s., gillyflower at 16s., flowered cinnamon at 5s. 6d., although more ordinary cinnamon only cost 20d. The household worked with local produce as well, grinding mustard seeds into that condiment or buying vinegar for the saucery.[55] Since much of Elizabeth's meat and poultry supply was slaughtered just before serving, spices were not to mask the taste of rotten meat, but to add variety to accompanying sauces. Elizabeth enjoyed confections, the medieval equivalent of candy, which were prohibitively expensive for ordinary consumers. Her purchase list typically included ginger and date confections, and others difficult to identify: madrian, pastry regal, festinade, and anise vermal.[56] She also bought enormous amounts of sugar, given its expense and scarcity: in 1344–45, 111 pounds of sugar, 144 pounds of sugar "babylon" and 414 pounds of sugar "taffetan." Probably sugar flavored the food and wine of important guests, officials, and family members, but rarely the fare of grooms and gardeners. Elizabeth did indulge her pet parrots, feeding them tidbits of almonds, which figured heavily in the spice accounts, with over 700 pounds purchased in 1344–45. Finding the annual cost for spices, confections, sugar, almonds, and rice is difficult, because the clerks changed accounting categories from time to time. In 1344–45 the spices and dried fruits came to £110 5s. 4d. ob., but that figure included wax from Lubeck. The 1337–38 accounts lump spices, confections, wax, and canvas together for an expense of £62 4s. 8d. ob., with little sugar or almonds noted.[57] The various foods and ample quantities suggest Elizabeth set a good table. Bread, meat, fish, and ale satisfied the hearty appetites of workers, while the palates of the favored few experienced menu choices embellished with fruits and spices from foreign sources.

The accounts rarely inform about cooking methods and never include recipes. No inventory of kitchen equipment has survived, but some items hint at preparation methods: a spit, ovens, griddles, and turners. Kitchen knives, forks, skewers, bowls, measures, funnels, a grater, a mortar and pestle, are mentioned, along with a flesh ax and a whetstone for sharpening. Inexpensive dishes and plates were purchased, tankards, cups, and costrels made from Elizabeth's timber, and towels furnished for cleaning chores. Paupers ate from their own dishes when bread and herring were distributed by the almonry.[58] Kitchen and buttery required many baskets, barrels, and chests for storing bulky commodities. Department heads must have suspected staff of larcenous desires, for containers from eel traps to candle chests were closed with locks that frequently needed repair, raising some question about their capability for deterring crime. When barrels required repairs, the staff bought ash trees and hired coopers to form the strips into new hoops; pantry personnel spent hours mending grain and flour sacks.[59] The accounts make clear that thrift and parsimony were prized virtues, at least in areas blocked off from public view.

Kitchen and poultry personnel rarely rate mention in the rolls unless they traveled as buyers whose journeys and expenses were carefully noted. Two poulterers worked at the establishment for many years: Robert for 20 and Hugh for at least 26. These men knew nearby market towns well, for they visited regularly for supplies. Hugh, for example, spent much of each week at Colchester, Sudbury, Bury St Edmunds, or even further afield. His superiors trusted him with finding fish, poultry, and meat, with arranging for transport back to the household, and with money to pay for his expenses.

Pantry, buttery, and kitchen required a constant fuel supply to produce for the table; the rest of the castle needed fuel for a modicum of warmth. East Anglian wood supplies came from Elizabeth's manors of Bardfield and Hundon, and from Wellok when the lady resided in Wales. Tallwood was collected for the hall and chamber fireplaces; peat and sedge were used at Anglesey, but apparently not at Clare or Bardfield. The household bought some sea coal, but it never figured as a major source for heating or cooking fuel. Whenever possible, wood resources of the lady's manors supplied the household needs, even when she resided in London.[60]

Medieval castles deserve their reputation for gloomy darkness, which perhaps accounts for the joy that medieval people found in light, both during their lives and during the waiting period between death and burial when they wanted to be surrounded by blazing tapers to ward off evil. Elizabeth honored Edward de Monthermer with such a display and she wanted 200 pounds of wax tapers to shine around her own body before interment.[61] Some candles used in Elizabeth's homes were manufactured with tallow from kitchen wastes and purchased wicks, with the markets of Clare or Bardfield supplementing the tallow supply. The chandlery department appears sporadically, sometimes with a resident chandler, sometimes with outside labor. The wardrobe supplemented the homemade stock with purchases of commonplace Paris candles.[62] Wax cost considerably more; that imported from Lubeck cost 38s. a hundredweight. Elizabeth designated part of her wax to light the chapel: a pound or two in ordinary weeks, ranging up to 64 and a half pounds for her favorite feasts, such as the Purification of the Blessed Virgin (Candlemas) or Christmas.

The lady of Clare wanted a well-lit home and a clean one. Dusting and sweeping cost nothing beyond staff wages; when Elizabeth moved to other residences, the advance party sent to clean the chambers incurred expenses the clerks duly recorded. A team of local women often did the actual cleaning, polishing, strewing rushes or straw, and ensuring the lady's chambers met necessary standards. Housekeepers at Clare and Bardfield changed the rushes frequently, especially before major holidays. Rushes came from Cattiwade in Suffolk or from Maldon near Chelmsford, collected and transported by scullery staff.[63] Routine latrine cleaning must have occurred, but the smelly task was recorded only when outside labor was hired.[64] Elizabeth's private quarters had a garderobe; presumably sanitary facilities for the rest of the household were more primitive and public.

The accounts say little about water. Clare Castle had a cistern and a well and easy access to river water; Usk possessed a well, but water also needed to be hauled laboriously by a yoke and pail system as the site lacked easy access to a river.[65] The pantry supervised the laundry workers: laundresses in earlier years, a William Loteby (or Loteller) in the late 1350s. Before Elizabeth reached the normal menopause age, laundresses received high wages of 3*d.* a day and were rewarded with gifts of squirrel furs, suggesting Elizabeth felt some modesty about her menstruation.[66] Maintaining white table linens, caring for Elizabeth's silk and woolen garments, and cleaning clerical vestments required skill. The rolls never mention methods of cleaning materials that would be sent to dry-cleaning establishments now, instead recording purchase of large laundry tubs and soap. The household bought potash for the laundry, suggesting much of the soap was manufactured domestically.[67]

Household members fell sick from time to time, secure in the knowledge that wages would continue during their illnesses and that the lady stocked medicines to alleviate their symptoms. John de Horsele and a professional hunter ailed in 1338–39; John de Stowe and William atte Stour were sick the next year; an almonry page fell ill in 1340–41. Alan of the saucery and Walter Derleston stayed in the Anglesey infirmary in 1337–38, and Suzanne de Neketon in 1346–47, when the place was called a hospital. Elizabeth responded to illnesses of her staff without much regard for status. The hierarchical tendency so common in the household seems missing here, except for services of university-trained physicians. They attended the lady or her family in response to some dire medical emergency, such as the impending death of Edward de Monthermer in 1339.[68] Elizabeth employed apothecaries for much longer periods and they must have treated those in the household who were sick. Aided by non-staff women, apothecaries concocted medicines from spices, such as the 1¾ pounds of cumin bought to treat "sick men." Traditionally, the lady of the household knew the rudiments of medical treatment and supervised care of the sick; in a large noble household, professionals often ministered in the lady's stead.[69]

The accounts yield more specific information on veterinary medicines than on specific nostrums used for humans. The marshalsea staff treated sick horses with honey, vinegar, ginger, salve, and onions. Horses became ill away from the castle, necessitating recuperative stays at some distant facility, attended by a groom. Sick or healthy, horses were a continuing costly feature of noble life. The marshalsea played a central role in the household, supplying transport for the various departments, operating a forge where cartwheels were repaired and new horseshoes fabricated, and caring for the riding mounts of the lady and her *familia*. Marshalsea staff provided the means of transportation and communication, key elements in household maintenance and seignorial power. When the lady's horses traveled in the countryside, they advertised her prestige, which required good grooming and some adornment to identify them with her house.[70] The marshalsea also accorded care to horses of important guests, who expected good treatment for their animals as part of the establishment's hospitality. To ease demands for pasture and fodder at Clare or Bardfield, manors often boarded marshalsea's charges, with the attendant costs credited to their annual accounts. In a typical transaction, the Hundon provost received credit of 10s. 6d. when the lady's destriers (medieval military horses) used three and a half acres of manorial pasture.[71]

It is difficult to determine just how many horses the marshalsea cared for even though manorial carting and farm animals were outside its purview. It stabled carting horses and traveling retinues of Elizabeth's friends for overnight stays, so when daily records show the marshalsea feeding 50 horses, some would have been temporary visitors. The clerks accounted for horses differently than for other commodities. The 1349–50 roll noted costs of 112 horses boarding at Hundon, tended by two men and two pages for 28 days. It seems unlikely so few servants could properly fulfill their obligations for such a large number. Dividing costs for 28 days into 112 results in four horses. The latter figure tallies more accurately with the next year's inventory, which listed six destriers, three palfreys, four sumpters, two hackneys, one affer, and 18 carting horses.[72] Naturally there was turnover in stock each year as new foals were born and older horses died from old age, ailments, or the dreaded murrain. The lady bought and sold horses in most years, upgraded her stock, gave horses as gifts, and received others in return. Horses were named in ways that described them and their donor: Grisel de Bassingbourn, Blanchard Conyers, Grisel de Walsingham, Morel de Lovayn. When a horse died, the staff ignored sentimentality and processed the horsehide for useful purposes such as cart-covers and repairs to departmental gear. In general, the marshalsea operated in a thrifty fashion, using drippings from the kitchen for greasing needs and selling its own surplus in local markets.[73] The staff practiced economies whenever they did not impinge on Elizabeth's outward show of wealth.

The marshalsea maintained a number of carts, which were not totally interchangeable: the dung cart would have been unsuitable for hauling salt. The cart supply was adequate for daily chores, but neighbors and friends lent carts for major moves.[74] The accounts suggest considerable cooperation among noble and ecclesiastical neighbors, which meant valuable capital was not allocated to equipment used occasionally. Carts broke down on the rough roads and tracks of fourteenth-century England; horses constantly needed to be shod. The 1358–59 inventory noted 1,668 horseshoes consumed when household horses numbered 34. Skilled farriers and smiths worked the forges of Clare or Usk, using old iron and Spanish or Swedish iron, which the household bought in large quantities. Using either staff-produced or purchased items, the smiths sheathed wheels with iron and fashioned iron devices to protect vulnerable parts of the wooden carts.[75]

Nobles of both sexes preferred to ride horseback rather than to travel in the uncomfortable carts of the period. Elizabeth rode, but indulged herself with two chariots built in London. Vehicles with suspended carriages were becoming fashionable for noblewomen on the continent, and presumably Elizabeth's chariots were suspended, improving passenger comfort. Elizabeth bequeathed the larger of her chariots to her daughter Elizabeth, along with its rugs, blankets, cushions, and gear. In a generous gesture, the lady left the smaller one to her chariot driver Richard Charer, knowing that possession of such a prestigious carriage would insure him good opportunities for employment after her death. Chariots of the period were usually brightly painted and decorated. They served the lady, her damsels, and her granddaughters, but also were called upon to transport wine or livery cloth.[76] Whether carrying passengers or goods, the chariots advertised Elizabeth's wealth along the roads between London, Clare, and the Norfolk coast.

The marshalsea department engaged in the widest diversity of tasks in the household. It followed the rhythms imposed by seasonal changes, finding pasturage for its charges in the spring and accumulating hay, oats, and horse bread for other months. Men from the department supervised breeding of the better horses to improve the stock. When Elizabeth traveled, the marshalsea organized the move, supplied transportation, and sent advance men ahead to arrange provisions and accommodation for mounts and carting animals, although occasionally non-staff guides were required in unfamiliar territory.[77] The department hired couriers to deliver letters and verbal messages throughout the realm. During the lady's long residences in London, a subsidiary marshalsea branch operated out of Tottenham, ready to respond to her transportation needs in the city. Manorial officials often transported their renders to the household, but the marshalsea fetched many items purchased by the buttery, pantry, and kitchen. When household saddles needed to be restuffed with wool, the marshalsea performed the repairs. The department purchased thread, hides, turpentine, and tallow to make repairs and to maintain saddles, bridles, and harnesses. Repairing or replacing broken cartwheels required the skilled labor of men such as Richard Wheelwright, who received 1*s.* 2*d.* a week for his services. Smiths and farriers were also professionals, sometimes meriting the title of "Master."[78] Probably the marshalsea was the largest household department: it hired skilled labor, requiring talents ranging from veterinary medicine to tanning to iron-working, and it was charged the wage bill for valets, grooms, and pages, the lowliest ranks of servants.[79] Because marshalsea personnel incurred expenses beyond their wages, their names appear more frequently in the accounts than larder or kitchen employees.

Robert Mareschal, who first appeared in the accounts in 1326 and headed the department from 1336 to 1360, was one of the lady's most trusted associates. He served on her council, but the accounts are more apt to mention his hunting activities. He received livery as a squire, and his wife as a damsel, in 1343. The Mareschals held a manor in North Weald, Essex, but spent much time in Elizabeth's service, Margery sewing and selling kitchen wastes while Robert hunted or directed the marshalsea.[80] Robert attended parliament in 1339 and 1340, but seems to have avoided other governmental tasks and devoted himself to Elizabeth's service. She responded generously and once illegally, when she maneuvered transfer of a manor near Standon to the Mareschals without royal license, and subsequently was fined for the infraction. She paid expenses of their son Thomas for schooling at Cambridge and showered their daughter Elizabeth with finery for her wedding. Margery may have died before Elizabeth wrote her will, for only Robert received a legacy; he also was a principal executor.[81]

Elizabeth's household included small specialized departments and single professionals. Presumably Matthew and Henry Scriptor wrote letters or copied books in the 1330s. Robert the Illuminator received robes as a "little clerk" (one of the categories in Elizabeth's livery list) in 1343, having appeared in the accounts during the preceding five years. Thomas le Purtreour, presumably a pewterer or portrayer (painter), received a small legacy in Elizabeth's will, perhaps painting banners which Elizabeth used in her hall and chamber. He may also have painted these rooms with scenes from Biblical or romantic literature, currently popular in northern Europe.[82]

In the 1330s Elizabeth maintained a goldsmith's department at Clare which fabricated new artifacts and repaired damaged ones. This department purchased gold, usually paying 10*s.* of silver for 10*d.* of the more precious metal. The goldsmiths were equipped with typical tools of their craft: bellows, pans for gilding, pots, and wire, suggesting a fully operating goldsmith's establishment. Five goldsmiths are named, some permanent staff and some hired for shorter periods for specific tasks. John de Markeby received 100s. for his year's work, as well as travel expenses for himself and his servants; later in the account he received £14 13s. 4d. for fashioning six images, supplemented by gifts from Elizabeth of 20s. and 30s.[83] Others on this roll were Robert de Tewkesbury, William atte Hall, Walter atte Verne, and Robert Losfever, the last being a Bury St Edmunds craftsman hired from St John's Day (June 24) to Easter for 20s. Her goldsmiths often traveled to London, underscoring the increasing supervision of the Goldsmith's Company of London over provincial craftsmen after 1327. Perhaps Elizabeth donated some artifacts to Anglesey and Walsingham, for the goldsmiths traveled to those houses for periods suggesting times for planning or installation. For example, Thomas Aurifaber made at least five trips to Anglesey in 1330–31 and 1334; Robert de Tewkesbury and other goldsmiths spent over a month at Walsingham before Elizabeth arrived there in 1334.[84]

Production for Elizabeth's domestic needs fill a large portion of the surviving goldsmith's account: spoons, saucers, belts, clasps, mazers, goblets, and a pax. The craftsmen also worked on jewelry, including a gold brooch, several gold rings, one ring incorporating a diamond, and another a ruby. They also produced a major religious work, requiring an enameler, hired for 28 weeks at 3s. a week, and several carpenters. The carpenters worked on a table, John de Markeby on the images which the enameler then decorated. Goldsmiths appear in the general household accounts in other years, especially Robert and Thomas Aurifaber, but disappear in the 1340s. The craft was becoming more professionalized so perhaps the Clare goldsmiths gravitated to London and a degree of independence. Elizabeth employed her goldsmiths for their professional skills, but they were expected to take on household chores if necessary. Thomas Aurifaber delivered a parrot to Lady FitzWauter although two boys were assigned to carry the bird; Robert de Tewkesbury bought lampreys for Elizabeth when he was near the Severn. Proud craftsmen could easily resent these forays into domestic chores. Cessation of domestic production was achieved amicably, for the lady called on the services of Thomas Aurifaber for her Walsingham foundation.[85] Good sources for precious artifacts and jewelry existed in London, and Elizabeth patronized several: Stephen Freynch, William de Burton, Richard Mundene, and Henry de Northampton. The lady, an avid purchaser of beautiful things, amassed an impressive collection of gold and silver domestic plate created by staff and by purchase: the 49 porringers, 95 saucers, 53 pairs of candlesticks and candelabra, and 64 bells mentioned in her will demonstrate quantity, while the jasper, beryl, and alabaster goblets show the richness and diversity of her possessions. Elizabeth equipped her private chapel with splendid silver chalices, holy water containers, and censers. Her three reliquaries, her painting of the Annunciation, and the three crosses with jewels or images may have been for the chapel or for personal devotions in her chamber. Purchases of silver, gold, and jewels figured prominently in the lady's actual expenditures but rarely in surviving accounts.[86]

Elizabeth's private chapels required resident chaplains as well as liturgical equipment. She may have stinted on the clerics' wages, but she spent heavily on their vestments. Elizabeth bequeathed six surplices to Peter Ereswell, with those remaining for Clare Hall; she left 19 vestments to various religious or educational institutions. The Minoresses received a vestment decorated with a thousand pearls, while the samite cope destined for Hereford Cathedral was embroidered with a design of images and archangels set off with pearls.[87] Others had crests and arabesques or checkered silk with silver-gilt. The more elaborate were splendid examples of *opus anglicanum,* embroidery work prized throughout Europe. Elizabeth maintained an atelier at Clare Castle, where some of the work may have been executed, for she purchased silk thread and cloths of gold which formed the base for much embroidery work. She also bought ready-made gold embroidery at 6s. 8d. an ell. (An ell was a measure of cloth, somewhat longer than a yard, but not more than 45 inches in length.) Thomas Cheiner, a London embroiderer, appeared on her 1343 livery list, so perhaps the more elaborate vestments were purchased.[88] Just as with jewelry and plate, the lady probably balanced domestic production with purchases from professional craftsmen.

One would expect to find a tailoring department, given the large amounts of cloth purchased for the annual livery. Only a casual mention of sheep hide and nails for the tailor hint at the domestic production entailed in cutting and sewing the colorful outfits that the lady gave her staff. The cloth was sheared outside the household, but Elizabeth's damsels probably were responsible for most sewing chores. Elizabeth's annual livery costs ranged from £100 to £200, excluding domestic labor, with larger sums expended in her later years.[89] Colors and textures of the livery cloth varied from year to year and within each household rank. In 1358–59 the household knights and Elizabeth's wards dressed in the same material chosen for the lady and countess of Pembroke. The squires were given outfits of azure blue and striped cloth; officials had green and striped medley. Clerks and damsels wore brown mabryn (a marbled cloth) outfits, with the women adding "bruskyn" medley belts or bodices. "Little clerks" had green costumes, which set them apart from the servants in their mixed, colored wool and tan stripes. Elizabeth's manorial bailiffs wore red and green livery, as did the household pages, although materials and shades differed. The assembled staff must have been a dazzling sight. Elizabeth probably expected some of the household would need more practical outfits, for she sent to Wales for 182 ells and 100 yards of russet.[90] Shoes and boots for Elizabeth and a few wards and grandchildren were purchased: 23 pairs of men's shoes and several pairs for damsels at 4*d.* a pair. Her own shoes cost more: three pairs of felt shoes for 2*s.* 6*d.* for example, or two pairs of shoes, one pierced (*penetre*) for 16*d.* Boots were more expensive: her grandson-in-law's pair cost 3*s.* 6*d.* Servants repaired shoes for a few of Elizabeth's closest associates; old shoes were purchased occasionally as gifts for faggot-stackers.[91] Overall, the household alternated between purchasing in urban markets and producing domestically, with no clear pattern emerging. Outside forces probably hastened closing the goldsmith department, but neither the tailors', embroiderers', or shoemakers' associations possessed enough national clout to change practices within the lady's household.

The Clare establishment had a chamber and wardrobe, each usually headed by a cleric, until the departments merged in 1355.[92] These units were superior to other household departments because they tracked income and expenditures, but their accounts offer no intimate details of the lady, in part because she received weekly money for personal needs, rarely enumerated by the clerks. Wardrobe and chamber rolls mention indentures, quittances, leases, expenses for pursuing legal remedies at Exchequer and Chancery, and costs for her great Christmas livery. Information on Elizabeth's private schedule and daily habits does not appear since she hired wardrobe and chamber clerks to administer establishment finances rather than to memorialize her activities.

Clerks heading the wardrobe and chamber belonged to Elizabeth's hand-picked council which deliberated policy issues for her enterprises. The council was Elizabeth's upper management team, whose purposes included maximizing profits and working for a favorable political and judicial milieu for the lady's business. Some members audited manorial accounts and visited individual manors to check on operations, while others scrutinized household accounts, which retain marginal notations of approval. Council members journeyed to the capital to look out for Elizabeth's interests at parliamentary sessions. Although the composition of her council changed over the years, the lady generally recruited men with special professional skills in law, competent administrators, or well-placed local men. The council was modeled on royal practice, but functioned in a more personal, local, and restricted setting. The accounts never list all council members, but rather economically note the name of one member, adding "and other members of the Lady's Council."[93] The strong local element in the council insured that Elizabeth's status among her neighbors remained undiminished by providing her with information and a strong network of clients whose own position prospered as a result of her successes.

Elizabeth's pleasure and purposes dominated and directed the council and the work of nearly 200 servants at her residences and scattered estates. She did not intervene in daily administrative duties of the departments, but she certainly kept her staff apprised of her wishes. The lady was well-informed, rewarding servants whose performance merited her appreciation, and she commanded exceptions to routine operations by the rubric "at the Lady's precept." She instilled a sense of loyalty in many of her servants, who chose to make service in the Clare household their lifetime occupation. Their accumulated experience smoothed the daily functioning of the household which served as their workplace and their home. The household was a complex entity, providing a sense of extended family to those who ate together daily and followed the same rhythms of fast and feast in their shared faith. Working for Elizabeth and wearing her livery gave servants enhanced status in the world beyond the castle walls, for the lady intervened to protect her men from the consequences of unlawful activities and from indignities meted out by surly villagers. However, protection, decent meals, and annual gifts were only by-products of the true *raison d'être* of the household. It functioned to serve and honor Elizabeth and to promote her good estate in this life, responsibilities it performed quite well.

CHAPTER 3

FAMILY AND FRIENDS

Family and friends figured prominently in Elizabeth's life. She gloried in her Clare heritage with its ancient and commanding place in English history. The division of Clare lands awarded her the honor bearing the family name, further identifying her with ancestors and the heart of their patrimony. Elizabeth was the lady of Clare, a title she claimed for herself (others occasionally called her the countess of Clare) and used for her last widowhood. She could have been the lady of Usk or Cranborne, Bardfield or Weymouth, but she chose Clare, prompted by pride in her lineage.[1] Elizabeth did not assume the title lady of Clare immediately upon Damory's death, still evoking relationships with Gilbert and Roger in her 1326 secret protest. However, a few years later household rolls begin to note the title. Her chantry foundation for Gilbert de Clare reinforced natal relationships and gratitude for the wealth her paternal connections brought her.

Family

The heritage from her mother, Joan, was equally important, for it provided links with English and Castilian royalty. The latter was mostly symbolic, but important enough to Elizabeth that one of her seals incorporated motifs from her grandmother Eleanor of Castile.[2] The English royal connection was practical, immediate, and advantageous throughout Edward III's reign, when she was routinely identified as the "king's kinswoman." Elizabeth's tributes to her mother included extensive building projects at Clare friary, where Joan was buried. The friary was quite literally across the street from Clare Castle, so projects dedicated to Joan had intimacy and proximity. In 1347 Bishop John Paschal preached an indulgence for those offering at the friary church for Joan's soul, an initiative probably inspired by Elizabeth, who had attended similar sermons in 1318.[3] A curious episode in Elizabeth's life concerns her mother. According to Osbern Bokenham, Elizabeth wished to see her mother's remains at the friary in 1359, 52 years after her death. Elizabeth found an incorrupt corpse, so she tested the body personally by pressing Joan's breasts and lifting her eyelids.[4] Bokenham gives no motive for Elizabeth's action, making any explanation conjectural. Perhaps the Clare friars had finally completed Edward de Monthermer's tomb and uncovered Joan's corpse when installing her son's memorial. They would have informed Elizabeth, who proceeded to her own examination. She was still paying for the tomb's fabrication in 1352, though Monthermer died in 1339, so a 1359 installation was possible. Two points are clear: Elizabeth's accounts do not mention the event, and Joan's reputation for sanctity probably had its origin at this time.

All the Clare sisters seemed dedicated to their birth family, though each demonstrated that commitment differently. Eleanor showered her donations on Tewkesbury Abbey, enhancing the church with stunning windows portraying males of the Clare lineage buried there.[5] Margaret Audley directed her energies toward seeking the Clare comital title for her husband. His ambitions seem obvious, but Margaret may have wanted to be a countess, a status she enjoyed in her first marriage.[6] With Eleanor guarding and glorifying the family burial church and Margaret aiding her husband in acquiring the Clare comital title, Elizabeth needed to exhibit ingenuity in exalting the family name, which she did by founding Clare College, a novel memorial to the family which perpetuated her ancestors' name among a constantly renewing corps of students. The Clare sisters were truly daughters of their house, showing that family pride was not solely a male preserve in fourteenth-century England.[7]

It is difficult to gauge the degree of intimacy or amity among the sisters during Edward II's reign. They shared a few childhood years, but carefree days for noble daughters were short at best. Their mother had been assigned quarters at Windsor Castle, so perhaps they spent time together there or resided with Joan and Monthermer. Later associations of Margaret and Elizabeth with Amesbury convent suggest some residence, which may have provided a time for sisterly interaction in a quasi-family setting with their aunt Mary, a nun there.[8] Each sister's childhood terminated at marriage, in 1306, 1307, and 1308 respectively. By 1311 Eleanor had joined Queen Isabella's court, where she undoubtedly saw her sister Margaret Gaveston. The sisters had ample opportunity to establish familial bonds by 1317, when their husbands were awarded the Clare inheritance and began jockeying for additional royal favors. Sibling friendships suffered when Damory and Audley allied themselves against Despenser. Undoubtedly the sisters supported and encouraged their spouses' ambitions, for none would have wanted to relinquish an acre or a knight's fee of their inheritance. Perhaps Eleanor sought to mitigate Despenser's greed against Margaret and Elizabeth, but little suggests she succeeded, if indeed she tried.[9]

The Clare sisters' situations altered dramatically after Isabella's 1326 invasion. Margaret's activities are poorly documented, but she left confinement at Sempringham and rejoined her husband as he was reestablishing himself. From 1326 to 1331 Eleanor exhibited audacity and recklessness and, above all, a firm resolve to maintain her Clare legacy by any means. Initially she was consigned to the Tower of London, a storehouse for many Despenser possessions which Eleanor managed to spirit away with outside assistance.[10] In spite of royal inability to recover the goods now rightfully escheated to the Crown, Eleanor was allowed possession of her lands, rendering homage in May 1328. Eight months later she lost her estates because she married William la Zouche after a supposed abduction and marriage without royal license. She was imprisoned again until she and Zouche arranged to pay a punitive fine in return for full pardon and restoration of Eleanor's properties. The couple got their pardon and lands, but never paid the fine. They were also successful in beating back John de Grey of Rotherfield, who claimed he married Eleanor before Zouche. This took years as Grey pursued his suit in both royal and ecclesiastical courts.[11] Bits of evidence suggest some rapprochement between Elizabeth and Eleanor before 1326. The youngest Despenser daughter was named Elizabeth and later appeared in her aunt's household. In 1329 the lady paid Eleanor and Zouche 500 marks for the farm of Usk and a payment of £170 for the preceding four years. The lady of Clare had recovered this Welsh property by 1329; it would seem a debt that might have been ignored with Eleanor under arrest. Most likely the Despensers had allowed Elizabeth to rent Usk by 1325, part of the lessened hostility mentioned in her 1326 secret testament. Though Elizabeth later responded to Eleanor's children, her last personal contact with Eleanor may have been in a livery of cloth she gave Lady Despenser in 1330–31.[12] Meanwhile, Eleanor and William la Zouche began a family. One son survived, choosing to become a monk at Glastonbury since he had few prospects for secular fortune. William's motives for joining the monastery perhaps lacked a strong religious impulse, as Glastonbury was more noted for its comfortable style than its zeal or piety in the late Middle Ages. Elizabeth's accounts confirm that William's thoughts ranged beyond the monastery, for in 1355–56 he leased her estate at Bletchingdon.

The Audleys experienced real domestic trauma in 1336 when their only daughter, Margaret, was abducted and forcibly married by Ralph Stafford.[13] Stafford's bold move founded his family's fortunes, since young Margaret was the only heir to her mother's Clare inheritance. The Audleys protested the abduction in vain, for Edward III supported Stafford. The Audleys reconciled themselves to their daughter's marriage, perhaps because the king awarded Hugh the earldom of Gloucester in 1337 or perhaps because a son was soon born to the Staffords. Elizabeth's household rolls are less informative in the 1330s than later, but they show messengers and letters being exchanged between the lady of Clare and her sister Margaret between 1338 and Margaret's death in 1342.[14]

The Clare sisters acted together when their interests required a common front, as shown by their joint petition to the king to be rid of their father's debts. However, little suggests they found joy in each other's company, for they seem to have been disinclined to exchange visits or gifts.[15] Medieval siblings often failed to establish amicable relationships, perhaps prompted by inheritance laws. These affected males more forcefully than their sisters, but women had grounds for rivalry as well. Early on, Eleanor saw one sister becoming a countess and one expecting that title. Later in Edward II's reign, her husband predominated while Elizabeth and Margaret suffered major reversals of fortune. The animosities inherent in these circumstances could be papered over but not necessarily forgotten.

The marital episodes of Elizabeth's parents left her with six half-siblings. There is no evidence of relationships with her two half-sisters, Gilbert's daughters from his first marriage.[16] Joan and Ralph produced four living children during their union: Mary, Joan, Thomas, and Edward. Only Elizabeth and Edward de Monthermer remained on close terms; he accompanied her son, William, at his knighting and she purchased a palfrey for him in 1338. Young Monthermer was ailing the next year when he joined Elizabeth's *familia*. She employed Master Martin to treat his medical problems, but Edward died, with Elizabeth and her staff attending to details of his funeral and burial. She informed Thomas de Monthermer, Queen Isabella, and Edward's knightly friends and assembled some of her children and grandchildren for the service.[17] Burial was at Clare friary near Edward's mother.[18] Candles and tapers were furnished for the service, trestle tables were prepared for the mourners' feast, laborers dug the grave, all at Elizabeth's expense. Later she paid the Austin friars of Clare to pray for his soul and construct his tomb.[19] Monthermer had done a bit of judicial work for the Crown; the height of his career was in the 1335 campaign against the Scots. Perhaps Edward applied to his half-sister Margaret for help, but it was Elizabeth who provided him hospitality, showing her firm sense of family duty.

After her sister Eleanor died in 1337, Elizabeth reached out to her Despenser kin. The eldest nephew was Hugh Despenser III, a young man who had suffered supporting the claims of his lineage. He defended Caerphilly Castle from royal forces, but even after its surrender he was imprisoned for four years. Only in 1331 was Hugh free of all charges against him.[20] Hugh did not need his aunt's material help by 1338, when her rolls first mention letters to him, for the lands he inherited from his mother were rich and King Edward added to his possessions. Elizabeth, however, could offer connections, friendship, and affection. Hugh visited Elizabeth at Bardfield in 1339–40; that year she sent him falcons and falconers and remained in contact by messenger. When the king commissioned him envoy to the pope in 1343, Hugh obtained papal indults for himself and his aunt. Their relationship was strengthened by his marriage to Elizabeth Montague, the lady's friend, and daughter of the earl of Salisbury. Hugh visited Elizabeth in 1347–48 in East Anglia and in Wales, before his death in February 1349.[21]

Eleanor's second son, Edward Despenser, died in 1342, leaving his widow, Anne, and Edward, his six-year-old son and heir. This boy, Elizabeth de Burgh's great-nephew, joined her *familia* in 1346. Her home offered good prospects for instruction in manners, conversation, and estate management. Such concern for a distant relative seems commendable on Elizabeth's part, but Edward was also Henry Ferrers's nephew, and welcoming the boy honored her son-in-law's memory.[22] Perhaps she also sought a connection for her Ferrers grandson, William, as both he and Edward Despenser expected central England to be the core of their landed estates. Edward Despenser accompanied his great-aunt to Wales in the summer of 1348, but then disappears from the accounts. The Black Death transformed the boy's status from one of expecting a good collection of estates to one with prospects for enormous wealth, for Edward was heir of his uncle Hugh Despenser III who died childless during the time of the plague. Earlier, Bartholomew de Burghersh, husband of one of Elizabeth de Burgh's Verdon stepdaughters, had arranged a marriage contract between Edward Despenser and his granddaughter; quite possibly the arrangements were made at Clare or Bardfield. The 1346–47 marshalsea account, during the period when Edward Despenser belonged to Elizabeth's *familia,* shows that Burghersh and Despenser horses were stabled in October and December of 1346 and January, February, March, April, May, June, August, and September of 1347.[23] A few of the entries could be messengers, but the frequent Burghersh visits are exceptional, even though friendship between the lady and the Burghersh clan stretched over many years. Did the parties consider themselves family, friends, or useful connections? Distinctions blur. Elizabeth reached out to young Edward because of his Despenser and Ferrers connections; she seems to have facilitated his future associations with her more remote Burghersh relations. The Crown disposed of its wards' marriages and Burghersh had to purchase Edward's, but Elizabeth provided the place where the families could meet, discuss, and negotiate in a congenial atmosphere. Her reward would have been the gratitude of all involved, a treasury of accumulated favors for herself and her family.

Elizabeth's youngest Despenser nephew, Gilbert, appeared in the household rolls between 1347 and 1349 as a member of the lady's *familia*. None of the accounts delineate his position or activities, except for frequent hunting at Trelleck and Caerleon.[24] He may have been stranded at Elizabeth's Welsh estates and decided to sit out the plague as her guest, for he vanishes from the accounts after 1349.

Eleanor and Hugh Despenser junior produced daughters, though ascertaining how many is difficult. The *Glamorgan County History* notes three: Isabella, Eleanor, and Joan; the *Close Rolls* mention a daughter, Margaret; another daughter, Elizabeth, married Maurice Berkeley in the 1330s.[25] Part of the revenge heaped on the Despenser family by Queen Isabella was to force Eleanor, Joan, and Margaret into Gilbertine convents where they were professed for life.[26] Elizabeth seems not to have had much contact with these Despenser nieces. Eleanor never appears in the accounts, though she was still alive in 1351. When Margaret died in 1337, her aunt sent religious goods for her sepulchre: wax images and a painting on buckram of the Four Evangelists. Joan Despenser died in 1351, so her aunt's gift that year was probably another funereal memorial.[27] Isabella Despenser escaped being dumped into a convent because she married Richard Fitzalan, heir to the Arundel earldom, a union that eventually faltered. Isabella Despenser sent a gift of fish in 1351–52, but otherwise received no mention in the accounts.[28]

One unmarried Despenser daughter escaped conventual life. Little Elizabeth was probably the youngest of the Despensers, since her future husband, Maurice Berkeley, was born in 1330, marrying her in 1338. Noble boys might marry older females, but with a reasonably small age gap favored. Elizabeth de Burgh took an active interest in this niece, who was delivered to her care in August 1338 by the prioress of Wix. The young girl was part of her aunt's *familia* for about a year and a half before she was sent to Tewkesbury, presumably to join the Berkeley family.[29] Elizabeth was a natural tutor for young girls on the eve of married life, especially in the absence of a mother to instruct in proper behavior and intimate expectations.

The lady cultivated contacts with male Despensers more assiduously than with their sisters. Partly this stemmed from political reality, for Despenser males were better situated than three nuns, a discarded wife, and a young bride. Despenser males had a freedom of movement denied to three of their sisters, so they could easily visit their aunt or join her *familia*. Beyond that, males were more important in alliance-building and influence than females. Elizabeth felt family ties with and obligations to her nieces and nephews, but the latter had more clout politically and therefore received more sustained interest.

Elizabeth's Audley niece, Margaret Stafford, does not appear in the lady's household accounts until after her mother's death, though aunt and niece may have visited earlier. Household clerks tended to note titled visitors rather than others; young or never-married women do not appear in guest notations unless titled. (Names of Elizabeth's granddaughters appear in her *familia* rather than as guests, except for the countess of Ulster). Also, Elizabeth reached out to nieces and nephews most clearly after their mothers were dead. Her Audley niece, Margaret Stafford, probably stayed at Clare in August 1346 while her husband, Ralph Stafford, fought at Crécy.[30] Margaret was Elizabeth's link to the Stafford family, but Ralph, eventually Earl Stafford, figured more prominently in the lady's rolls. Contacts with him continued after his wife's death, in part because his control of Clare properties gave Ralph common concerns with Elizabeth, and in part because he had the ear of the king. Both reasons fit with Elizabeth's pattern of cultivating family and friends who could be useful allies. Ralph visited Elizabeth in East Anglia and London; one of the last household rolls recorded letters to Ralph. The relationship profited both parties. Ralph was an earl and an original member of the Order of the Garter. Elizabeth was the king's kinswoman, an important landed noblewoman in East Anglia, Wales, and Ireland, where Ralph also had landed interests, and she patronized the Augustinian friars, as did Ralph.[31] Their interests meshed, and neither would have viewed the continuation of their tenuous family tie as manipulative.

Elizabeth's natal family mattered to her for several reasons. She owed the bulk of her lands and castles to her paternal relatives, and her connections to royalty to her mother. Gratitude and pride prompted remembrances of them, augmented by ecclesiastical exhortations to honor parents.[32] Attitudes toward her siblings are problematic, but friendly interchanges seem minimal. Only Elizabeth survived after 1342 and she responded to her surviving nieces and nephews from duty, self-interest, and perhaps affection. These young people offered potential for expanding her alliances and those of her children and grandchildren, always key for the lady. Promoting her children's interests involved Elizabeth with their paternal kin, especially the Burgh and Verdon families, and eventually with her children's spouses. Her attitude was not wholly altruistic, for her own interests were advanced by maintaining good relationships with her former husbands' families, and the children's spouses offered new avenues for constructing advantageous networks.

In the years after John de Burgh's death, Elizabeth and Earl Richard of Ulster remained on cordial terms, but she had fewer contacts with her son's paternal uncles and cousins. Nevertheless, the Burghs respected Elizabeth, for they continued to pay rents to her for nearly 50 years. The lady kept herself informed of Irish conditions, both for herself and her son's political future. William had remained in Ireland during Elizabeth's Verdon interlude, but joined her when he was about seven. Under her tutelage, William learned about his eventual inheritance, as well as being taught on matters of faith and behavior. Sharing his mother's imprisonment at Barking, and knowing of her subsequent misadventures, educated the boy in stark political realities. As a single mother for most of William's youth, Elizabeth would have enlisted men to teach her son gender-specific skills necessary for his future career.[33] Unfortunately we do not know much about affective mother-son bonds beyond her desire to raise the boy in his formative years. These ended soon, as Earl Richard died in 1326 and his grandson inherited the earldom of Ulster. William was quickly catapulted into adult life when the earl of Lancaster bought his marriage rights and interceded with the Crown for his early inheritance. William married the earl's daughter Matilda in 1327 after receiving papal permission, since they were related within prohibited degrees. The newlyweds were teenagers and William's comital revenues took a while to materialize, so Earl Henry and Elizabeth de Burgh supported the couple at first. The young people spent time at the earl's Kenilworth and Higham Ferrers residences and may have had a house at Caythorpe provided by Elizabeth. Some provisions came from the earl, but Elizabeth paid the bulk of the newlyweds' expenses until at least July 1328. William tarried in England for several reasons: he was not knighted; he needed military training before meeting the Irish challenges; he needed military backing from the Crown to be instrumental in asserting English interests in that turbulent land. This program had been recommended by Elizabeth's trusted counselor, Thomas de Cheddeworth, who visited Ulster on his lady's orders in 1327. Urgency attended William's program, for Robert Bruce of Scotland had intervened in Ireland that year, landing in an Ulster still racked with disorder after Earl Richard's death. There was fear the area might look to another lord, possibly Bruce himself, if William did not claim his Irish inheritance quickly.[34]

Since Elizabeth was financing her son before he assumed his Irish responsibilities, an account of his expenses is included among the Clare accounts. In 1326 she began equipping William for knighthood, hiring Adam le Heannier to fabricate his armor and purchasing ten horses for her son, including one that cost £52 12s. More utilitarian equipment was needed for his traveling entourage and knighting ceremony: napery, baskets, wall hangings, cooking dishes, tankards, two baboon (babbewing) chairs, cloth, and furs. The lady paid out £859 15s. 9d., between one-third and one-half of her annual income, easing the burden by collecting a feudal aid. Her costs were actually higher, for the accounts ignored wages of her staff delegated to attend William: Alan de Medefeld, keeper of the wardrobe; Robert de Stalyngton, receiver of Clare; Thomas de Cheddeworth, her clerical advisor; Henry de Colyngham and Robert Mareschal, trusted squires; Hubert de Burgh, clerk of her wardrobe; and John de Horsele, an old retainer. Servants with specialized abilities, valets, and grooms were sent along too. Elizabeth assembled a knightly group to add honor to his entourage, among them her son-in-law Henry Ferrers, her half-brother Edward de Monthermer, and John Sturmy. Finally, William's retinue included a contingent of Poers and Irish Burghs, who had fled to England.[35]

William did homage to the king for his lands in November 1327, attended his first parliament at York in February 1328, followed by tourneying at Blyth. William went north in style, with his falconer, hawks, and hunting dogs. Elizabeth purchased cloth for William and his friends, to be made into yellow, hooded coats at a cost of 54s. 4d. William was not yet knighted, but this did not preclude joining in military games, for youths who would soon be in knightly ranks were welcomed.[36] Military exercises offered training in skills needed in warfare, so the Blyth tournament was educational as well as social. There were other celebrations in the spring, culminating in William's formal knighting in June 1328, probably by Edward III. Elizabeth did not attend the ceremony, which seems to have been a masculine affair, but she assured her son a glorious experience. She called in favors from monastic friends: the prior of Stoke sent carting horses and the abbot of Tewkesbury provided a cook.[37] The lady gave her son a competent staff to organize the military games and to hire the necessary laundress, carpenters, grooms, and the more colorful herald and minstrels: Patrick and Richard Vidulator playing viols, Adam Harper, W. Taborer, and Martin Trumpe, whose horn was adorned with banners.

Soon after the ceremony, William was due at Berwick for the wedding uniting the Plantagenet and Bruce families, to be followed by his passage to Ireland. Elizabeth's counselor Thomas de Cheddeworth had recommended that the new earl of Ulster make his progress into Ireland with military backing from the English Crown, yet no English troops accompanied William. Rather, Robert Bruce, the Scottish king, escorted William. This must have humiliated King Edward for the message was clear: "that the English king was unable to do for one of his own subjects what the Scottish king was both willing and able to do." Robert Bruce and William de Burgh were related, as Bruce's wife was William's aunt, perhaps glossing over the political implications.[38] Nothing in the Clare rolls indicates that William desired a Bruce escort, for his uncle's name was mentioned only once in the 1327–28 roll. William and the Scottish king landed in Carrickfergus in July, with Bruce staying until mid-August.

Elizabeth continued to send her son supplies and perhaps worried about his youth as he was only 17 when he reached Ireland. Three years later he was dead. Elizabeth may have grieved, but the accounts are silent on her emotions. In later years she sponsored masses for his soul, but she left a chantry foundation to his widow. The lady's 1355 will gives the impression she still resented his failure in Ireland, for she bequeathed his daughter "all the debts that my son, her father, owed me on the day that he died."[39] Quite possibly, in the brashness of youth William had ignored maternal injunctions, contributing to the hatred that motivated his murder. For Elizabeth, protecting one's heritage demanded responsibility and sacrifice. She may have loved William, while doubting that he had met those challenges.

William's murder in 1333 left his widow, Matilda, and his daughter, Elizabeth, in an extremely vulnerable position, terrorized and threatened by his enemies. The widowed countess and her daughter fled to the security of England, where Matilda fought to obtain her dower. Little Elizabeth de Burgh was a Crown ward, but Edward allowed the girl to stay with her mother and even paid Matilda for her maintenance.[40] Matilda visited her mother-in-law in June and July of 1334, and Elizabeth demonstrated affection for Matilda by sending her two spaniels in 1340. Edward III, always eager to enrich his own children with minimal expense, intervened in the lives of Matilda and her daughter by the 1340s, for young Elizabeth's vast Irish and Clare inheritance tempted him. In February 1342, Matilda's custody ended when the little girl and the king's son Lionel were betrothed and she joined the royal nursery.[41]

If Ireland were to be a financial asset for Lionel, it needed to be pacified and made profitable. The king needed a trusted military commander to represent royal interests and chose Ralph Ufford, the earl of Suffolk's brother. Edward III reasoned that Ralph's position would be strengthened by marriage to Matilda, countess of Ulster, who wanted to reclaim control of her Irish dower lands. Ralph and Matilda were married before August 1343, reaching Ireland about a year later.[42] In the end Ralph's military initiatives faltered because of illness and he died in 1346. Matilda again fled to England, accompanied by her infant Ufford daughter.

The lady of Clare's granddaughter Elizabeth had not gone to Ireland for she was established in the royal household. Her grandmother entertained her for two weeks in December 1344. At this juncture the young girl was called the lady of Ulster, but by 1347 she appears in the rolls as countess.[43] The shift in the girl's status reflected her husband's assumption of the title of earl and changes in her mother's situation. Matilda was cautioned in May 1347 not to marry without royal license, but another wedding was far from Matilda's mind. By October Matilda had endowed a chantry at

Campsey Ash convent for her two husbands, her daughters, and others, and professed there as an Augustinian nun. Matilda truly felt called to her vocation. While at Campsey she withdrew even more decisively by becoming an enclosed anchoress within the convent. Finally she realized her childhood dream of becoming a Minoress when her son-in-law, Lionel, established a Franciscan community for her at Bruisyard.[44]

After her mother entered conventual life, little Elizabeth regularly visited her paternal grandmother, especially when she could interact with her Ferrers and Despenser kin. Young Elizabeth also maintained ties with her half-sister, Margaret Ufford, who came with her to Clare in 1350. When the lady began spending time in London, her granddaughter visited her there.[45] Perhaps Elizabeth even had an opportunity to enjoy her great-granddaughter Philippa, child of the countess of Ulster and Lionel.[46] The lady gave her namesake gifts in her lifetime—cloth, a silver needle, for example, but nothing personal in her last will except the debts of her father. As heiress to the Clare and Ulster lands, she would not need the beds and coverlets and silver dishes the lady's less wealthy granddaughters required, but Elizabeth had ample jewelry and plate for a testamentary gesture. Perhaps Earl William's supposed mistakes and her own failure to divert some Clare lands to other heirs still rankled, but this granddaughter would receive the lady's residual personal property, so the will's omission need not be vindictive.

The lady's two surviving daughters, Isabella de Verdon and Elizabeth Damory, spent most of their childhood with their mother. They shared Elizabeth's imprisonment in 1322 and were living with her in 1327, when Elizabeth had to find care for them while she attended Edward II's funeral. Their whereabouts in the interim are unknown, though a stint at Amesbury convent seems possible before their marriages in the late 1320s. Isabella's husband, Henry Ferrers, claimed his marital rights around 1330. She conceived quickly, for Elizabeth sent her a book costing £36 for her purification in March 1331, and showed maternal concern by checking on Isabella's condition in February and April. Another pregnancy followed quickly, with son William born in February 1333.[47] By that time, Elizabeth had instituted a use for the Ferrers, assuring Isabella and Henry a fairly large estate at her death. The lady had lost her own son and may have projected a filial role on to Henry, rather than seeing him only as Isabella's husband.

Henry's career from 1332 to his death in 1343 demanded long stretches in the king's service. He participated in Scottish campaigns before joining royal forces on the continent in July 1338, where he acted as royal chamberlain and undertook various diplomatic assignments. Elizabeth and Henry maintained close contact, exchanging typical noble gifts. Hers were practical: food, horses, equipment repair, and money; he gave her food and wine. The lady's staff supervised some breeding of his horses; Henry had a chamber in Elizabeth's London residence.[48] Certainly these two developed a close rapport, though he needed her support less and less as his favor with the king brought him grants, respites from taxation, and acknowledgments of "special grace." The degree of trust may be measured in part by Henry's choice of Elizabeth's Irish lawyer to watch over his interests there, hers by an additional license for a use in 1337 to place Tregrug Castle in the eventual possession of Isabella and Henry.[49]

Elizabeth's daughter Isabella seems lost in these arrangements between the lady and Henry, but his predominance reflects fourteenth-century realities. Elizabeth, as a widow, had a legal standing that her married daughter did not, requiring that business be transacted in Henry's name even when Isabella's properties were involved. Isabella is rarely mentioned in Crown documents, but she appears in the Clare accounts. She visited her mother briefly in 1337 and for three months in 1338. Both Ferrers were at Clare in May 1340, and Isabella was back for the Christmas holidays, arriving in November and staying until February. By the summer of 1342 Henry was weak and sick, according to King Edward. After his death the following year, Elizabeth remembered him with commemorative masses. She opened her home to Isabella and her children, renovating her daughter's rooms in Clare Castle. Isabella often stayed at Clare and her mother reciprocated with visits to the Ferrers manors of Stebbing and Woodham Ferrers, suggesting a loving relationship between the two. In 1347 Isabella joined Elizabeth's pilgrimage and triumphal foundation progress to Walsingham. Their last meeting was in early 1348, before Elizabeth departed for Wales, where she later learned of Isabella's death during the plague.[50] The rolls present a bare-bones picture of mother and daughter, ignoring matters of the heart. The lady's gift of a £36 book implies love for her daughter, the sum indicating that Elizabeth not only spent generously but invested thought into the gift, probably an illuminated volume.[51] The book and the castle chambers were private tokens, not the normal parading of status, so they denote affection rather than ostentation.

Long before their parents' deaths, the Ferrers children spent time with their grandmother. William attended the Monthermer funeral; Elizabeth spent part of the winter of 1341 with the lady. Philippa went to Wales later that year, spending the summer at Usk, except for a stint at Amesbury convent in June. Grandmother paid her expenses, provided servants and suitable retinue for the conventual retreat.[52] By September Philippa concluded her Welsh interlude and went home. After news of Isabella's death reached Elizabeth in Wales, she immediately acted on her grandchildren's behalf. Philippa and Elizabeth were with their grandmother in 1349–50, but apparently William was not.

Henry Ferrers had arranged the marriages of Philippa and Elizabeth, following the typical pattern of making marriage contracts for daughters well before they were expected to function as wives at the sexual level, though they assumed their spouse's name at the time of the contract.[53] Philippa anticipated a brilliant union with Guy de Beauchamp, son and heir of the earl of Warwick. Elizabeth Ferrers also would be a countess, though of a less grand earldom. Because Philippa was considered part of her grandmother's *familia* after Isabella's death, it is difficult to estimate if her position there was constant or intermittent. In any event it was short-lived, for Philippa last appears in the accounts in May 1351, when she was ready for adulthood as a wife. The earl and countess of Warwick visited Elizabeth that spring, possibly to take Philippa to her husband. Philippa de-livered a child in 1352; she and her husband, Guy, had another child be-fore his death in 1360. Katherine, the eldest, was professed as a nun at Shouldham before she was seven; the next child, named for the lady of Clare, may have entered Shouldham convent at an even younger age.[54] Daughters in many noble families were named for the reigning queen, their mothers, or grandmothers. Certainly this fashion was typical in Eliz-abeth's family and in those of her children. Philippa chose her grand-mother's name for one daughter, suggesting that the lady of Clare provided Philippa's strongest maternal image. Philippa emulated her grandmother by taking a vow of chastity when Guy de Beauchamp died in the spring of 1360. She may have abhorred the married state or treasured Guy's mem-ory too dearly to contemplate another union, but more likely she admired her grandmother's model. Philippa's vow entailed greater courage then Elizabeth's, because the young widow's only material assets were two Nor-folk manors held jointly with Guy. We do not know if Philippa and her grandmother experienced any reunions after Philippa's marriage, but Eliz-abeth knew about her two Beauchamp great-grandchildren because the countess of Warwick visited her in 1357 and 1358, an example of the ex-panded social contacts marriage alliances produced. Philippa stayed close to her natal family; her brother, William, remembered her with legacies of silver dishes.[55] Elizabeth bequeathed nothing to Philippa, seeing no need to endow a granddaughter expected to be countess of Warwick. That ex-pectation was dashed at Guy's death, but apparently Elizabeth failed to change her testament.

Philippa's sister, Elizabeth, grew up under her grandmother's tutelage, appearing in the Clare accounts from 1341 to 1358. The young girl was a Crown ward after 1343, but her grandmother had retained custody of her own children during their minorities and seems to have kept her grand-daughter as well. The lady provided generously for her granddaughter, buying her shoes and clothing and giving her gifts of gloves, a knife sheath, and accessories. In 1352 she was grouped with the children for the festivities and frivolities of the Boy Bishop's reign.[56] Young Elizabeth learned manners and social graces as she watched her grandmother's activities and expanded her contacts as she interacted with her relatives and her grandmother's guests.

The marriage arranged by Henry Ferrers promised a title for his daughter Elizabeth, but the arrangement lacked the potential brilliance of her sister's marriage contract. Elizabeth was married to David de Strabolgi, the earl of Athol's heir. David's title sounded grand, but much of his inheritance was in Scotland or Northumberland; his claim to the Scottish inheritance was never realized, although he benefited from being one of Earl Aymer of Pembroke's heirs. Young David first visited Elizabeth de Burgh in 1344–45, with two return trips in 1346–47; his brother-in-law, William Ferrers, and his mother-in-law, Isabella, were in attendance for the later visits. The lady provided many opportunities for interaction of prospective marriage kin as she understood the value of extensive kinship and friendship networks, so David's visits integrated him into his wife's family. Elizabeth heaped clothing gifts on David in 1351, outfitting him with buge fur and skins for his sleeves, a pair of leather boots, spurs, belts, laces, three pairs of gloves, a hat, a saddle and bridle.[57]

It is uncertain when Elizabeth moved from her grandmother's *familia* to her own household with David. It should have occurred in 1355 when Edward III ordered his escheators to give the earl of Athol his lands. David then accompanied the Black Prince to France, and his wife reappeared in her grandmother's *familia* in 1357–58. In April 1358, the lady supplied a small retinue for the countess when she went to Langley and Windsor, presumably visiting the royal court.[58] The countess returned to Clare but then vanished from the remaining accounts. Elizabeth de Burgh showed affection for her namesake by bequeathing her two elaborate beds and a green coverlet. (William Ferrers left his second sister some silver plate and a religious triptych.) Probably the older woman was apprehensive about this granddaughter's future or was responding to close emotional ties.[59] The alacrity with which the grandmother reached out to the orphaned youngster and provided nurture over the next decade shows a deeply affectionate bond between the two.

William Ferrers, born in February 1333, was identified as a member of his grandmother's *familia* in 1339; for some years after, he depended on his grandmother for stabling his horses and for new horseshoes, though he may not have resided with her continuously.[60] Before 1344 he married Margaret Ufford, daughter of the earl and countess of Suffolk. After Henry Ferrer's death, the earl likely brought his young son-in-law into his household, where the boy could receive education in knightly skills. About the time of William's marriage the Uffords began to visit Elizabeth. Both parties now had a slender kinship tie and both were interested in the outcome of Ralph Ufford's Irish expedition. The Uffords and the lady of Clare performed the niceties typical of the magnate class: the earl sent her a cask of Vernach wine and she supplied his horses with an extra reward when he visited.[61] Apparently no deep friendship developed, but both families could appreciate another linkage of interests.

When Isabella died in 1349, William received part of his inheritance, with the bulk falling in after proof of age in 1354. William fought in France under various commanders in the late 1350s. These campaigns enriched many English soldiers, as they helped themselves to booty or collected ransoms of captured French nobles, but William seems not to have profited handsomely from his military service. He possessed sufficient funds to lend £400 to his brother-in-law the earl of Athol in 1357, but by 1360 William experienced financial problems. He borrowed from Elizabeth and remained over £130 in debt to her when she died; he also owed a sizable debt to the executors of his brother-in-law Guy de Beauchamp. Finally, in 1364, he sold all but one manor of his Irish Verdon inheritance, although this may have shown astuteness rather than financial desperation.[62]

William's military service in France precluded many meetings with his grandmother. She did stop over at Stebbing in 1358 on her journey to London. William had a son by then and perhaps daughters as well. His daughter Elizabeth professed at the London Minories, but the date of her enclosure is unknown. The lady of Clare's generosity to the Minoresses assured the great-granddaughter a cordial welcome, whether she entered during her great-grandmother's life or later. William received no personal bequests from Elizabeth as she followed her pattern of omitting legacies for grandchildren holding or expecting reasonably comfortable estates.[63] Philippa and Elizabeth Ferrers enjoyed closer associations with their grandmother than did William, attributable to gender differences and his early marriage into a comital family. The accounts tell us nothing of emotional ties, but naming his child after his grandmother suggests some filial regard as perhaps does his daughter's entry in an establishment favored by the lady.

Although Elizabeth spent only five months of married life with Theobald de Verdon, associations with two Verdon stepdaughters persisted much longer. Margery lived briefly with Elizabeth when Damory held the girl's wardship. Margery later married William le Blount, whose family figured prominently among Earl Henry of Lancaster's retinue. In the 1330s, Blount briefly joined Elizabeth's staff as keeper of the wardrobe, so Margery again lived at her stepmother's home. William left Elizabeth's staff by 1336, but was murdered within a year. By 1339 Margery married Mark

Husee, who died about six years later. Just before his death and again be-fore her marriage to John de Crophull, Margery returned to see Elizabeth. The Crophulls were allowed to rent Newbold in 1355, part of Margery's anticipated purparty in Elizabeth's Verdon dower.[64] Margery probably spent little time in East Anglia and though Elizabeth responded at some moments in Margery's life, the nature and depth of Elizabeth's commit-ment to her stepdaughter seems minimal.

Elizabeth de Burghersh, another Verdon stepdaughter, visited the lady more frequently, probably because both moved in the same social circles and because the younger woman's husband, Bartholomew de Burghersh, of-fered an avenue of political favors as his fortunes flourished under Edward III. Moreover, Burghersh's brother was Elizabeth's friend Bishop Henry of Lincoln. Elizabeth de Burghersh accompanied her stepmother on the grand progress to Walsingham; one of the Burghersh sons joined the lady of Clare's *familia* briefly.[65] A comparison of the associations of Elizabeth de Burghersh and Margery le Blount with their stepmother shows differences and similarities. Both rented their Verdon purparties by 1355 and both seemed welcome at Clare or Bardfield, but the situations of their husbands were quite different. Burghersh stooped to violence on occasion, but he had the good fortune not to be murdered and to find royal favor; once William le Blount was dead, Margery experienced downward mobility through her marriages.[66] The Burghershs moved in noble East Anglian circles, while Margery did not after 1337, and Burghersh contacts offered potential po-litical influence to which Margery's husbands had no access.

Ties to the Damory family go almost unmentioned. A namesake of Roger's appears as a ward from 1331–36, but the accounts note only a few supplies and his escort to London, not the boy's identity. Nicholas Damory, perhaps a relative of Roger Damory, played a major role in the lady's house-hold, but the kinship was so distant he can hardly be classified as family.[67]

The lady's daughter Elizabeth Bardolf and her husband, John, appear more frequently in the accounts than her other children. The Bardolfs lived longer and presumed frequently on the lady's hospitality since they resided in East Anglia and Lincolnshire. Elizabeth assisted the Bardolfs in main-taining their social position and gave John livery as a knight, but she attempted no grand transfer of properties to them. Probably Elizabeth re-alized that this son-in-law never could aspire realistically to a premier place in national politics. The king included Bardolf in the 1345 royal banneret list, and Bardolf fought with royal forces in Scotland, Brittany, and Ger-many, but either failed to distinguish himself or missed key engagements. For the most part, John served at home in various local defensive roles: in 1338 he was commissioned to array the men of Norfolk and guard its coast, functions he still performed in 1360.[68] John received parliamentary summons, but his primary work for the Crown was serving on various oyer and terminer commissions, as justice of laborers and of peace after 1350, and as commissioner to survey "the dykes, ditches, gutters, sewers, bridges, causeways, weirs and trenches of sweet water . . . in county Norfolk." Such duties enhanced one's local status but were not the stuff of chivalric prowess nor the route to extensive royal favor.[69]

Before his death, John's father had attempted to secure some of his manors to John and Elizabeth through the device of the use, but John's mother felt cheated and successfully demanded full dower and control of jointure lands. Since she lived until 1358, John and Elizabeth had to make do with the remainder of John's inheritance. To aid the Bardolfs, Elizabeth exchanged the manors of Kennington and Vauxhall for the manors of Ilketshall, Clopton, and Claret, which would later come to the Bardolfs. She also lent money to John Bardolf, still owed to her when she died.

Elizabeth was generous to the Bardolfs for 30 years. Before John received his inheritance, the couple spent time in Elizabeth's *familia*. Later the lady dispatched game to them, provided John with robes, and gave her daughter expensive gifts of ermine and cash.[70] The relationship between the Bardolfs and Elizabeth lacked the reciprocal gift-giving that characterized the lady's ties with the Ferrers. John sent Elizabeth bream in 1352, but most of the gifts went to him rather than came from him. Elizabeth Bardolf was the lady's only surviving child but also the one with the least secure financial situation, for she inherited little from her father's estate, and John Bardolf's management record was less than exemplary. Elizabeth demonstrated affection for her daughter by leaving her several personal bequests: a green velvet bed, bed coverlets trimmed with fur, and hangings decorated with parrots and blue cockerels. The younger Elizabeth also received her mother's large chariot with its assortment of gear. Not many noble households could boast such a vehicle, quite fashionable for female transport. It also recalled memories and shared pleasures. Elizabeth showed concern for her Bardolf granddaughters as well, leaving both Agnes and Isabel bequests "in aid" of their marriages: beds and coverlets and silver dishes. Elizabeth knew the centrality of marriage for females and wanted to enhance the opportunities of prosperous unions for these little girls.[71]

Elizabeth Bardolf usually visited her mother at Christmas and again in the summer, with John often present for the winter festivities, enlivened with music from a portable organ.[72] Elizabeth paid her daughter's travel expenses on these journeys to Clare, including stopovers at Anglesey or Barnwell priory. The accounts mention Bardolf chambers at Anglesey, which Elizabeth repaired in 1340. Familial connections were enhanced by a shared devotion to Franciscan spirituality, so naturally the couple joined

Elizabeth on the trip to Walsingham as she founded the friary there. Affection dominated the mother-daughter relationship, for few political or economic benefits accrued to the lady from this association, nor did social convention demand close ties. She had no need to pay expenses for the Bardolfs' visits unless she truly welcomed their companionship.[73]

The lady of Clare cared for all her children and wanted to nurture them. Here, maternal love triumphed over self-interest and social norms, for her custody precluded contacts they could develop by living at royal court or with some magnate. She maintained her love after each child married, bringing new spouses into the family circle. Royal ambitions inhibited her ability to enrich her daughters and sons-in-law, but her caring toward them persisted in less grand ways. The lady reached out to her grandchildren, especially the girls. She became the dominant maternal figure for her Ferrers granddaughters, and perhaps for the little countess of Ulster as well when her mother entered Campsey Ash convent. Elizabeth's affection included each grandchild, but she provided most lavishly for those with the smallest material prospects.

The lady was devoted to the Blessed Virgin and perhaps consciously tried to imitate Mary's maternal role in nurturing her children and grandchildren. By the fourteenth century, motherhood was receiving renewed honor, and increasingly society applauded joy in infants and young children. Religious teachings, especially of the friars, emphasized the sweet intimacy of the family and love of the young as service to God. Elizabeth was attuned to contemporary religious thought, which would have enhanced her own affectionate responses to children and grandchildren.

Friends

Love may have predominated in Elizabeth's family connections, but duty, responsibility, and societal norms figured as well. Even pride in lineage could not minimize the inherently involuntary obligations imposed by families. Friendship had a different dimension. Friendship meant individual choice for fourteenth-century magnates and nobles, an exceptional opportunity for those at the pinnacle of secular society. Custom circumscribed occupational options for noblemen and often limited their pool of marriage partners. For noblewomen, even more than their male counterparts, freedom to choose in the intimate aspects of life was a rarity. Noble females never selected their spouses unless they gambled on placating their families or overlords after the fact, as Elizabeth's mother had. Women rarely could embark on spiritual vocations of their choice. Elizabeth's daughter-in-law Matilda endured two marriages and two widowhoods before being allowed to follow her childhood dreams of conventual life. But women could choose their friends, following the dictates of their hearts rather than being wholly constrained by rigid social demands. Yet the need to preserve status and promote one's well-being did intrude, so Elizabeth's friendships often contained an element of self-interest as well as affection. There is no evidence that she crassly exploited her friends or that utilitarian ends determined her choices—mutual assistance formed a normal part of medieval friendship. Friends insulated friends from political fall-out, promoted them for favors, and introduced them to others in broadening webs of association.

Social class often determined general parameters of interaction, but within that broad rubric choices were made. In examining Elizabeth de Burgh's friendships, circumstances that created possibilities for affection are more evident than the personal traits that animated mutual admiration and attraction. Since Elizabeth mainly avoided royal court and her sex precluded parliamentary and military activities, her circle of intimates had a local, neighborly flavor. Her closest friends resided in East Anglia for much of their lives, so contacts were frequent, and maintaining ties was simple. Many of the lady's dearest friends shared kinship ties with her; some were her cousins, with the countess of Surrey and the Bohun earls prime examples.[74] Elizabeth's dearest women friends experienced long widowhoods: Queen Isabella, Countess Mary de St Pol of Pembroke, and Countess Joan of Surrey. They, too, came from the highest noble ranks and lived in eastern or southern England.

More than in other areas, absence of personal documents hides the dimensions of individual friendships. The accounts mention numerous letters from Elizabeth, but none are extant; she apparently kept no journal. Therefore, identifying her friends depends on records enumerating visitors, noting messengers dispatched with letters to specific people, and gifts that Elizabeth gave or received. Expenditures on food and wine, and even the specific food served, offer hints of her assessment of the guests' standing, though she may have judged on political circumstances as well as affection. Friendships strengthened by the spiritual ties between godparent and godchild are not illustrated by the accounts, but Elizabeth's social position and reputation for piety must have made her a popular baptismal sponsor. Undoubtedly she enjoyed spiritual affinities that deepened links of kinship and personal affection. Some twelfth-century monastic writers emphasized the spiritual dimension of friendship, likening it to an encounter with God.[75] Elizabeth would not have phrased her experiences in those terms, but spirituality infused her most intimate friendships, especially with Mary de St Pol, Duke Henry of Lancaster, and Edward the Black Prince. Mutual religious feelings may not have initiated friendships but could strengthen them over time. Religion was only one factor in these friendships, which were cemented by class ties, shared circumstances, proximity, and love.

Friendship with Mary de St Pol, the earl of Pembroke's young French-born widow, lasted nearly 40 years and was broken only by death. As a young widow with few natural protectors in England, Mary and her estates were vulnerable to the machinations of Hugh Despenser junior and Edward II. Hugh was intent on expanding his Welsh holdings, targeting the late earl's Pembrokeshire properties. As victims of a common aggressor, Mary and Elizabeth may have been drawn together. Both sided with Queen Isabella as she prepared and successfully managed her invasion of England; Mary was in her company in Paris during the queen's self-imposed exile, and Elizabeth welcomed the invasion itself. Although few of Mary's household accounts are extant and Elizabeth's tend to be fragmentary in the late 1320s and early 1330s, the lady's show the women were good friends by 1327. One of Mary's residences was at Anstey where Elizabeth visited in 1327 and 1328; Mary came to Elizabeth in January 1331.[76] More indicative of their growing affection was the custom of sharing similar outfits for their Christmas holidays. Elizabeth often included identical material for Mary when she bought her personal cloth for the annual livery, and Mary reciprocated at least once. One year the custom expanded, with the women gowned in tawny for Elizabeth's autumn birthday. These exchanges seem quaint to modern eyes, but in the more visually-attuned fourteenth century, wearing identical robes signified closeness and attachment. Ordinarily wearing another's livery denoted dependence, but with reciprocal gifts, the message intended was equality and affection.[77] Females in the fourteenth century had few rituals or occasions for celebrating their friendships with other women, quite in contrast to masculine experience: King Edward III's Knights of the Garter encouraged male bonding in an atmosphere of fantasized equality. Here clothing liveries of similar costumes emphasized membership in the group of peers, selected for their courage, martial skills, and friendship with the king, but noblewomen had nothing comparable. Elizabeth and Mary found formal occasions and appropriate symbols to express their female bond and repeated the exchange of identical robes often between 1331 and 1358. They also exchanged visits, interrupted by Mary's trips to France, where she had family and estates. The Clare accounts show that Elizabeth honored Mary when she visited, serving swans and herons, game and pike, always signs of an important guest. Between visits, messengers from one searched out the other to deliver letters or verbal messages.[78]

Widowhood conferred independence on females, but maintaining that status when one controlled extensive landed estates required ingenuity or luck. Elizabeth's vow of chastity precluded her overlord from rewarding a favorite at her expense. Mary could have done the same, but had not by

1327 when her marriage rights were awarded to Roger Mortimer. Later
the countess employed some strategem—a vow of chastity, buying her own
marriage rights, or negotiating some arrangement with Edward III—for
she remained a widow. Elizabeth and Mary always properly honored former husbands, safely dead, but showed no interest in exchanging their widowed state for a new spouse. Both women enjoyed having control of their
lives and properties, and both took an active interest in estate management.
Each had manors in several English shires and in Ireland, so they probably
compared practices and personnel policies. Each eagerly used the courts to
protect her lands and appreciated favors dispensed to her as king's
kinswoman. Each in her own way scrambled to maintain or expand her
holdings. Initially, Elizabeth possessed more property, but Mary equaled or
surpassed her friend's wealth when she acquired a life interest in the English lands of her relative, the earl of Richmond. While Mary had no children, she may have been pleased that some of her estates would descend
to Elizabeth's granddaughter, who married David de Strabolgi, one of Earl
Aymer's heirs.[79]

Elizabeth and Mary shared the pleasures and pastimes of their class
and perhaps savored a good gossip about mutual acquaintances. Both indulged their tastes for luxurious clothing and jewelry. Mary's will gives
some hint of her plate and relic collection: saints' statues and their relics,
a piece of the True Cross in a jeweled setting, gold and silver plate. Elizabeth seemed less devoted to relic collecting, though she cherished her
own fragment of the True Cross. Both women amassed magnificent
church equipment and clerical vestments, and possessed beautifully illuminated books as aids to devotion.[80] Each explored patronage avenues
less appealing to the other. Mary poured great effort and wealth into
construction of her late husband's tomb in Westminster Abbey; Elizabeth seemed content to remember her spouses with prayers on anniversaries of their deaths. Mary supported Cistercian and Carthusian
orders that evoked little enthusiasm from Elizabeth. Elizabeth appreciated the female anchoress, while Mary's support of the religious solitary
involved one male hermit in London. While these women had spiritual
causes uniquely their own, their generous impulses and religious development converged in their love of Franciscan piety and in educational
benefactions. Here they stimulated each other's interest and creativity in
collaborative ways: both founded Cambridge colleges and both funded
and joined in the spirituality of the Second Order of the Franciscans,
the Minoresses.

A relative of Mary's husband had founded a house of Minoresses at Waterbeach. Mary succeeded to the patronage and decided to relocate the
convent to her neighboring manor at Denny. She received proper licenses

to effect the transfer, but encountered entrenched hostility from some sisters who preferred familiar surroundings to the new accommodations built or refurbished by the countess. Mary probably consulted Elizabeth and may have used her active intervention to persuade the recalcitrant nuns to conform. Elizabeth frequently traveled to Waterbeach and Denny between 1336 and 1345. Naturally she wanted time with Mary, but two of the trips included both convents, as if the lady were engaging in shuttle diplomacy between the foundress and the rebellious Minoresses. Mary's designs triumphed because she understood the advantages of tapping secular and ecclesiastical power to attain control of her foundation. Both women enjoyed directing projects where their control and decisions were paramount. Moreover, Denny provided a spiritual dynamic for Mary and probably for Elizabeth as well. The countess may have been associated with a French Minoress house during residency in France, but the visits to Waterbeach and Denny may have been Elizabeth's first encounter with the best in contemporary female conventual spirituality.[81] Mary's quarrels with her Waterbeach/Denny nuns may have contributed in an unintended way to her friend's spiritual growth. Later both women joined in the Minoresses' devotional life and both chose to be buried among them.

While Mary sorted out problems with her Minoress foundation, Elizabeth proceeded with her endowment of Clare Hall. Just as Mary redirected an earlier foundation to her own ends, Elizabeth took over a faltering institution and made it her own. In fact, Elizabeth's success in transforming old University Hall could have encouraged Mary's determination to transfer the Waterbeach sisters to Denny as the years of frequent visits between the two friends coincided with Elizabeth's growing involvement with Clare Hall. Just as Mary helped introduce Elizabeth to female conventual piety, so Elizabeth stimulated Mary's interest in educational foundation, little valued by noble contemporaries. Mary began collecting properties for her collegiate foundation of Pembroke College (originally Marie-Valence Hall) about 1345 or 1346, acquiring one from John Bardolf, suggesting Elizabeth's encouragement and help. Elizabeth seemed more genuinely devoted to pursuing intellectual and moral goals in her foundation, personally savoring the "sweetness of learning," which she hoped to promote. Mary was interested in keeping places for French scholars at her college, introducing strong Franciscan administration, and legislating tight personal control with the right to expel fellows at her pleasure.[82] Perhaps her experience with the Minoresses made her suspicious of institutional independence. The friendship of Elizabeth and Mary challenged the thinking and generous impulses of each, widening their charitable urges in directions neither may have ventured without external support. They discovered in their foundations at Cambridge a niche where female initiative influenced generations of students long after glamorous masculine chivalry was dead.

Elizabeth's friendship with Mary was not exclusionary, as both had other dear friends. These two, along with Queen Isabella and Joan of Bar, formed a coterie of wealthy, independent widows. Joan and Elizabeth were cousins; Isabella was Elizabeth's aunt by marriage and godmother of the lady's oldest daughter. Joan, Mary, and Isabella were all born on the continent and had family ties there. These three spent time together in Paris in 1325, and Joan and Mary attended the dowager queen as she neared death.[83] Elizabeth and Joan may have known each other as children. Joan became a ward of her grandfather Edward I at the death of her parents, the count and countess of Bar. King Edward arranged for the girl, then nine or ten years old, to live in England. In 1306 she married another of his wards, John de Warenne, heir to the earldom of Surrey. Elizabeth would have participated in those celebrations, as her sister Eleanor married the same day. Arranged marriages often worked well, but trouble surfaced early in this one, as John, now earl of Surrey, found happier company and sought to terminate his legal union. Earl John and Countess Joan never enjoyed a compatible married life and spent little time together as the earl attempted to have his marriage annulled so that his bastard offspring could inherit his patrimony. In his last desperate and unsuccessful effort he claimed a sexual liaison with Mary, nun at Amesbury and aunt of Joan and Elizabeth. Under the circumstances, Joan needed to be constantly alert to protect her material interests. With a living spouse, she had no dower lands, but lived on income wrested from the earl. Joan frequently traveled abroad, occasionally acting as a royal agent or visiting various shrines.[84]

While Joan and Elizabeth were good friends, their relationship was not nurtured by the frequent personal interaction that prevailed between Elizabeth and Mary. The Clare accounts note occasional letters or messages received or sent between 1337 and 1359, as well as Joan's visits to Elizabeth mainly in the 1350s. Joan had papal permission to enter Minoress houses and may have joined Elizabeth in Franciscan devotions in London.[85] Two instances indicate the depth of their friendship. In 1346 and 1347, Joan's chaplain resided for several months with Elizabeth. Initially this would seem a courtesy to one of the countess's staff; however, the chaplain was Garner Bertrandi, a goldsmith. His visits coincided with Elizabeth's preparations for her Walsingham foundation, so it is likely that Joan was lending a valuable artisan to help fabricate altar equipment for the friars. Elizabeth's affection for Joan appears in her will, where she bequeathed the countess a gold statue of St John.[86] Aside from family and staff, only four friends were remembered in this testament, underscoring an abiding fondness for Joan. These examples show reciprocity in sharing valued personnel or personal treasure, neither ever offered lightly. Their relationship began because they were cousins, but it was strengthened by adherence to Queen Isabella's cause after 1325 and a continuing closeness later to Mary de St Pol and the dowager queen. The friendship of the foursome was paired—Elizabeth and Mary, Joan and Isabella—but each enjoyed the company of the others.

The bond between Elizabeth and Queen Isabella had been forged early in their lives. Probably each attended the other's marriage festivities.[87] The queen visited when Elizabeth was pregnant with Isabella de Verdon, and she served as godmother for that namesake baby. During the turbulent period between 1317 and 1321, the queen supported the faction to which Roger Damory adhered and viewed the growing Despenser ascendancy with alarm. Elizabeth and Isabella suffered from Hugh Despenser's power in a more personal and intimate way than did Joan and Mary. Isabella was humiliated by Eleanor Despenser's surveillance, while Elizabeth was dragged through the patently unfair Usk/Gower exchange. Their victimization by a common enemy was bound to strengthen their alliance. After her successful invasion, Isabella supported Elizabeth's efforts to reassemble her properties and settle her children's futures. The lady's attendance at Edward II's funeral probably was dictated by affection toward his widow rather than grief over his death. Elizabeth maintained contact with the dowager queen, visiting her at Hertford and Kenninghall in the late 1330s. The two women exchanged letters over the years and may have met in London or homes of mutual friends. Elizabeth sent Isabella bream in March 1358; presumably there were other gifts, letters, and visits unrecorded or on lost rolls.[88]

The early experiences of these two women brought them into close friendship, but not as intimate an association as Elizabeth shared with Mary. Isabella and Elizabeth shared a love for Franciscan piety; both supported the Walsingham canons and made pilgrimages to that Marian shrine. But as the years progressed, each woman emphasized different spiritual interests. Isabella enjoyed pilgrimages more than Elizabeth, but seemed indifferent to expending for pious foundations and chantries. Both supported paupers, but Isabella's outlays, on an income greatly exceeding Elizabeth's, were less generous.[89] In short, Elizabeth chose to direct her riches toward more good causes than did the queen. Elizabeth never stinted on clothes, furs, or jewels, but her expenditures on these luxuries lacked the prodigality of Isabella, perhaps because of disparity in income. They each possessed splendid breviaries and Bibles, but their tastes in nonreligious literature diverged over the years, with Isabella retaining her predilection for romances, while Elizabeth pursued a more serious reading program.[90] Isabella eagerly rejoined court life in her middle years, while

Elizabeth was content to entertain royalty without seeking out the king's hospitality. The women aged differently: Elizabeth enjoying control she never had in her 20s; Isabella losing the power and influence she once possessed. Their friendship persisted, but perhaps more on memories than current involvements.

The small glances available into the lives of Elizabeth, Mary, Joan, and Isabella preclude grand generalizations about the outlook of medieval noblewomen. They shared a common pool of societal norms—family concerns, pride of lineage, interest in maximization of profits, high aesthetic standards, and the appeal of mendicant piety—but they cultivated individuality as well. Elizabeth was the most thoroughly English of these women, not having continental ties nor engaging in foreign travel. She involved herself more with family issues because she was the family "head," where the other women were not or had no offspring to promote. Perhaps this is why Elizabeth seems the most serious of the four, though her intellectual interests contributed here as well. Elizabeth and Isabella showed great concern for their servants, according them generous treatment, and both reached out to the needs of women. All four women articulated causes which they supported with some generosity.[91] All delighted in female companionship without excluding men from their circles of affection.

Among her many male friends, Elizabeth cherished Duke Henry of Lancaster and Edward the Black Prince, above all others. They embodied chivalric ideals dear to the nobility, combining military courage with pleasing charm and courtesy. The lady responded to their personalities, adding perhaps maternal affection and admiration for the spiritual aspects of their lives. She introduced them to her Minoress friends and singled them out for testamentary bequests of religious artifacts. Her love was returned as each man often included Elizabeth in his trips back from the continental wars.

The lady of Clare had ties of family and friendship with Duke Henry's father, Earl Henry of Lancaster. He hunted on her estates and they jointly launched William de Burgh and his wife, Matilda of Lancaster, on their married union. Elizabeth maintained contact with the earl as he slipped into blindness, and welcomed his son as he shouldered the old earl's responsibilities, although the younger Henry only appeared in the Clare accounts once before his father's death in 1345. Son Henry, first earl and later duke of Lancaster, served his king as a leader in military enterprises, a trusted diplomat, and a seasoned administrator.[92] People saw Lancaster as a valiant and successful war captain and as a gallant Christian in crusading ventures in North Africa and Prussia. Magnates must have vied for his company to add stature to themselves. Very often he chose to spend time with Elizabeth just before leaving for the continent or soon after his return. Lancaster returned from abroad in January 1347, visiting the lady that same month. Before he sailed again for France in May 1347, he made a trip to see Elizabeth and he sent messengers to her in May and July. When the earl returned to London in May 1350, he came to Clare that same month and twice later in the year. When he visited Elizabeth in March and June 1351, he bore the newly created title of Duke of Lancaster. During his Prussian crusade and his continental diplomatic missions in late 1351 and 1352, he wrote Elizabeth and sent her venison. In the midst of his heavy duties, he wrote a confessional autobiography in 1354, a very personal expiation for his sins. Perhaps Henry presented her with a copy in October, when he was her guest at a dinner with the Minoresses.[93]

Elizabeth's feelings in this friendship seem rather transparent. Henry was the same age as her murdered son and displayed qualities she would have wished for in William. Henry Ferrers substituted for William in Elizabeth's affections once, but he died in 1343, so Henry of Lancaster may have stepped into that role. He found a kindred spirit in Elizabeth, in spite of differences in age, gender, and occupation, perhaps responding to Elizabeth's maternal outreach for he lost his own mother relatively early. Lancaster's opinions were valued by the king, allowing him to support his friends' causes in royal court and also at the papal court, where he often visited on diplomatic missions. Henry was well-versed in European affairs and could recount stories and report on current events to an interested audience. He was literate, perhaps even well-read, and steeped in the religious currents of his day. The lady shared his interests in religion and reading; both devoted a good portion of their possessions to worthy causes. His crusading experiences in Africa and Prussia may have initiated the concern for fighting the infidel, which surfaces in her will. She left Henry her piece of the True Cross, recognizing in him the warrior for Christ. On a homelier note, she fed him well, often including his favorite dish of salmon, her favorite as well.[94] Friendship with Elizabeth offered Henry no political gains or openings for social advancement. She could inform him on local conditions, but he had ample staff and contacts with comparable information. The lady lacked continental experience and military knowledge, so she could not contribute to his diplomatic efforts or warfare. Neither the element of courteous flirtation so prominent in medieval romances nor a bid for sexual favors played a part in this association. Henry must have loved Elizabeth for herself.

Prince Edward also developed a deep friendship with Elizabeth, in spite of the 35-year difference in their ages. Though his first recorded visit to her only occurred during the Christmas season of 1344, she sent him messages in 1340. He shared the festival of the Conception of the Blessed Virgin with her in 1347, fresh from his initiation into martial glory at Crécy. Edward was with the lady shortly before the English triumph over the Castilian fleet in 1350 and just ten days after. John of Gaunt accompanied his brother on summer visits in 1350 and 1351, but Edward came without him to Bardfield in March 1355.[95] The friendship between Elizabeth and the young prince seems rather conventional and unexceptional until 1357 when the dynamic changed. Edward returned to England that year after the stunning victory at Poitiers. He had rallied the outnumbered English, showed good strategic and tactical insights, and was the architect of that victory rather than merely a brave participant, as he had been at Crécy. His honorable treatment of the defeated French monarch displayed the finest chivalric sentiments, appreciated by the nobility and applauded by the London populace on his triumphant return. He certainly did not need the adulation of an aging woman to cap his successes, but he needed her company for some reason. The prince sought out Elizabeth's hospitality 23 times between December 1357 and August 1359. Naturally Elizabeth served him fine food, often herons, bitterns, or egrets, accompanied by ample wine. They may have hunted together near London, for Elizabeth sent for her sparrow hawks and coursing dogs, which required renting facilities for their boarding away from her London residence.[96]

Elizabeth was more intellectually inclined than her young friend, who left no books in his will other than devotional works. Perhaps she was trying to broaden his outlook, for the lady introduced the prince to Bishop John Paschal of Llandaff, a Carmelite friar noted for erudition and religious commitment. The common religious thrust for Edward and Elizabeth was their devotion to the Blessed Virgin and the prince joined Elizabeth for several Marian festivals. Although the Trinity ranked highest in the prince's devotion, he wanted memorial masses for himself "on all the feasts of Our Lady." In Elizabeth's will, two of the bequests for Prince Edward featured the Blessed Virgin: a gold tabernacle with the Virgin's statue and a large cross flanked by Mary and St John. On August 15, 1358, Elizabeth celebrated the Assumption of the Blessed Virgin with a banquet, where Prince Edward and the Minoresses were her guests. He had given the convent gifts of wine earlier, but Elizabeth may have wanted to enlist Edward as a protector of the London nuns, as such patronage would be invaluable if he succeeded to the throne.[97] He predeceased Edward III, however, and directed his testamentary bequests elsewhere, so if Elizabeth's motives were to enrich and protect the convent, they failed.

The lady enjoyed the young man and must have been flattered that this popular royal hero wanted her company so frequently. His rewards from Elizabeth are harder to assess. He had a loving mother, though Queen Philippa may have been distracted from single-minded concern for her eldest son, simply because 7 of her 11 children survived to adulthood, the last being born in 1355. He could have been looking for sympathy about his love-life, for his great love was a married woman, Joan of Kent. Elizabeth would not have encouraged any secret trysts at her London residence, but she could have been a good listener and adviser.[98] Fourteenth-century princes had few opportunities to discuss matters of the heart. Their confessors would have expounded on themes of adultery and lust, while royal parents expected to dictate marriages that promoted family welfare not personal choice. A man could hardly be so love-sick as to confide in his companions-at-arms if he expected to be their sovereign. Choosing Elizabeth as a confidante made eminent sense under the circumstances. Of course, all this is speculation; Prince Edward may just have delighted in her company and wanted to spend as many days with her as possible as she neared the end of her life. Even if the true nature of this friendship cannot be fathomed, its solidity is certain.

Elizabeth cared more for the prince than others in the royal family. The prince's younger brother Lionel visited often as husband of the lady's granddaughter and heir, but the association seems infused with duty rather than affection. Queen Philippa and Elizabeth were friends at the social level: the queen visited occasionally and once sent her harper to entertain the lady. The household accounts often fail to differentiate between the reigning Philippa and the dowager Isabella, but nonetheless give the impression that the relationship between Elizabeth and Philippa lacked intimacy.[99] Elizabeth respected Edward III as her lord, the king; he often deferred to his kinswoman. Soon after becoming king, Edward stopped over at Caythorpe to see Elizabeth, and he visited her infrequently over the years. He was expected in late 1337; he was entertained magnificently at Clare in late May 1340. The king hunted at Elizabeth's manor of Trelleck in 1349 and she moved from Usk to Hereford to entertain him that autumn. On June 24, 1357 Edward enjoyed game and herons at Elizabeth's London home, their last recorded meeting. The fact that Elizabeth avoided royal court limited opportunities for intimacy with the king. She paid him the requisite homage, she sent a gift to his collegiate foundation at Windsor, and she remembered that foundation with a gold cup "for the body of our Lord" decorated with three silver-gilt angels. That bequest typified her attitude to the king, supporting one of his cherished projects rather than leaving him something personal. He deferred to her, often postponing her Irish tax burdens or issuing mortmain licenses without the usual fee.[100] Elizabeth had reasons for a muted dislike of the king. Edward's failure to send an expeditionary force to Ireland in support of her son, William, may have contributed to his early death. The king negated her use, directing some of her estates to other descendants, a move she would have found distasteful. The king tolerated Elizabeth, but she provoked him several times: by insisting on the full term of her Hastings wardship, and by assuming her kinship with the king would exempt her from paying full taxes on wool at a time he desperately needed funds for his military enterprises. She lacked the ability to further his continental projects, except through ordinary taxation. The familial bond between them, and the formal respect she accorded her king, prevented any major confrontation, but neither sufficed to create permanent ties of affection.

Her Bohun cousins were among her dearest friends. Elizabeth bore the name of her Bohun aunt, daughter of Edward I and favorite sister of Joan of Acre. The lady's Bohun uncle, the earl of Hereford, had fought at Bannockburn and had been the principal leader of the Welsh Contrariants between 1320 and his death in 1322. Cousin John de Bohun was given his revived earldom in 1326 after Queen Isabella's invasion. In the lady's one surviving goldsmith account, Earl John received a small gold ring and other items. He visited Elizabeth twice in 1334 and she sent representatives to his funeral in 1336, remembering him 15 years later with masses for his soul. The lady's prayer list for deceased family and friends was rather short, so John's inclusion suggests an abiding affection and also underscores her practice of a kind of "spiritual economy," concentrating memorial prayers on those who had no surviving progeny to take up the obligation. After John's comital title went to his brother Humphrey de Bohun, Elizabeth sent horses and servants to London in November 1336 to escort Earl Humphrey to Pleshey. Apparently neither John de Bohun nor his brother Humphrey followed the normal noble occupations of war and politics, an aberration probably caused by physical disabilities.[101] Neither did Humphrey marry. Humphrey de Bohun and Elizabeth exchanged visits, she going to his residences at Pleshey and Walden, and the earl visiting her in return, with his horses given an extra reward. Humphrey showed his concern for Elizabeth by providing transport and personnel for her 1350 trip from Usk to Clare, and by sending her gifts of game. Both patronized Augustinian friars and both responded to the appeal of the Holy Land in their wills.[102]

Elizabeth's associations with William, brother of John and Humphrey, lasted more than 20 years. Edward III created the new comital title, earl of Northampton, for William in 1337, acknowledging his assistance in the overthrow of Mortimer in 1330 and his potential as a military leader. The cousins' friendship was complemented by Elizabeth's affection for William's wife, Elizabeth, one of Bartholomew de Badlesmere's daughters and widow of the lady's Welsh neighbor, Edmund Mortimer. Because of Earl William's frequent campaigns in France or on the Scottish frontier, he and Elizabeth maintained contact by messengers and letters

with Elizabeth's staff searching out the earl at Cheshunt, Harwich, Colne,
Norwich, Rochford, and London. The cousins exchanged gifts and visits as well. The earl and countess came to Clare or Bardfield more frequently than the lady visited them, but Elizabeth went to Rochford in
1352 and gave the paupers, maintained there by the earl, a gift. The earl's
concern for his cousin deepened in the years just before her death. He
came to see Elizabeth in 1356 in London and also managed visits at
Bardfield or London between December 1357 and August 1358. Along
with her other friends, he wanted to spend as many hours with her as
possible in those last years. Actually, William died in September 1360, two
months before Elizabeth.[103] On the surface, the differences between the
earl's brilliant military career abroad and Elizabeth's decidedly English
environment would seem to make a close friendship unlikely. Even their
spiritual predilections were different: Elizabeth favoring Franciscan and
Augustinian friars, while the Bohuns tended to sponsor Dominican establishments. They were neighbors, but more important, both William
and Elizabeth de Burgh shared a link with royalty through their grandfather Edward I. A consciousness of royal descent set them apart from
many other nobles, for they were kin of the king. They shared an interest in English politics, a keen awareness of estate exploitation, and some
cultural interests.

The earl and countess of Oxford were another married couple with
long-standing ties to the lady of Clare. John de Vere succeeded to the earldom in 1331; John's wife, Maude, was another of the Badlesmere heiresses
and so may have initiated the friendship with Elizabeth. When the earl visited Elizabeth, his horses received the extra reward reserved for the mounts
of special friends. The countess came to Clare or Bardfield in 1339, 1347,
1351, and twice in 1358. The list is probably incomplete, for the Veres were
close neighbors in their castle of Sibyl Hedingham, which Elizabeth visited at least once.[104] There is little on which to judge this friendship other
than that it persisted over time. Perhaps it was only a linkage between fellow magnates and neighbors, strengthened by the Badlesmere connection.

Many other titled or noble personages appear in the household rolls,
underscoring Elizabeth's hospitality, though not necessarily real friendship: the earls of Arundel, Salisbury, and Ormond; Walter Mauny; the
countess of Devon; the earl and countess of Suffolk; Roger Mortimer (d.
1360).[105] The earl and countess of Warwick exchanged letters and visits
with Elizabeth, probably drawn to her company by joint interest in the
marriage of their son Guy and Elizabeth's granddaughter Philippa. Lady
de Roos, another Badlesmere daughter, appears in the rolls in 1344 and
1347.[106] Elizabeth maintained a relationship with the Percy family, even
though its interests were primarily in northern England. Robert Percy

was awarded livery as a squire in 1343, appearing in 1347 in her *familia*. Thomas Percy, a younger son, appears in the rolls after his election to the bishopric of Norwich. Elizabeth went to some effort to stock the fishpond at Clare for Henry Percy in 1331 and 20 years later made offerings for his soul.[107] Lady FitzWauter was a step below the magnate class, but sufficiently important to rate mention on the Clare guest list. Lady FitzWauter may have been an overly solicitous mother, for Thomas FitzWauter belonged to Elizabeth's *familia*. Still, Elizabeth felt enough ties of friendship to send her a gift of a parrot or popinjay.[108]

Two women outside or at the fringes of the nobility won Elizabeth's friendship. Katherine de Ingham, abbess of the Minoress convent in London, was the widow of John de Ingham, who received arrears of a fee from Elizabeth in 1326. Katherine does not appear in the rolls, but she had many opportunities to see and to know Elizabeth once the lady built her London residence next door to the convent. Elizabeth's generous bequests to Katherine underscore a genuine friendship.[109] The other woman was Katherine or Katrina de Haliwell, whose relationship with Elizabeth is something of a mystery. This Katherine accompanied William de Burgh to Scotland in 1327–28. Elizabeth sent her bread and malt, felled timber for her house in Cambridge, and occasionally paid her expenses, all of which point to a subordinate supported by the lady's generosity. Conversely, Elizabeth's gifts to Katherine of wine and game were typically given to noble friends. Elizabeth's pattern was to send palfreys to Cambridge for Katherine's trips to Clare or Bardfield, where she often spent several weeks with expenses paid by her hostess. Katherine was sufficiently important to have her own chaplain, who was brought to Clare once. Yet Katherine never appeared in notations of Elizabeth's *familia* nor in the marginal entries of guests. The last recorded expense for Katherine was in 1340, showing that Elizabeth felt a need for her company for 12 years, for reasons which are never clear.[110]

The young women (*damoiselles* in the rolls) who received livery from Elizabeth seem to have been drawn from aspiring merchant families or from the ranks of the neighboring gentry. Placing a daughter in Elizabeth's household would be a family asset, for Elizabeth provided for them generously. Anne of Lexeden progressed from Elizabeth's household to an anchorhold supported by the lady. Elizabeth Torel, the daughter of Robert and Margery Mareschal, received a party and expensive outfits at the time of her betrothal. All the *damoiselles* living in 1360 benefited from Elizabeth's will. These young women had close relations with the lady, but probably fell outside the circle of her friends, except perhaps for Suzanne de Neketon, who was a companion of the lady for nearly 20 years.[111] Elizabeth also treated the wives of her chief administrators with affectionate indulgence.

The household accounts fail to yield information on the full richness of Elizabeth's friendships, but they do provide enough material to show her extensive contacts. Elizabeth must have had the gift of friendship, ranging from a royal prince to the local gentry, from cousins to an abbess. Even the routinized and often dull accounts show a woman capable of bridging generational gaps, gender, and status differences, in attracting people who liked or loved her and found in her a true friend.

Her friends and family connections gave Elizabeth the security she lacked in 1322 when she was relatively isolated and vulnerable. Then her friends were dead, imprisoned, or powerless against Edward II and Despenser. Thirty years later the prince, the dowager queen, and her comital friends could intercede on her behalf with Edward III, for all enjoyed his favor. In 1322 Elizabeth's children were very young, dependents rather than companions. Later, as they married, they and the families of their spouses accorded the lady respect and, in some cases, real affection. Her Despenser kin enjoyed her hospitality rather than greedily coveting her estates as Hugh Despenser junior had done. Naturally with the passage of time political actors changed, people died, and children matured. Elizabeth's later networks of friends and family illustrate her ability to cope with new circumstances and construct new ties.

Associations with friends and family also reveal some facets of Elizabeth's character. For example, she reserved her rancor for her persecutors, not their children. Her friendships had solidity and staying power, as evidenced by the continuing affection among Elizabeth, Queen Isabella, and the Countesses Mary and Joan. Although their original ties partly related to their victim status, continuing closeness shows other common interests. Elizabeth worked out agreeable personal associations where she had no voice in creating ties. Others determined her children's marriage partners, yet the lady cultivated amicable relations with them and their families, just as she did with two of her stepdaughters' husbands. Elizabeth's generosity is often depicted in terms of her piety, but she was generous to family and friends as well, with gifts, hospitality, and time.

Remembering Elizabeth's trials in the 1320s, it is easy to assume she was using both friends and family to protect herself and her heritage, that her motives were basically selfish. Certainly she gained prestige from her kinship with royalty and visits from military heroes. Her cordial dealings with the Despenser nephews and Stafford nephew by marriage aided her protection of landed interests in Wales and Ireland, while John Bardolf could assist Elizabeth in his local assignments on royal commissions. Undoubtedly Elizabeth's friends and family were valuable allies, and she did not hesitate to use their good offices for her ends. The total situation was more complex, however, for her friends must have perceived a mutuality in their relationships with Elizabeth. It is hard to credit the duke of Lancaster or the earl of Northampton docilely accepting exploitation at her hands. Countesses Mary of Pembroke and Joan of Surrey had other options yet they remained fond of Elizabeth for over 30 years. Political, social, and economic benefits that might accrue through familial or friendly relations should not obscure the less obvious emotional dimension. The lady would have garnered more prayers had she left the legacies bequeathed to Countesses Mary and Joan and Prince Edward to religious institutions. Her children and Ferrers' granddaughters did not need to spend their childhoods with Elizabeth as they were royal wards, but she chose to open her heart and home to them. A half-brother, a Despenser niece, and a host of friends were welcome guests, which suggests delight in their companionship and concern for their well-being. Self-interest was a factor, but genuine affection probably dominated Elizabeth's care for family and friends.

CHAPTER 4

POLITICS AND PATRONAGE

Despite her landed wealth, kinship with the king, and friendship and family ties with important nobles, Elizabeth assiduously built connections with lesser men, especially royal officials and prominent lower nobility and gentry. She cultivated good will wherever she thought it would increase her security, enhance her prestige, or expand her influence. Though barred from official positions, Elizabeth developed a rather astute political sense, buttressed by a consciously constructed framework of dependencies, patronage, and associations. She needed to do all of this. Edward II's vengeful retribution after the failed 1322 revolt had taught her that wealth could be confiscated, that kinship with royalty was no defense against execution or imprisonment, and that the prevailing judicial system often acknowledged power rather than right. Elizabeth also realized that, as a female, she needed good relationships with influential men to maintain her independence and status. Consequently she developed connections where each party perceived some advantage worth commitment and loyalty, a practice typical of fourteenth-century society. It is difficult to understand what motivated each set of associations, or to see the true nature of each. George Holmes addressed this dilemma: "If we could penetrate into the real world of relationships which hide behind the lists of liveries and annuities, 'bastard feudalism' and much of fourteenth-century society would be clear."[1] Information from Elizabeth's accounts fails to meet Holmes's full challenge, but offers insights into ways in which a female could build a political base.

Officials

The events of Edward II's reign accented the importance of good relations with the king. Elizabeth had found little favor with her uncle, but fared better with Edward III. She may not have loved the king, but she believed in hierarchical values and she honored him. Moreover, she had an abiding affection for Queen Isabella and the Black Prince, which the king would have appreciated. Edward also valued family ties, which insulated the lady at critical moments when his own ends were not jeopardized. While ties to the king were valuable, there were practical limits to imposing on his favor. The lady needed many associates throughout royal government who would look kindly on petitions, taxation issues, and lawsuits. Elizabeth thus followed a policy, typical of her class, of cultivating royal officials. Some received her livery as knights, squires, or clerks, depending on their importance to her needs and their status as laymen or clerics; others were rewarded with monetary gifts and hospitality. Ties between royal officials and individual nobles, which today would be labeled corrupt, were an accepted part of Elizabeth's environment.[2] She wanted friendly justices to hear her suits and protect her interests, so she identified and rewarded men who sat on the courts of King's Bench or Common Pleas or who seemed likely to receive such appointment in the future. Not only did these justices hear the great cases of the kingdom, but they served as commissioners in suits at the county level where they could offer even more useful service to their patrons. When an attack on their properties or servants occurred, nobles would petition for an oyer and terminer commission, fully expecting to name the trial's venue and the justices to hear the case. The procedure could be expensive, for beyond the cost of gifts to justices the plaintiff normally paid the commissioners' expenses during the hearings.[3] Elizabeth judged the costs worthwhile, developing a patron-client relationship with several important royal justices.

John Stonor was a justice of the Common Bench who figured in several cases involving the lady in the 1320s and 1330s, including a complicated suit over the manor of Steeple Cleydon in Buckinghamshire. She probably had a strong case in the Steeple Cleydon affair, but by 1326–27 she also had a friendly justice in Stonor. That year she purchased cloth for him "against Christmas" (meaning that she awarded him livery), which may have been sufficient to influence his outlook. A little later, Elizabeth paid a huge expense bill for Stonor and her counselors when they traveled to Dorset to hear cases where she was an interested party. Stonor's career culminated in two stints as chief justice of the Common Bench: 1336–40 and 1342–54.[4] He does not appear on the one surviving livery list of Elizabeth's household, dating from 1343.

By then, however, she had a neighbor on the Common Bench perhaps even more amenable to her concerns. This was John de Shardelowe, first appointed a justice of King's Bench in 1329; by 1332 he transferred to Common Pleas, where he served until 1340 and again from 1342 to 1344, the year of his death. Shardelowe held land in Norfolk, Suffolk, Essex, and Cambridgeshire, including a messuage in Berton by Mildenhall, where he was Elizabeth's tenant, owing service of a twentieth part of a knight's fee.[5] He had been a narrator in the Common Bench by 1318, steward of Bury St Edmunds by 1323, and a commissioner of oyer and terminer in Suffolk by 1325. Any of these positions might have alerted Elizabeth to his potential. Perhaps he was especially useful in 1331, when the king commissioned him to investigate the "oppressions of the ministers of the late king" in Norfolk, Suffolk, and Kent. The lady and the justice probably entered some formal arrangement fairly early, but it is only with the 1343 livery list that Elizabeth's estimate of her neighbor is documented; Shardelowe appeared as one of her knights, the most distinguished category of those wearing her colors and receiving her robes. He played his role as a client should, for in the Hilary term of 1342–43, when Elizabeth's suit "prayed the aid of the King," Shardelowe concluded the proceedings with a decision in her favor: "Let her have the aid." He was one of several judges dismissed briefly in 1340, accused of taking bribes. A fourteenth-century patron would have been more concerned with a justice's loyalty than with his judicial ethics, and Elizabeth correctly estimated Shardelowe. His position allowed him to serve Elizabeth's needs, and she responded by according him honor and gifts.[6]

Shardelowe's heir failed to sustain the amicable relationship with Elizabeth. In 1357 this later John Shardelowe seized her cattle, carried away her goods, and caught her servant and clapped him into stocks until she fined for him. Elizabeth secured an oyer and terminer commission to investigate the trespass; William Shareshull, chief justice of the King's Bench, was among the commissioners. Shareshull then appeared in Elizabeth's accounts, when he, another justice on the commission, and one of her counselors spent two days in Stoke, "on the lady's business," with expenses paid by her.[7] She provided food, covered their horses' costs, and sent servants to attend to their comfort. Presumably after this hospitality, the justices understood the merit of the lady's cause. The case was important to Elizabeth, both for prestige and costs. Elizabeth had paid the younger Shardelowe a 100s. fine for her servant's release, and paid 20s. to the Crown for forming the commission. Obviously she would not scant on generosity toward Shareshull. This commission already had personnel partial to the lady. One was her close confidante, Nicholas Damory; another was John Cavendish. Cavendish's career on the Benches peaked long after Elizabeth's death, when he was appointed a chief justice, but she evidently identified his potential earlier. Cavendish was a pleader before the courts by 1348 and a tax collector for the levies of the tenth and fifteenth in 1352 in Suffolk and Essex; consequently he was a good contact for Elizabeth. She employed him on some business at Usk in 1351–52, rewarding him with a handsome gift of £6 13s. 4d. He undertook some of her business in 1357, the same year he served on the oyer and terminer commission with Shareshull.[8]

Robert Thorpe first appeared in Elizabeth's accounts as a recipient of legal fees in 1340, the year he began to act as an advocate before the courts. By 1343 she awarded him squire's livery. He was on the commission appointed to survey Clare Hall in 1353, probably the reason for Elizabeth's letters to him the preceding year. Thorpe's major appearance in the accounts was in the spring and summer of 1359, when he was chief justice of Common Pleas. She paid for his three boat trips on the Thames from Westminster to London Bridge, accompanied by men of her council. While these were surely not pleasure excursions, the purpose of Elizabeth's interest in the chief justice then is obscure. He received a recognizance touching her manor of Sandhall in August; she paid for Thorpe and his retinue of ten horses to go from St Edmunds to Wynbergh that month.[9] In some fashion, she was profiting from her recognition of a young attorney 19 years earlier.

On St Thomas' day in 1351, Elizabeth presented Richard de Kelleshull with a gift of 40s.; his clerk received 3s. 4d. Kelleshull was a justice of the Common Bench and had held assizes in Norfolk in 1349. By 1351, justices were forbidden to receive robes and fees from their patrons, but as Kelleshull ignored this prohibition in other cases, his acceptance of her generous gift was typical behavior.[10] Even with the gaps in existing documentation, Elizabeth's cultivation of judicial contacts on the major Benches is impressive. Stonor, Shardelowe, and Thorpe received her livery. Cavendish worked for Elizabeth before his grander appointments; Kelleshull was a justice of the Common Bench when he accepted his gift from her. Shareshull was less in Elizabeth's debt, though he enjoyed her hospitality.[11]

Other major royal officials attracted Elizabeth's patronage as well. Robert de Sadington, a knight on Elizabeth's 1343 livery list, was appointed king's chancellor that year. Sadington was no novice in governmental circles, having served as chief baron of the Exchequer since 1334. Perhaps it was his tenure in that powerful position that led the lady to write him in 1339–40, for undoubtedly the two developed some trust before 1343. In any event, giving livery to the chancellor of England enhanced Elizabeth's chances of influence.[12] Other chancellors had ties to Elizabeth. Bishop Henry Burghersh served Edward III as treasurer and chancellor; Elizabeth utilized his London quarters and he visited her at least twice.[13] Sir Robert Parving was already a skillful legal counselor in 1339 when Elizabeth sent falcons and a falconer to him in Carlisle. In 1340 and early 1341, she needed Parving's support for some project, for after an exchange of letters in October and January, Elizabeth directed her advisor John Bataille to prolong his London stay to oversee her business with Parving. The accounts furnish no clues about the issues involved in this flurry of gifts, letters, and meetings, but Parving's career was about to blossom: the treasurership, chief justice of the King's Bench, and finally the chancellorship in 1342. Bishop William Edington of Winchester received cloth costing nearly £8 from the lady about the time of his 1356 appointment as chancellor of England.[14]

Elizabeth sought out men in lesser government positions, such as four clerks who received her 1343 livery. David Wallore (or Wollore) was keeper of the Chancery rolls from 1345 to 1371 and often one of the custodians of the Great Seal. Before he became archbishop of Dublin and chancellor of Ireland, John de St Pol worked as a greater clerk in Chancery for 16 years. William de Stowe had East Anglian roots as archdeacon of Colchester and holder of half a fee in Finchingfield, Essex; later he became baron and eventually chancellor of the Exchequer. A fourth clerk on the lady's 1343 livery list, William de Everdon, had his first appointment as baron of the Exchequer in 1324, serving into Edward III's reign. Elizabeth had known Everdon for some time, as her marshalsea shoed his horse during the Christmas season of 1330.[15]

Through livery and gifts to men of the central courts and the great royal administrative departments, Elizabeth improved her opportunities for favorable judgments and prompt attention to her affairs. Since some of these officials formed the professional element on royal council, she might anticipate a friendly reception to her business likely to be discussed there. The lady felt no need to buy the favor of every justice or major official, but sought out those most amenable to her gifts.

Royal household officials lacked the power to intervene in matters touching Elizabeth's interests in the same direct way that justices and chancellors might, but these men regularly interacted with the king and had influence that could be extended favorably on her behalf. Consequently Elizabeth pursued a deliberate policy of building ties with men in household government, though occasionally family connections aided that policy. From 1337 to 1340, her son-in-law Henry Ferrers was the king's chamberlain; her step-son-in-law Bartholomew de Burghersh held the position in 1344 and 1345. Several stewards of the king's household were aristocratic friends or quasi-family: Robert Ufford (1336–37), Ralph Stafford (1341–44), and Guy Brian (1359–61), who received squire's livery from her. Richard Talbot, another steward (1345–49), does not appear in Elizabeth's accounts, but Lady Talbot visited. The keeper of the Privy Wardrobe, John de Flete (1323–44), probably was the man who received Elizabeth's livery in 1343.[16]

The 1343 livery list is a marvelous document, but it focuses on a single year of the 30-odd annual liveries bestowed by the lady.[17] Her livery fluctuated with changing conditions, deaths, and probably by replacement of men who failed to serve her interests wholeheartedly. Because of the singularity of the 1343 list, it is impossible to know if a recipient supported her causes for many years and received ongoing awards, or if she gave livery in relation to a particular matter and lost interest at its conclusion. Given the contemporary emphasis on loyalty, one presumes some continuity. Several officials disgraced and removed from royal government in 1340–41 appear on her 1343 list, but by then most had been rehabilitated by Edward III. Was Shardelowe dropped from Elizabeth's favor because he failed to meet royal standards? Given the neighborly and vassalage ties between the two, it seems doubtful.

Overall she chose her knights from men well-known to her personally and, similarly, she knew the servants who served her each day. Clerks and squires in the middle range of her livery classifications present the greatest puzzle, because of their diversity in background, including merchants, attorneys, even valets of cherished friends or family members. East Anglian neighbors figured prominently among the liveried squires, as did key men from other shires where she held lands. John Wake of Dorset is a good example of the latter. He had held various commissions in Dorset before 1343: array, peace, oyer and terminer, all of which gave Wake the local power Elizabeth wanted available on her behalf. She also favored sheriffs and escheators in districts where she had property, either awarding them livery or providing more subtle inducements in hospitality and favors. Another Dorset man receiving livery was Thomas Cary, who held lands from her in that shire. More importantly, Cary served as both sheriff and escheator for Dorset and Somerset between 1343 and 1353.[18] Elizabeth rarely visited her Dorset estates, but with Cary and Wake in responsible local offices, she could assume her interests would receive friendly attention.

The 1343 livery listed few men whose primary shire identification were in areas where Elizabeth's holdings derived from her Verdon marriage. Possibly she assumed her relationships with Henry Ferrers or Bartholomew de Burghersh were sufficiently strong to afford her security. Similarly, men from Lincoln are missing from this list, but John Bardolf, her son-in-law, had major holdings there.[19] Richard de la Bere, who received a squire's livery, had lands in Shropshire and Herefordshire, though his shrievalty began only in 1354. Another squire, John de Horsele, in her service since at least 1317, held fees in Somerset. Walter Colpeper, who received robes from Elizabeth in 1340 and 1343, came from a prominent local family in Kent and held lands of Elizabeth there.[20] Through her livery, Elizabeth maintained connections to important local men in districts where she had estates; conversely, she wasted no robes on men from Devon or Durham. London is a special case, as the sheriff's offices were served by citizens of the merchant class. Elizabeth patronized at least 11 of the merchant-sheriffs between 1328 and 1358, but none received livery in 1343. That year she gave robes to Bartholomew Thomasyn, an alien merchant from Lucca, and to Robert de Eynesham, a skinner, men never elected sheriff.

Neighbors

Because her principal residences were in East Anglia, Elizabeth concentrated on building her strongest connections there, through hospitality, fees, and employment. She selected inducements to fit the individual rather than relying on a uniform pattern. While several sheriffs, escheators, and tax or subsidy collectors were among her recipients, the favors each received differed markedly. In 1351–52 Elizabeth gave a gift of 26s. 8d. to William Middleton, sheriff and escheator of Norfolk and Suffolk from 1349–1353, critical years because of the high mortality rates. The size of the lady's gift suggests he had proved useful to her, probably in his official duties. John Coggeshall received wages from her for some task in Norwich while he was sheriff in nearby Essex and Hertfordshire.[21] Another sheriff of Essex and Hertfordshire, John de Wauton, held land from Elizabeth. He may have been satisfied with the prestige attached to being her representative at the earl of Hereford's funeral.[22] In 1343 Elizabeth gave squire's robes to John Dengayne, who had served earlier as commissioner of array and collector of subsidies and wool for Cambridgeshire; by 1345 he was escheator and sheriff for Cambridgeshire and Huntingdonshire. There is no evidence that he suborned his offices in her interest, but their association persisted for 20 years, so one assumes that any bias might be in her favor.[23] Another sheriff and escheator in those shires, Thomas de Grey of Cavendish, was also an important landholder in Kent, Norfolk, Suffolk, and Cambridge. Elizabeth responded to his higher social status by entertaining him at a hunting party at Hundon and sending his wife a dish of boar, the type of food gift the nobility favored for their own class.[24] Through a variety of gestures, Elizabeth managed cordial relationships with key officials in the East Anglian shires that were her home base.

Other recipients of her favors are more difficult to categorize. A few went to parliament, but it seems doubtful that was a major factor for Elizabeth. Robert Bousser went to parliament from Essex for five sessions and the lady wrote to him at least twice during his last term, but since Bousser held land from her the timing of the letters may have been coincidental. She also sent letters to Edmund Durem, her neighbor in Dunmow, during his parliamentary stints.[25] John Dyn, sent to parliament from Essex during the reigns of Edward II and Edward III, accepted a gift from Elizabeth. Another East Anglian landholder, John de Goldyngham, received squire's livery from Elizabeth for several years. Later he attended parliament and acted as justice of laborers for Essex, positions that provided opportunities to remember his patroness.[26]

Building a network of deferential and friendly neighbors mattered to Elizabeth. She utilized livery robes to bind some more closely and they benefited by having a prestigious friend with important contacts. For example, Walter de Finchingfelde and William de Clopton received squire's livery in 1343. Both had lands in Essex, and Clopton held in Suffolk and Cambridgeshire as well.[27] Neither seems to have been selected for judicial or political posts. Rather, their recruitment by Elizabeth signified that they were sufficiently important to cultivate for their potential office-holding or as part of a network of friendly neighbors. The Loveyn family, with manors in Essex and Suffolk, received more prestigious favors. Thomas Loveyn received a knight's livery in 1343; Elizabeth had communicated with him for at least seven years, given his wife food gifts, and extended hunting privileges to their son.[28] John Sturmy placed his son Robert with Elizabeth for part of his childhood. Elizabeth and John traded favors: he gave her a palfrey; she awarded his son squire's livery. Elizabeth may have felt the greater obligation in this instance, as John Sturmy had belonged to Edward II's council and worked as seneschal and steward of the royal chamber. These positions placed him in a position to mitigate royal vengefulness, and perhaps he did, for he appeared at Elizabeth's castle in the week of Isabella's 1326 invasion.[29] The favors extended to various East Anglian men provided Elizabeth with a comfortable milieu, secure in the knowledge that many individuals there were obligated to her in some fashion.

Members of Elizabeth's council received the widest array of rewards for themselves and their families, and from them she demanded faithful and trustworthy service. She recruited men of substance, who served in advisory positions on her council that left them time to enhance their own estates. Robert de Cheddeworth served as constable of Clare during Elizabeth's Damory marriage, and his brother Thomas was her closest clerical confidant until his death in 1351. Elizabeth trusted both brothers: Thomas witnessed her secret protests against the Despensers in 1326; Robert was dispatched to the queen soon after her invasion. Robert prospered under the new regime with appointments to responsible posts, mainly in Essex, where he collected taxes and subsidies and served on peace and oyer and terminer commissions. In the 1330s he represented Essex in four sessions of parliament while he belonged to Elizabeth's council. Although he served the lady well, his deepest loyalties were to the Vere family, apparent in his chantry foundation where prayers were to be offered for the late earl of Oxford.[30] There was no need to compromise his commitments to the Veres or the lady of Clare, for they were close friends. Cheddeworth had obligations to the Crown and two noble patrons and presumably aimed at furthering his own status and wealth. Noble patrons hoped to harness these ambitions of the knightly class to their own ends.

Andrew de Bures enjoyed a closer relationship to Elizabeth than did Cheddeworth. The household clerks labeled him *familia;* he received robes of a knight in 1343. During the 1340s, Bures acted as chief household officer, important enough for Elizabeth to successfully seek a royal pardon from overseas duty, allowing him to prosecute her business in East Anglia, Wales, and London. His royal service was local: in 1343 as collector of wool in Suffolk, and as justice of laborers and the peace from 1350 to 1355. Undoubtedly Bures' conduct in the former office helped Elizabeth evade some royal demands for wool. She rewarded him with robes and a pony, and leased some lands to him. He had other properties in Norfolk, Suffolk, and Essex, making him the kind of knightly gentleman she preferred for her key staff.[31]

An exemption from military service was also secured for Warin de Bassingbourne, a staff member who was about Elizabeth's age and, like her, anti-Despenser in the 1320s. He received royal livery as a squire in 1330; Elizabeth gave him knight's livery in 1343. As a landholder in Cambridgeshire, Wiltshire, Hampshire, and Lincolnshire, Warin was prominent enough to represent Elizabeth at the Earl Marshal's funeral. He also garnered a number of offices in the 1330s and 1340s, representing Cambridgeshire in parliament, acting as peace commissioner of that shire for several years, and occasionally serving on oyer and terminer commissions. While belonging to the lady's *familia,* he served two stints as escheator of Cambridgeshire and Huntingdonshire and was sheriff there in 1332, 1338–40, 1341–45, and 1347–48.[32] Undoubtedly he protected her interests at Clare Hall and, as a member of her council, witnessed several of her grants to the college, including the first in 1336. There was a certain level of reciprocity between Elizabeth and Bassingbourne: he gave her a horse, Liard Bassingbourne; she provided squire's livery for two of his relatives, Robert and Thomas de Bassingbourne. Elizabeth probably helped him in other ways but one was especially critical. As keeper of Cambridge Castle, Bassingbourne was responsible for prisoners housed there. Twelve escaped in 1348, an embarrassing occurrence and one that exposed the keeper to the Crown's punitive powers. Elizabeth secured a royal pardon for her friend, which exempted him from consequences of his dereliction.[33] Obviously there were rewards for loyal service to the lady.

John Bataille belonged to Elizabeth's council, receiving squire's livery
in 1343. Often he transacted Elizabeth's legal work in London, but also
went to Standon, Farnham, and Wales in her service. Apparently his careful audits of manorial accounts and service as her attorney led Elizabeth
to name him a principal executor of her estate and leave him a generous
legacy of silver.[34]

The Waldens were an Essex family with long-standing ties to Elizabeth.
Andrew de Walden, who held an Essex manor from her, probably is among
those knights whose names are illegible on the 1343 livery list. She trusted
him sufficiently to represent her at the earl of Cornwall's 1337 funeral and
to transact her business with the earl of Northampton in 1339–40. Most
of Walden's career was spent in the lady's service, with a short stint as justice of laborers and the peace. She gave him venison and hunting privileges
in her Tonbridge park and when he died in 1352 she paid the Austin friars of Clare to pray for his soul.[35] Humphrey de Walden, who joined Elizabeth's staff in 1347, was probably Andrew's cousin. Previously Humphrey
had collected subsidies and various taxes in Essex and represented that shire
in parliament; in 1349 he served a brief term as escheator and sheriff of
Essex and Hertfordshire. Humphrey de Walden first appeared in the accounts on buying trips to Wales or Stourbridge Fair, but by 1350 he was
receiver of Clare. His work must have pleased Elizabeth, for he received silver plate in her will and was appointed a secondary executor of her estate.
Nevertheless, the sense of familial intimacy that Andrew de Walden enjoyed seems not to have extended to the younger man.[36] Elizabeth had lost
many of her favorite advisors by the 1350s and perhaps lacked the energy
and will to develop close ties with a new generation. Certainly Theobald
de Monteneye and William Talmach, members of her council in the late
1350s, never became part of the household dynamic in the fashion of Andrew de Walden or Warin de Bassingbourne.

Neighbors who served on her council differed from men who accepted
Elizabeth's gifts, but who were employed primarily by the Crown. The latter dealt with problems throughout the realm, while the former concentrated on village, shire, or region. Those who served on her council might
receive appointments to commissions or offices from the king, but their positions focused on the local community where they held lands. Most were
married and intent on building their own estates while serving Elizabeth
loyally. Consequently, they also differed from the household staff, whose
employment and income depended on the lady.[37] Andrew de Bures, Warin
de Bassingbourne, and others utilized their positions in the community in
Elizabeth's interests, and her prestige was enhanced by recruiting important
local men. Their jobs as sheriffs, collectors, and commissioners increased her
expectations for favorable treatment in legal and financial affairs, while their

standing as landowners gave them experience on a small scale which could be transferred to her grander enterprises. They could act as her eyes and ears in situations where a noble widow would receive deference rather than candid opinions. Elizabeth honored and rewarded these men in return for their professionalism, bias, and loyalty.

Other neighbors held their land from her, creating a continuing inter-change, such as suit at the Clare honor courts. In other instances, her agents purchased grain and goods in the countryside from small landholders, noble friends, village parsons, and knightly neighbors. Some families placed children or relatives in her care or service for short periods, beneficial to them and Elizabeth.[38] The young men and the few young women learned proper behavior and received household administrative experience, while forming contacts that would serve them well in adulthood. In turn, Eliza-beth developed gratitude and obligations from her neighbors. The lady of Clare possessed a deep sense of the superiority of her own class, but she lacked petty snobbishness toward the growing merchant class. She main-tained cordial relationships with East Anglian merchants, who received a good portion of her custom and other recognition. Wearing Clare robes and insignia served as a noble endorsement of the merchants' reputation and products. Thomas Cotellar of Ipswich and Nicholas Thebaud of Sud-bury, both merchants, received her squire's livery in 1343. Cotellar was a self-made man, beginning his career as a servant and then parlaying a small inheritance into considerable wealth and local prestige. One Thebaud son became a wine merchant patronized by Elizabeth, while son Simon en-tered the Church, where as an ambitious young cleric, he briefly joined Elizabeth's *familia*.[39]

Many males found long-term employment as servants in Elizabeth's household while others were recruited for casual labor. Often pairs of men received stipends for cutting wood, or teams of women helped in brewing, larder jobs, and cleaning tasks as Elizabeth moved from one establishment to another. The lady built rather extensively during her tenure, hiring local labor to supplement the professional builders and servile laborers' custom-ary works.[40] Elizabeth fed local paupers and dispensed charity in the com-munity. Her chariot driver's son attended Clare grammar school at her expense; an anchorite living on the bridge at Clare received 2s. in Octo-ber 1351. The next year, the lady presented two babies, baptized in her presence at the Clare church, with gifts totaling 5s., and two infants named for her received gifts as well. Elizabeth frequently attended church in Clare, supporting it to benefit the whole congregation. In 1351 she gave 40s. to provide lights and perhaps did so other years when no documen-tary evidence survives. She bequeathed the parish churches of Clare and Bardfield each 60s. and a cloth of gold.[41] None of these benefactions in

Clare promoted Elizabeth's interests as her noble or knightly contacts might. At best, she encouraged a few prayers for her well-being from grateful recipients. However, she garnered good will, which reduced any local hostility while fulfilling the traditional demands of her station.

Free and servile peasants comprised the bulk of population on Elizabeth's lands, but she made no great effort to placate or oppress them. She possessed economic and judicial power over her serfs; their only power was the latent threat of riot and destruction. She was aware of this potential as she had lived in East Anglia in the late 1320s during the mob attacks on Bury St Edmunds' abbey, where the conflict was initiated by townsmen, but where peasants caused the major losses. Consequently Elizabeth's attitude toward her peasant neighbors aimed at their quiescence, since they were already dependent on her in some fashion. Her stately progresses from one manor to another were meant to evoke awe and deference. Her friendships with officialdom left little doubt about the outcome of legal cases a freeman might want to pursue. Still, Elizabeth's reputation for piety gave the peasantry some hope for minimal kindness in time of destitution. Although her Cambridge hall kept spaces for poor boys, probably few charity students were recruited from the farm. Her officials always extracted fines and rents due her, but nothing suggests they exploited the peasantry beyond the usages inherent in the system. At harvest time she gave modest tips to the work crews, at least in 1352.[42] It would be instructive to know if this generosity existed before the plague decimated the countryside and put a premium on keeping a work force intact. The lady's great wealth stemmed from the land, which was worthless without labor, so in that sense, she was dependent on the peasants. It is somewhat ironic that the deepest economic ties resulted in the most distant social relationships.

Ties with churchmen were complex, because of the wide spectrum of clerical occupations. Some appeared in Elizabeth's accounts because of their associations with her friends or royalty: Bartholomew Bourne, canon at Lincoln where his kinsman Henry de Burghersh was bishop; Roger de Chikewell, special secretary to Queen Philippa and later king's clerk; William de Culpho, associated with Queen Isabella; Simon Clement, who became a chaplain for the Black Prince; Master Richard de Evesham, chaplain to Laurence Hastings, earl of Pembroke.[43] As noted above, clerics employed in high governmental positions enjoyed Elizabeth's generosity, extended to them for her own ends. Other ecclesiastics who appealed to her for intellectual or spiritual reasons will be considered in the next chapter. Some clerics worked for Elizabeth, in her chapel, on her council, and even in the homely duties of buying and selling household supplies, while others were simply neighbors.

Although she traveled to Canterbury several times, only one account entry indicates any sort of personal relationship with a reigning archbishop. In December 1343, she sent Archbishop John Stratford 30 gallons of ale during his stay in the Norwich diocese. The gift hardly seems appropriate to his status or her reputation for generosity. In contrast, Henry de Burghersh, bishop of Lincoln from 1320 to 1341, received a gift of four bucks and she gave supplementary feedings to his 28 horses when he visited her at Anglesey in 1337.[44] At least two London bishops visited Elizabeth: Steven Gravesend, in 1331 and twice in 1334; Ralph Stratford, twice in 1346–47 when his mounts received a reward. Stratford later dispatched a horse and boy to help her move from Wales to East Anglia, a gesture suggesting closer ties than the accounts document.[45] Bishop Thomas de Lisle of Ely was a nearby episcopal neighbor who stopped with the lady in the fall of 1346. While Elizabeth entertained him and his entourage honorably, she could not have been enchanted by his reputation as a robber baron and employer of thugs. Closer ties developed between the lady and the priors of Ely. John of Crauden and Alan of Walsingham were builders, constructing the fourteenth-century glories of their church. Both visited Elizabeth and corresponded with her.[46] The accounts reveal little about the bishops of Norwich: the lady sent representatives to William Airmyn's funeral; a few carting horses belonging to William Bateman were fed; Bishop Thomas Percy visited her in October 1357.[47] As neighbors, these bishops shared some common concerns with the lady, but fewer than she shared with nearby nobles, knights, and gentry. She was not overawed by the episcopal dignity and looked to the pope for privileges and indults. Unlike many monastic houses, bishops did not need to cultivate Elizabeth for material gain. Any real friendship Elizabeth felt for a bishop depended on his personal qualities and connections rather than ecclesiastical status.

Since their arrival at the time of the Norman Conquest, the Clares had founded monasteries and patronized specific churches. Ecclesiastical patronage was split when the Clare estates were divided among the sisters, but this did not preclude Elizabeth's continued interest. For example, the Tewkesbury house fell within Eleanor's share, but Elizabeth maintained ties with the monastery. The abbot sent assistance for her son's knighting and helped her move from Usk to Clare in 1350.[48] Tonbridge Priory was located near Margaret's major estates and its patronage was hers. Elizabeth rented some nearby property from the prior, who contacted her several times between 1338 and 1341, probably hoping for aid after a disastrous 1337 fire. The lady may not have donated then, but she bequeathed the house 100 shillings and two cloths of gold and also provided funds for prayers for Margaret's soul.[49]

Elizabeth showed special interest in three East Anglian Clare family houses where she was patroness. From her castle, Elizabeth could see the church she built for the Clare Augustinian friars, where her mother and half-brother were buried. She also financed other buildings in the friary precinct, leaving her personal mark in windows glazed with Clare, Ulster, and Bardolf arms. Over the years she entertained clerics who offered indulgences for the faithful to visit and donate to the church's fabric fund. In 1320, Elizabeth and Roger Damory and the friary reached an agreement calling for two friars to celebrate daily mass at Clare Castle during the lifetimes of the Damorys in return for an annual render of wheat and malt. Elizabeth showed generosity beyond this contractual exchange, giving habits, sandals, and gifts to individual friars. Small gifts of hens and pittances were sent to the convent, and she bequeathed £10 to the house in her will.[50]

Patronage of another Clare foundation, Stoke by Clare, a dependency of Bec in France, belonged to Elizabeth. The monastery was in a vulnerable position during the Hundred Years' War, for like his father and grandfather, Edward III decreed that alien houses be taken into royal custody in 1337. To avoid earlier custodies, Stoke had paid a £200 fine or as much of that sum as the house could find to satisfy the Crown; again in 1337, it was assessed for £200. Stoke benefited from the staunch defense of its patroness, who argued that the lay community would lose the prayers and charity of the monks if they were forced to pay this sum. The king was sufficiently moved by his kinswoman's testimony that he halved the annual assessment.[51] The prior of Stoke and Elizabeth were already on friendly terms before her spirited intervention on the convent's behalf. She gave him a gift of boar in the Christmas season of 1336; the priory often assisted Elizabeth on her major relocations by sending cart horses to convey household members or supplies. For example, when she left London in 1355 for Clare, the prior dispatched carts to aid in the transport. There must have been other non-spiritual financial dealings between the lady and the prior, because she paid him £20 in 1350–51 to cover a debt. Elizabeth worshiped at the chapel of Stoke twice in 1352 and bequeathed the house 12 silver-gilt bells, two cloths of gold, and a silver-gilt comfit dish.[52]

That same blending of the religious and the worldly appears in her relationship with the small house at Anglesey, where she founded a chantry and constructed a range of buildings to accommodate herself and her traveling household during frequent visits. Her Lenten retreats at Anglesey imply a religious dimension in her ties with these Augustinian canons, but the house was also convenient to Cambridge and the countess of Pembroke. Often some member of the house purchased turves or sedge for Elizabeth's use or even traveled to London on her business, perhaps in connection with her chantry foundation.[53] After 1335–36 her chantry priest assumed many of the commercial duties formerly handled by Walter de Yevelden, canon and eventual prior of Anglesey. William Arderne, the chantry priest, first appeared in the accounts selling kitchen surpluses at Clare. Later Elizabeth outfitted him with furred robes, and by 1343 he received a clerk's livery from her, along with 21 other clerics. When he was free of chantry duties, Arderne acted as a household agent, having the Anglesey stable cleaned, buying supplies, and preparing Elizabeth's quarters before her visits. The lady was generous to the convent, for besides building a chantry chapel, she added to the canons' endowment. From the convent she received religious benefits, help with local purchases, a corrody for a clerical friend, some sort of medical intervention for a few household members, and a convenient stopover for visits by herself or her family.[54] Elizabeth rescued Anglesey from financial problems but at a cost of distracting the house from its spiritual routine and intruding a secular element at her convenience.

Although Anglesey, Stoke by Clare, and Clare friary all enjoyed Elizabeth's patronage, she treated them quite differently. She gave more to Anglesey and demanded religious and commercial services, including some inn-keeping chores. Stoke seemed primarily a neighbor, with minimum obligations on its part or hers. The lady respected the Austin friars' eremetic tradition, asking little beyond their spiritual role, although her generous building program at the Clare friary raised her prestige within the order and among her neighbors. In sum, she molded patronage rights to the nature of the house and her own requirements.

Horses from neighboring houses appear frequently in the marshalsea records, but the accounts divulge little on relationships with monastic personnel.[55] Given the rules of medieval hospitality, the carting horses of neighbors, lay or monastic, naturally received overnight accommodations. Some houses probably gave Elizabeth carting assistance on her progress to Walsingham in 1347; Tewkesbury, Evesham, Walsingham, Dereham, and Ely convents supplied horses and servants to ease her 1350 trip from Wales. A few houses must have hoped that her generosity would extend to them, for some of her monastic neighbors were feeling extreme financial distress by the mid-fourteenth century.[56] A woman with great wealth and a pious reputation would animate even great monastic centers, always eager to enhance their environment. All these efforts may have been initiated through neighborliness or Christian caring, but the suspicion lingers that Elizabeth was a prize prospect to be developed in the same manner that charitable and educational institutions utilize today. Overall, Elizabeth's ties with neighboring houses differed little from those with her secular neighbors. In a few instances, a monastery might hold all or part of a fee from her or she might hold lands from a monastery.[57] As landholders, both the lady and her ecclesiastical neighbors shared economic and social concerns. Monastic officials could enjoy a hearty meal with her, hope for a generous gift for their house, ensure competent stabling for their horses, or even have a voice raised in their defense at the highest reaches of government. They supplied Elizabeth with neighborly assistance and the promise of continuing prayers for her good estate and eventually for her soul.

Elizabeth constructed a complex network of officials, associates, and neighbors, which augmented ties to her family and noble peers. She aimed at protecting her security, economic well-being, comfort, and prestige, and she was quite successful despite the disadvantages of her sex in fourteenth-century England. Being female was not an enviable condition even if one controlled great wealth. In building her network, she lacked the inducements of glamorous tournaments and the lure of war booty and chivalric opportunities. She competed with her noble neighbors for the services of well-placed men and governmental officials, and many prospective associates probably preferred to align themselves with an earl rather than an untitled woman. Elizabeth managed to circumvent these disadvantages. Naturally, her wealth was critical to her success, but her friendships with great magnates helped as well. Continuing visits from the Black Prince, the duke of Lancaster, and the Bohun and Vere earls advertised her importance to them and mitigated any uncertainty among lesser men about enlisting in a female's circle. Elizabeth's reputation for piety probably served her well, as one would not suspect a pious person of dishonesty or double-dealing. Content to operate in areas surrounding her estates, she lacked overweening ambitions elsewhere. Even her recruitment of justices aimed primarily at protecting her local concerns. Above all else, she understood that the long-range achievement of her objectives required lasting loyalty rather than sullen acquiescence. The key to her success was the mutuality of reward to her recruits as well as to herself. Elizabeth provided generously for those who served her, and they responded by promoting her interests and her prestige.

CHAPTER 5

PIETY AND PRESTIGE

Two of Elizabeth de Burgh's major goals are reflected in her chantry foundation formulas: her good estate in this world and her salvation after death. She pursued her earthly good estate masterfully through shrewd exploitation of her lands and cultivation of ties of affection and dependency with family, friends, neighbors, and clients. Elizabeth carefully developed those secular relationships at the same time she explored ways to improve her chances for salvation, subscribing to contemporary religious norms and giving generously to charitable causes. These, in turn, deepened her piety and stimulated her intellectual interests.

Chaucer immortalized the fourteenth-century penchant for pilgrimages in his *Canterbury Tales*. These excursions offered both the excitement of travel and the awesome presence of certified sanctity. Elizabeth was not immune to the lure of pilgrimage, going at least three times to Canterbury, the premier destination for English pilgrims. Her first was a pilgrimage of thanksgiving after the birth of her daughter Isabella.[1] She traveled with her aunt Mary and Lady Isabella of Lancaster from Amesbury convent, on a journey financed by Edward II. The trip was leisurely and circuitous, with visits from friends, a five-day stopover at Windsor, a few days in London, time for Mary to run-up gambling debts. The women did include worship at Marian shrines in Caversham, Canterbury Cathedral with its Becket sites, and the nearby monastic church of St Augustine, which honored missionaries who began the successful Christianization of England. Later the women proceeded to St Albans, whose shrines were dedicated to British martyrs of the Roman period. Mary and Isabella donated at each site, and Elizabeth probably did as well, from personal funds not covered in the royal clerk's rolls.

The lady's later pilgrimages to Canterbury lack key details: no mention of alms, oblations, visitors, gaming, or specific shrines. The 1340 pilgrimage from

East Anglia to Canterbury and return took about three weeks, lengthened by avoiding travel on Sundays, Pentecost, and Corpus Christi. In 1353 her three-week pilgrimage included eight days in London, two nights in Canterbury, and no Sunday travel.[2] Elizabeth traveled in grand style in 1340, with about 70 horses and ample household staff. Although the rolls are very explicit about consumption expenses, they ignore Elizabeth's spiritual purposes. The second greatest English shrine, at Walsingham, honored the Blessed Virgin. Elizabeth journeyed there four times, including the magnificent progress in June 1347, associated with her friary foundation. The lady, her staff, family, and various clerics spent three days in Walsingham, where Elizabeth hosted a splendid feast. Afterward she went to Bromholm, whose shrine housed a relic of the True Cross. Her pilgrimages suggest she must have felt some impulse for closeness to holy artifacts available through pilgrimages.[3]

The lady's spirituality shows more clearly in her homes, with their devotional books to sustain her personal faith and chapels for the household's collective worship. She enhanced the drama of the mass with beautiful silver and silver-gilt altar equipment, splendid clerical vestments, and devotional statuary such as the gold image of St John the Baptist, later bequeathed to Joan of Bar. The accounts never mention wages for choir boys, but perhaps music accompanied some services, for her own breviary was "well-noted."[4] If she stinted on religious expenditures, it was in her chaplains' wages. Sir William Ailmer, resident chaplain at Bardfield in the 1350s, received only 1s. a week beyond room and board, though he may have benefited from chapel offerings.[5] Elizabeth was more generous to visiting clerics who preached in her chapels. In 1351–52 ten friars gave sermons for the lady and were rewarded with compensation ranging from 5s. to 10s. for a day's work, presumably because she found their sermons more compelling than those of her resident staff. The accounts and her testament show that Elizabeth loved the beauty of the mass, liturgical music, and the inspiration to her faith and intellect of a good sermon. She also subscribed to the merit of masses for deceased family and friends, remembered on anniversaries of their deaths.

The genuine nature of Elizabeth's piety permeated her life, creating an environment conducive to the spiritual development of her companions, best illustrated by Anne de Lexeden. In 1343 this young woman received livery as a damsel; several years later, Anne found her vocation in the anchoritic life and convinced Elizabeth to sponsor and support her choice. Anne opted for a life of voluntary poverty, giving up the variety of the lady's table, colorful clothing, and social interchange for simple, black outfits and quiet solitude away from the vibrant world she knew. This could have been done only with Elizabeth's encouragement, conviction of Anne's resolve, and ecclesiastical permission. The local bishop determined the applicant's sincerity, suitability of living accommodations, and source of sustenance.[6] Anne was enclosed at Radwinter near the home of John de Lenne, Elizabeth's former clerk. John could give priestly direction to Anne, while the lady supplied her daily needs. Elizabeth paid for a porch and a wall in Anne's house in 1351–52 and had paid Anne 110s. the year before, perhaps to cover other building costs.[7] Entries in the accounts show Elizabeth supplied Anne's needs, which were minimal, given her anchorite profession. She received black cloth, an occasional money gift, along with bread, wine, ale, and fish for herself and her maid, which cost about 20d. per month. Elizabeth also paid for Anne's charitable initiatives, refunding 5s. Anne doled out to two nuns from Rowney. In her will, Elizabeth tried to guarantee Anne's religious withdrawal by bequeathing her £20, her black outfit, a chalice, and various silver dishes. Anne was still living in 1374, sustained by her sponsor's bequest, which underscored Elizabeth's abiding concern for women's spirituality.[8] The lady gave to others in the anchoritic life, but only Anne was totally dependent on Elizabeth. A female recluse in Norwich received a gift in 1328; in 1351–52, another in Hereford received 20s., and a hermit at Brandon was given 5s., while an anchorite in Thaxted had his roof repaired through the lady's generosity.[9] Gifts of money, goods, or services to those following a reclusive religious life enabled them to sustain their calling while opening another charitable avenue to donors.

In the fourteenth century, neighbors and clergy expected those entrusted with riches to share their bounty with the poor through almsgiving. This obligation was sweetened by the donor's knowledge that true charity provided the most secure route to salvation. Gifts to prisoners became a specialized and rather common form of almsgiving. Certainly those incarcerated needed charity, for they were required to pay their enforced room and board charges. Elizabeth gave to prisoners in neighboring towns during 1351–52.[10]

When she was in residence, Elizabeth established a routine of feeding the poor at her homes. Early accounts indicate she employed an almoner and had established two major yearly distributions, on All Souls' Day (November 2) and St Gregory's Day (March 12), a pattern which continued through her life.[11] Typically the pantry baked over 3,000 loaves of bread, and the kitchen furnished several thousand herring for the poor on these days. Elizabeth's distribution days differed from religious houses, which typically chose Maundy Thursday for their spring feeding, and though she occasionally gave a supplementary Maundy feeding and another on her birthday, neither became standard.[12]

In the last decade of her life and perhaps before, Elizabeth gathered a group of paupers who could expect feeding throughout the year. Her friend the earl of Northampton maintained 15 paupers and probably Elizabeth had a similar company. She purchased cloth for paupers, more likely for a small group than for the mobs that thronged in for major distributions.[13] Once the poor enjoyed bacon, and sometimes the almoner dispensed small quantities of wine, but no pattern emerges, except the wine allowances do not coincide with the major spring and autumn feedings.[14] The best evidence for a small, designated group of paupers appears in 1357–58. The roll notes 5,390 paupers cared for at Clare and Bardfield for six months, at a cost of £22 9s. 2d., amounting to 1d. a day per pauper. Later 848 paupers are mentioned in a 28-day reckoning that cost 70s. Costs of horses and paupers were recorded differently from other categories, so it appears Elizabeth supported 30 paupers, giving each 1d. a day rather than feeding them from stock. The accounts suggest that funds for charitable distribution increased in the lady's last decade, a period coinciding with the aftermath of the plague's first visitation.[15]

In addition to the spring and fall distributions and the cadre of paupers maintained on a continuing basis, Elizabeth made special gifts to the poor at her pleasure. Fifty received 9d. apiece on Maundy Thursday in 1351–52; a poor woman with two children received only a penny. Almsgiving to paupers usually accompanied upper-class funerals. When Elizabeth's half-brother died in 1339, she expended 69s. on bread and herring for paupers, who were expected to pray for his soul. A few years later, 3s. 6d. was distributed for the soul of John le Hosteller, formerly of the hall and chamber staff. Elizabeth believed in enlisting prayers from the poor, allocating £200 toward this cause for her own burial. Here, as with other charities, she provided more generously than her peers.[16]

Aiding the poor figured annually in Elizabeth's expenditures, but less prominently in her will, where they received alms at her burial, but otherwise only benefited if a residue remained in her estate after bequests to named beneficiaries. Still, directions for that residue allow insight into the lady's concerns. She remembered poor prisoners, merchants ruined by risk-taking, persons who lost their homes, and gentlewomen burdened with children. She hoped to aid needy parish churches and religious men and women with scant resources. Naturally she remembered the poor scholars who needed funds for school; the 40s. legacy to the Hospital of St John, Cambridge, where students often lodged, probably helped them too.[17] Elizabeth sought to garner prayers for her salvation and gratitude, which would perpetuate her memory, but even with these caveats, her testamentary language shows sympathy for the misfortunes of others. The wealthy were judged by the generosity of their alms, so the lady surely gained prestige and enhanced her reputation for piety while earning the gratitude of the poor.

Just as widowhood allowed Elizabeth to dictate her alms schedule and testamentary bequests, widowhood enabled her to endow foundations and initiate building programs for religious institutions. After Ballinrobe's foundation, following her first husband's death, no great benefactions appeared until her third widowhood. The Verdon union was short; the few accounts from her Damory marriage do not record alms, though presumably there were some. Damory founded a single chantry where prayers were to be offered for himself and Edward II, but none for Elizabeth.[18] Although it must have been satisfying to move into major ecclesiastical funding, she began rather tentatively. In March 1327, Elizabeth gave life interest in messuages, lands, rents, and a fishery to the prior and convent of Ely, reserving the reversion to her heirs. Ely Cathedral was embarked on a building campaign since the church crossing had collapsed in 1322 and needed replacement; perhaps her grant was in aid of that. A year later she procured a royal license allowing Angelsey's prior and convent to acquire £20 of lands and rents in mortmain. She then granted Lakenheath manor to the prior and convent of Ely (which they had rented previously), for twenty pounds annually, which she assigned to Anglesey. The transaction fit the needs of each party: Elizabeth secured an annual income for Anglesey without administrative burdens for her staff; Anglesey was enriched; and Ely added to its holdings with a continuation of the rental amount.[19] Gifts to Anglesey served several purposes. Her ancestors had patronized the house, it was convenient for visiting Mary de St Pol, and it offered a retreat for religious exercises, such as the eight Lenten periods she shared with the canons. Elizabeth was generous to the house, founding a chantry there dedicated to the Virgin and building a chapel to house it. The chantry required two secular chaplains, whom the canons promised to support. Really, Elizabeth paid, for she increased their endowments with rents, rights, the advowson, and appropriation of Dunmow church. Later Elizabeth's interest in Anglesey flagged as she found other charitable causes, but she made a small grant to them in 1355. Now the canons were to support only one chantry priest while absorbing a 100s. annual pension for Robert Spaldyng, an aging fellow of Clare Hall.[20]

In the late 1330s and 1340s, Franciscan work began to capture Elizabeth's imagination, though she moved slowly and deliberately toward major endowments. Her pilgrimages to Walsingham alerted her to poor pilgrims unable to afford the housing fees demanded by the Augustinian canons who guarded the town's Marian shrine. Elizabeth believed a Franciscan house with a hospice for the poor would alleviate the problem, so she founded a friary there. When the Walsingham canons learned of her intent, they wrote her a vehement protest against the intrusion on their monopoly.[21] They appealed to traditional and familial ties that Elizabeth's forebears had with their house and reminded the lady of her own generosity to them. The canons recited the typical fourteenth-century monastic attack on the friars for inroads on their incomes: loss of tithes, offerings, payments for burials, and women's purifications, adding that parish churches would be harmed as well. The letter assumes Elizabeth was cognizant of contemporary ecclesiastical debate. Opposition did not deter Elizabeth from her foundation, though she remembered the canons' work in her will. Elizabeth began building the friars' housing and church, enabling their quick occupation.[22] The Walsingham friary never was large, but it met her goal of broadening opportunities for participation in Marian devotions. The foundation also underscores Elizabeth's belief in the efficacy of pilgrimages, devotion to the Blessed Virgin, and appreciation of Franciscan piety.

By her early forties, Elizabeth had founded an Augustinian friary and a Franciscan house, funded building programs for both friars and canons, instituted chantries, donated gifts to monastic recipients, and begun her interest in Cambridge University. Naturally her generosity attracted professional men of prayer who hoped to direct her efforts toward their own causes and institutions. Fourteenth-century clerics knew that funding was more difficult to wrest from donors than in earlier years. Though they lacked statistical data, the drop from nearly 300 new foundations in the thirteenth century to just 45 from 1300 to 1360 must have been obvious to monastic and mendicant leaders, who saw Elizabeth as a prize prospect worth developing for the greater glory of their work.[23] Many clerics were eager to include her in their prayers in exchange for donations—a kind of reciprocal exchange. Even as the lady garnered clerical prayers, her generosity enhanced her standing among her contemporaries, always desirable for the nobility. Being female limited possibilities for prestige in circles where the male chivalric ethos thrived, but Elizabeth modeled a role for herself, which added to her secular reputation while improving her standing among the arbiters of religious virtues. Her piety and generosity eased gender limitations as clerics muted their traditional distaste for females in the face of her wealth and its potential for them. Finally, Elizabeth gained entry into intellectual circles of academics and churchmen normally closed to women and of little interest to most of her male peers. Her decision to rescue University Hall and transform it into the well-endowed Clare Hall only expanded the list of intellectuals happy to promote her love of learning in tandem with their own purposes.

University Hall had been founded by Richard Badew, but his faltering financial situation, mounting quarrels with the master and fellows of the Hall, and destruction of the buildings by fire demanded intervention by a wealthy benefactor if the Hall was to survive. Probably Walter de

Thaxted, master of the Hall and farmer of the rectory at Great Bardfield, appealed to Elizabeth for assistance. She responded by giving the Hall the advowson of Litlington church in 1336. The master and fellows repaid that generosity by naming her receiver, Robert de Stalyngton, as Litlington's rector, though he remained on her staff.[24] Elizabeth was an appropriate prospective donor since she had already shown interest in studies and students. In 1327–28 she provided the salary of a master and living expenses for boys studying at Oxford, continuing in this endeavor for at least four more years; by 1330–31 she supported students at Cambridge and at the royal law courts. Perhaps her motives were not wholly altruistic, for, by 1336–37, one of the former Oxonians, who may have followed a business course, was measuring malt in her household. By the time of her gift of Litlington, Elizabeth was sending a contingent of little clerks to study at Cambridge. The boys spent holidays with her, escorted to and from the university by her household staff. Interaction with the little clerks gave Elizabeth an intimate view of the university and its curriculum.[25]

Elizabeth wanted full rights of patronage before she devoted more of her substance to the college, and it required ten years of negotiations before Badew fully renounced his interests in University Hall in 1346. She moved quickly after this, renaming the college Clare Hall and transferring two other advowsons, which provided it with about £60 annually.[26] Once Elizabeth controlled the patronage of Clare Hall, she procured papal license in 1348 to erect a chapel. The plague decimated Cambridge University so the king authorized a commission to investigate Clare Hall, "reported to be grievously wasted and dilapidated." This probably was instigated by Elizabeth to determine what material possessions needed attention and to restore collegiate discipline, which seems to have faltered with the plague.[27]

Founders set their stamp with governing statutes; Elizabeth's were delivered to the master and scholars in 1359. Her preamble stated three goals for her foundation: to promote the advancement of divine worship, the welfare of the state, and the extension of sciences. These ends were to be achieved by a company of fellows, headed by a master. Legal specialists were limited to three and medicine to one, showing her interest in broad learning. In this, Elizabeth followed the fourteenth-century trend toward improving intellectual life, but her preamble goes beyond current fashion, for in it she speaks from her heart.[28] She extols the sweetness of learning, a phrase drawing on her love of ideas and also on her passion for sugary treats. Her spirit also appears in the injunction to the fellows "to give light to them that walk in the dark paths of ignorance." Biblical allusions can be found in the phrase, but again the lady's own experience made the reference her own. She drew on her background in cherishing the "bond of peace and the benefit of concord," conditions she missed in her earlier years. Educational opportunities were extended to poor youth "chosen from amongst the poorest that can be found." They were to be younger than the master and fellows, but eligible for a fellowship if they merited advancement. The lady obviously believed that education should be open to promising boys from impoverished backgrounds. It is easy to assume that clerics and learned men could mold the college statutes with minimal deference to an aging widow who might manage to insert a few scattered phrases. The statutes tell a different story, for the foundress reserved for herself the interpretation and amendment of the rules during her life, pointedly observing that "we ought . . . to know better than others what our intentions are."[29]

One compelling reason for fourteenth-century charity was the earnest desire to collect intercessory prayers, and Elizabeth's statutes underline this concern. Daily and holiday masses were to include special mention of her during life and after death, while the anniversary of her death was to be celebrated with the service of the dead. Each day after dinner the fellows were to pray: "May the life of Elizabeth de Burgh our foundress, by the grace of God, be directed to salvation;" after her death the prayer was to be amended to "May the soul of Elizabeth de Burgh our foundress, and the souls of all faithful departed, by God's mercy, rest in peace." The perpetual prayers of the Clare scholars were also solicited for others she selected. Prayers were enjoined for Edward III at the daily and holiday masses and for his soul on the anniversary of his death. At the daily requiem mass, the souls of past kings, Elizabeth's husbands, children, parents, benefactors, and all faithful departed were to be remembered. These recipients fit conventional style, although the reference to benefactors is puzzling. Perhaps it included three men whose anniversaries Elizabeth wanted celebrated with a sung mass: Gilbert de Rowbury; John Salmon, late bishop of Norwich; and Thomas Cobham, late bishop of Worcester.[30] Each of these clerics had been a donor to Cambridge University or University Hall, now Clare College. That alone did not qualify one for inclusion as she ignored Badew. Gilbert de Rowbury had been a clerk of the royal council during the reigns of the first two Edwards, serving on King's Bench for nearly 20 years before a 5-year stint at Common Bench. Late in life he founded loan chests at Cambridge and Oxford. John Salmon was a Benedictine monk and prior of Ely before his selection as bishop of Norwich. He participated in politics during Edward II's reign, as an Ordainer, a council member, and chancellor, apparently trusted by both king and barons. He was an early benefactor of University Hall, giving it 100 marks. Bishop Thomas Cobham of Worcester achieved an enviable reputation for his character and learning after studying at Paris, Oxford, and Cambridge, receiving doctorates in both canon law and theology. His major benefactions went to Oxford, but he donated to Cambridge University or Clare Hall.[31]

Their reputations as Cambridge benefactors prompted Elizabeth's decisions to have the Clare scholars mark their anniversaries; possibly she knew these men personally as well. Salmon was politically active when Damory was a royal favorite; after Damory's death the bishop and Elizabeth spent some days in York in late 1322.[32] It is unlikely she would have honored Salmon if he had behaved poorly toward her when she was at Edward II's mercy. Cobham held a benefice in the gift of Elizabeth's brother before his elevation as bishop. If Elizabeth did not know Cobham earlier, she became acquainted in April 1318 when he preached at Clare, offering indulgences for Joan of Acre at the friary.[33] However, the remembrance at masses probably depended less on friendship than on honoring others who contributed to learning at Cambridge and whose reputations added a prestigious dimension to her foundation.

Her statutes call for daily mass and holiday celebrations in the hall's parish church. She expected three daily masses (some "with notes"): a mass of Our Lady, a requiem mass for the souls of persons listed, and a high mass. Dictating this program to a neighborhood parish seems presumptuous, but was common. Elizabeth's bequests to Clare Hall suggest they were destined eventually for the college chapel rather than a parish church, but Elizabeth's hopes for the chapel building were not fulfilled before her death; Mary de St Pol built the first college chapel in Cambridge for her Pembroke foundation, sometime after 1357.[34]

Collegiate foundation afforded Elizabeth a number of benefits: prayers for herself and others, a unique glorification of the Clare family name, prestige in the eyes of contemporaries, and participation in the cause of learning. Moreover, her foundation expanded the lady's connections with intellectual life through conversations with Clare scholars obliged to respond to their foundress. By selecting higher education as her prime benefaction, Elizabeth became a serious figure who merited attention, rather than a mere female, so other academics were drawn to her as well. The lady was aware of the main currents of learning because they were tightly interwoven with religious topics in contemporary scholarship; some were aired in sermons for the laity. Her book collection affirms her broad curiosity, now supplemented with conversations and correspondence with learned men. Others in the nobility had access to bishops and educated clerics, but none seemed as devoted to deepening their spiritual life intellectually. She loved learning and sought holiness; the men with whom she developed ties often could offer both.

Long before the initiatives at Clare Hall, Elizabeth showed an interest in learning. Her first known book purchase, in 1324, was a copy of the *Vitae patrum;* in 1327 she borrowed three volumes on surgery from the royal collection. For the next 30 years she bought books or paid to have them copied and illuminated. Though she borrowed four romances in 1327, none appeared in her testament, where the titles were devotional, legal, or theological: service books, a book of legends, a Bible, two collections of decretals, a book of questions, and *De causa Dei contra Pelagianos* by Archbishop Bradwardine. Some people build a library with little interest in reading; not Elizabeth, who would have collected different titles if she wished to impress her noble friends. She could read French and probably knew some Latin, a competency common among fourteenth-century nobility.[35] If her Latin failed in law or theology, she had a clerical staff to read to her and discuss the texts.

Magnates employed learned clerics in their entourages, so Elizabeth may have developed intellectual interests early in life through exchanges with household clerics, or with visiting royal officials and church dignitaries.[36] When recruiting her own staff, she included several men of learning. Richard Blithe, who performed important errands for her in the late 1330s and received livery as a clerk in 1343, had a master's degree from Cambridge. John du Boys, also liveried that year, purchased parchment, so perhaps he was a scribe or copyist. Earlier he had studied at King's Hall in Cambridge. Robert de Stalyngton, rector of Litlington after Elizabeth's donation to University Hall, probably urged Elizabeth to rescue it, because of his recent academic experiences at Cambridge. He served Elizabeth as chamber clerk and receiver, and represented her at the funerals of the earl of Hereford and the Earl Marshal. Naturally he received a clerk's livery before his 1347 retirement and, since her will does not include him, he probably died before 1355.[37] John de Lenne may have been the most trusted cleric on Elizabeth's staff, save for Thomas de Cheddeworth. In 1337 John was keeper of the wardrobe, later appearing as a liveried clerk, member of the *familia,* and purchaser for the household as late as 1358–59. Elizabeth's trust shows in several ways: he was the first clerk listed in her will and one of its principal executors. Elizabeth was chary of renting her lands, but she made him a life grant of Ilketshall manor, which he held until his death in 1376. Anne de Lexeden's anchorhold was built next to John's home, for Elizabeth appreciated his spiritual qualities as well as his managerial talent. The accounts portray Lenne in his staff role, but he had an interest in learning though apparently no university degrees. At his death he bequeathed a breviary, a missal, and a quire (*quaternus*) of learned tracts to Clare Hall and also gave the college the silk checkered vestment left to him by Elizabeth.[38] She described the vestment as "for confessions," so perhaps

Lenne served as her own confessor, though she may have been thinking of his supervision of Anne de Lexeden. Clare Hall also benefited from a gift by Henry de Motelot, Elizabeth's Usk receiver for 18 years. Some sources list him as a fellow of the college, but this is doubtful. Since Wales was his normal venue, he probably had little impact on her spiritual life or intellectual ventures.[39]

The lady's episcopal friends were learned men.[40] Two London bishops who visited her several times had studied in England and abroad: Steven Gravesend at Paris and Ralph Stratford at Bologna. Bishop Henry de Burghersh of Lincoln studied canon and civil law at Angers, after pursuing a master's degree in arts, possibly at Oxford. He helped Oriel College there, coming to its assistance in 1326 after its earlier founders failed to provide sufficient funding. Burghersh visited Elizabeth in 1336–37 and perhaps discussed his experience at academic rescue with her just as she was beginning her support of University Hall.[41] William Bateman, bishop of Norwich, was Elizabeth's neighbor and the two shared academic interests at Cambridge, but there is no evidence for real association. However, Elizabeth had fairly close connections with some of his household. Simon Sudbury was the son of one of Elizabeth's favorite merchants, Nicholas Thebaud, who sent him to Paris for a doctorate in canon law. Though on Bateman's staff, Elizabeth's clerks labeled Sudbury part of her *familia* in 1351–52, when she gave him an allowance of £10 10s. Sudbury, who later became archbishop of Canterbury, was well educated, but probably more interested in ecclesiastical administration than in intellectual pursuits.[42] John Paschal, Bishop Bateman's suffragan by 1344, was a learned Carmelite with a Cambridge doctorate in theology. By 1347 he was named bishop of Llandaff, but he was at Clare that July, when he preached an indulgence for Joan of Acre and Edward de Monthermer. He remained in contact with Elizabeth, visiting her at Usk during the height of the plague and later at Bardfield.[43] Paschal, noted for his preaching, seems the epitome of learning, spirituality, and pastoral care. Other clerics with advanced degrees enjoyed the lady's hospitality when they traveled in her neighborhood. Master Walter de Baketon and Master Nicholas de Baggethorp (or Bakethorp), canon lawyers belonging to Bishop Bateman's household, visited in the mid-1340s. Master John de Bliberg clerked for the bishop of Winchester in 1359, long after he visited Elizabeth in 1338–39. The lady may have found him tiresome, for she booked lodgings for him in the town of Clare. Elizabeth was more gracious to Master William Bergavenny, theologian and former chancellor of Oxford University, when he arrived in 1347–48.[44]

Elizabeth's most learned ecclesiastical friend was Thomas Bradwardine, briefly archbishop of Canterbury during the plague in 1349. He studied at

Merton before becoming chancellor of St Paul's in London, where Elizabeth sent him a gift of game in 1338. The man wrote extensively in several fields: history of science, history of logic, geometry, and theology. His most famous work was the *De Causa Dei contra Pelagianos,* a book in the tradition of St Augustine, emphasizing God's omnipotence and the limitations of human free will.[45] The work failed to achieve instant fame so Elizabeth's possession of the work suggests either a personal gift from the author (unlikely before the printing press) or a compelling interest in the subject on her part.

Master Richard Plessys was a distinguished churchman below the episcopal rank. He first appeared in Elizabeth's accounts in 1326 when she gave him a book worth 40s., which suggests she encouraged and supported his education. He was trained in canon and civil law by 1348 when appointed archdeacon of Colchester, a position he held until 1362. Plessys attained other church offices: dean of the Peculiars, canon and prebendary of St Paul's in London and Wimborne, clerk for Archbishop Islip of Canterbury. Elizabeth sent him letters, involved him in appropriating Litlington to Clare Hall, and sent him a tun of wine in fondness or appreciation. The lady of Clare was not his only noble contact: he lent money to the earl of Northampton, held land from the earl of Oxford, and impressed the countess of Pembroke, who petitioned the pope for additional benefices for him.[46] Either he moved in noble circles or Elizabeth's patronage gave him entry there. His learning and position in ecclesiastical government made him useful, but some characteristic beyond utility informed their association.

Naturally Elizabeth's intervention at University Hall and her refoundation of that failing institution into Clare Hall involved her with the college. She knew all the masters who served in the years of her donations. Walter de Thaxted, master from 1326 to 1342, leased the rectory at Great Bardfield, so he knew the lady. The next master, Ralph de Kerdyngton, appeared only once in the accounts. He may have annoyed Elizabeth by ousting fellow Robert Spaldyng for selling property owned by the Hall. Spaldyng somehow attracted Elizabeth's interests, for she arranged an annual pension from Anglesey priory for him. Spaldyng had donated books to Clare Hall, so her support for him could have been appreciation rather than an outcome of a Kerdyngton/Spaldyng quarrel.[47] Nicholas de Brune became master of Clare Hall in 1359 and accepted Elizabeth's collegiate statutes that year.[48] These men were well-educated, but administrative duties rather than great ideas defined their relationships to the foundress.

John de Harleton, a fellow at Clare Hall, was fetched by the lady's servants, who also sought out Master William de Wynelingham at Cambridge the same year. John de Stratton, who had a master's degree from Cambridge by 1349, received escort to and from Elizabeth's residences several times in the 1350s. She had written him as early as 1337–38 and rewarded him with a gift of 13*s*. 4*d*. in July 1352.[49] The accounts are silent on the purpose of these visits, but her searching out men from Cambridge shows at least a continuing desire for conversations with educated men. In other cases there at hints of her aims. Elizabeth contacted Cambridge Franciscan John de Fulburn in 1338–39. A few years later the accounts mention his chamber at Bardfield, so presumably he was employed as a copyist, illuminator, or confessor. Elizabeth wrote to Hugh de Duton in 1338–39, just as he received his appointment as vicar general of the English Dominicans. Duton came from Cambridgeshire, taught at Oxford University, had written a book detailing the various academic controversies, and was a man respected for his understanding of theology. Robert Godewyk visited Elizabeth in 1347 and probably more often, as he was provincial prior of the Augustinian Friars of England and Ireland. Godewyk studied at Cambridge before taking his doctorate in theology at Oxford.[50]

Friars, especially Franciscans, appear often in the accounts, perhaps for their learning or perhaps their spirituality. About one-third of fourteenth-century Cambridge scholars were friars, whose houses also had internal systems of education, creating a learned and spiritual community. The friars specialized in theology, and one modern supporter claimed that the Franciscans "gave its Faculty of Theology" to the University.[51] Elizabeth's interest in Franciscan spirituality and intellectual bent pre-dated her Cambridge foundation. In 1326 she sent servants to Cambridge to fetch Richard de Conyngton to Clare. This old Franciscan with an Oxford doctorate in theology had retired to Cambridge after a career teaching at Oxford and Cambridge and serving for six years as the provincial minister of his order (1310–16). The Franciscans were struggling over the issue of poverty within their order, with the attendant controversy sparking a pamphlet warfare between those defending a literal imitation of their founder and others more amenable to papal direction. Conyngton took a moderate approach, applauding the ideal but deferring to papal authority. His current reputation rests on his treatises on poverty, exploring the problem both as it affected his order and later to counter the arguments of William of Ockham. Conyngton also commented on Peter Lombard's *Sentences* and other authoritative texts and wrote a work on the penitential psalms. The lady's staff again brought Conyngton to meet with Elizabeth twice in 1330, shortly before his death.[52] The initiative for the visits came from Elizabeth, but her purpose is not clear. Whether for spiritual guidance or out of interest in the question of poverty, she looked to a man of learning to satisfy her needs.

In 1351 John de Alby, head of the Franciscan Cambridge custody, received 5s. in January, 6s. 8d. in February, and 6s. 8d. in March when he preached for Elizabeth. She heard sermons by Franciscans on the Purification of the Blessed Virgin and at Pentecost and gave the provincial minister of the order 20s. on January 13, 1351. Walter de Bykerton, former master of the Cambridge friary, preached for Elizabeth in June and August that year, with a reward of 6s. 8d. on each occasion. She looked to a Cambridge Franciscan when she wanted a manuscript illuminated. The lady's ties with this house went beyond associations with a few individuals, for her Walsingham foundation belonged to the Cambridge custody and she loaned the house her portable organ in 1340, reclaiming it for her Easter retreat at Anglesey. Her special appreciation of the Cambridge Franciscans is apparent in her will, where she bequeathed them 40s., typical of her legacy to several friaries, but she also left them 100s. for their work, a more generous legacy than the other Cambridge orders received.[53] The Franciscans' advantage may have come from their Augustinian theological outlook, a position also championed by Bradwardine. Theological and scholastic topics were once assumed the province of learned clerics, but topics such as predestination and free will appear in a fourteenth-century treatise explaining issues on which parish priests ought to instruct their congregations, suggesting lay interest.[54] Elizabeth's uniqueness came from her situation, which allowed personal consultation and conversation with scholars versed in the latest intellectual and spiritual movements.

Support for education traditionally belonged to clerics and kings, who endowed colleges, assisted poor scholars, and augmented book collections at Oxford or Cambridge colleges. With her foundation of Clare Hall, Elizabeth joined earlier benefactors and initiated the idea that the nobility might care about and fund the spread of knowledge, and demonstrated that females could play a key role in the learning enterprise. Elizabeth viewed her foundation support as making her an agent of God: "We have caused it [Clare Hall] to be enriched with resources, out of the property given us by God."[55] While Clare Hall was a testament to Elizabeth's intellectual side and a monument to her earthly prestige, it only augmented her more conventional generosity to religious orders and the poor.

embrace some chivalric ideals: pride, tenacity, courage, loyalty, generosity, honor. Pride and tenacity were at the heart of her defense of her heritage, for she gloried in the Clare and royal associations, but, at the same time, she tempered tenacity in the face of superior power, remaining courageous while not indulging in futile dramatics. When her own position was stronger than that of her opponents, she persisted for years in seeking redress against those who seized her holdings.[1] In her daily life, Elizabeth demonstrated an abiding loyalty and generosity to her friends and family, extending them hospitality, affection, and gifts during their times of trial and triumph. Loyalty was expected from her staff and servants, and she reciprocated by being loyal to them in life and death, providing many with satisfying positions on her staff and instituting a day for the annual remembrance of the deaths of household members. At her own death, she left generous bequests for the men and women who served her in life. It seems only fitting that two churchmen, whom she probably supported in their academic careers, honored her with chantry foundations after her death. Master Richard Blithe never moved very high in ecclesiastical circles, but he devoted some of his small substance to Elizabeth's memory in daily masses. Master Richard de Plessys belonged to the staff of the archbishop of Canterbury when he made his foundation honoring Elizabeth and Archbishop Islip. His broader resources allowed him to designate two priests to celebrate in Standon and two more to celebrate in London.[2] Blithe and Plessys remembered a caring benefactress with a tribute to the generosity that she had bestowed on them in their youth.

Fourteenth-century chivalric notions featured display that advertised individual honor and prestige, conceits that Elizabeth indulged in enthusiastically. For most nobles, parading of prestige was common in the areas of their most important holdings and at royal events or in royal court. During her Damory marriage, Elizabeth spent time in court, and after Queen Isabella's successful invasion Elizabeth used the royal library. She attended Edward II's funeral in 1327 and visited the royal residence at Woodstock as late as 1334.[3] Afterwards she turned away from court functions and festivities. Perhaps she recollected earlier court intrigues or perhaps she disliked the environment in and around the court. More likely she found herself outranked at court, falling in behind the titled earls and their countesses. Elizabeth preferred center stage in her own surroundings where the lady of Clare title never took second place. She advertised her prestige with powerful visual images: improvements to her already impressive residences; stained-glass windows bearing her arms at the Clare friary; the colorful livery worn by her servants, favorite merchants, and some obliging royal officials; the grand chair from which she presided at meals. Her contemporaries knew she was the kin of royalty and that the greatest nobles in the land were her friends and frequent guests. Her reputation for piety and generosity to charitable causes made her something of a paragon among both laity and clergy.

Divine judgment cannot be fathomed by mortals. Even with that qualification, Elizabeth's outward faith embraced and exceeded the Church's prescriptions for the laity. She devoted a greater proportion of her treasure to alms and institutional causes than did her peers. Her interior spirituality is more difficult to fathom, but apparently she sought to grow in God's grace by deepening her faith through worship and intellectual understanding. Her reading program changed from the romantic literature of her youth to theology and canon law. She sought to stimulate her faith by reaching out to clerics of deep spirituality and learning, who could help her master the intellectual dimensions of Christianity.

In her later years she became increasingly devoted to female spiritual potential, though she never abandoned her support of male religious. After years of sharing Lent and Easter with the Anglesey canons, in her last decade she found a more satisfying spirituality with the Minoresses. Their formal services were conducted and led by male clergy, but her residence within the Minories precinct gave her an opportunity for corporate devotions with women religious. The necessity of divorcing spiritual growth with the Minoresses, from the intellectual challenge offered by educated males, reflects a pervasive feature of the fourteenth century. Women in the institutional Church might cultivate inspiration from the sweetness of Christ's love, but they were discouraged from a comparable devotion to the sweetness of learning informed by faith. Consequently, if Elizabeth wanted to explore faith through an intellectual route, she needed to interact with men, even while her devotional practices might benefit from a collective female experience.

The lady joined in other activities that are more distasteful from a modern perspective: she exploited the servile system for her own advantage; she accepted inequality for her own children; she sought to buy judicial outcomes; she capitalized on her familial relationship with the king whenever possible—actions and outlooks that were typical of her class in the fourteenth century. Otherwise, she never sought to revolutionize her world. Yet in two areas, albeit unconsciously, she began to change attitudes. Over the years, Elizabeth expanded her own ideas on the purposes of education. Initially she paid for the education of young men with a view to using their added training to benefit the smooth operation of her household. At the end of her life she wanted her Clare scholars to improve the workings of the state and the Church and to banish ignorance in the world, moving from her earlier utilitarian ends to a broader and more humane vision of education. Elizabeth's foundation of Clare College broke the near-monopoly of clerics and royalty on collegiate endowment, suggesting another avenue for noble benefactions. That foundation also demonstrated that one woman's work could impact education for over six centuries.

Being female was not only a biological determinant but also the element that conditioned and circumscribed Elizabeth's social and political opportunities. Certainly she was not oblivious to gender, but it never became an obvious focus for her, probably because she found a way to become virtually independent through the vow of chastity, eased by the cushioning comfort of ample wealth. Most women lacked this option, but Elizabeth never pretended to be a pioneer for female emancipation. Neither did she apologize for her subordinate sex. Fourteenth-century legal and ecclesiastical theory denigrated women, but Elizabeth ignored those implications when she could and worked around them at other times. Nothing in the documents where her own voice can be heard indicates submissiveness or acknowledgment of inferior status. One of the seals for Clare College depicts Elizabeth offering her statutes to her hall: a woman dictating the rules for academic males.[4] This iconography ignored contemporary sensibilities in its reversal of traditional gender norms. That image of female prestige was remembered by another collegiate foundress in the next century who was inspired to emulate Elizabeth and her friend Mary de St Pol. Queen Margaret of Anjou, foundress of Queen's College, spoke to the lasting achievements of these women and, except for a more diverse student body, her observations remain true today: " . . . and to laud and honneure of sexe femenine, like as two noble and devoute contesses of Pembroke and Clare founded two collages in the same universite called Pembroke halle and Clare halle the whiche are of grete reputacon for good and worshipful clerkis that by grete multitude have be bredde and brought forth in theym . . ."[5]

In practicing good stewardship of her resources, deploying imaginative philanthropy, and providing an example of female potential, Elizabeth de Burgh left a legacy more meaningful and precious than most of her more famous noble contemporaries.

ABBREVIATIONS

Classifications cited from Public Record Office, London:

E101/   Exchequer, Accounts Various
S.C. 1/   Special Collections: Ancient Correspondence

Published Sources and Authorities:

BIHR   *Bulletin of the Institute for Historical Research*
BRUC   A. B. Emden, *A Biographical Register of the University of Cambridge to 1500* (Cambridge, 1963)
BRUO   A. B. Emden, *A Biographical Register of the University of Oxford to A. D. 1500*. 3 vols. (Oxford, 1957–59)
CAFC   *Cartulary of the Augustinian Friars of Clare,* ed. Christopher Harper-Bill (Woodbridge, 1991)
CCW   *Calendar of Chancery Warrants.* Vol. 1 (PRO, 1927)
CChR   *Calendar of the Charter Rolls.* Vols. 3 and 4 (1898 and 1920; reprint, 1972)
CCR   *Calendar of the Close Rolls.* Edward II, 4 vols.; Edward III, 14 vols. (PRO, 1892–1913)
CFR   *Calendar of the Fine Rolls.* Vols. 3–7 (PRO, 1912–23)
CIM   *Calendar of Inquisitions Miscellaneous (Chancery).* Vols. 2 and 3 (PRO, 1916 and 1937)
CIPM   *Calendar of Inquisitions Post Mortem.* Vols. 4–11 (PRO, 1908–35)
CPapR   *Calendar of Entries in the Papal Registers relating to Great Britain and Ireland.* 3 vols. (PRO, 1895–97)
CPR   *Calendar of the Patent Rolls.* Edward II, 5 vols.; Edward III, 16 vols. (PRO, 1893–1916)
DNB   *Dictionary of National Biography,* eds. Leslie Stephen and Sidney Lee. 22 vols. (1885–1901; reprint, London, 1949–50)
EHR   *English Historical Review*

GEC   G. E. Cokayne, ed., *The Complete Peerage,* new ed., rev. V. Gibbs
       et al. 13 vols. (London, 1910–59)
HMSO   Her/His Majesty's Stationery Office
LE   *List of Escheators for England and Wales* (London, 1971)
LS   *List of Sheriffs for England and Wales* (London, 1898)
MA   William Dugdale, *Monasticon Anglicanum,* ed. John Caley et al.
       6 vols. in 8 books (London, 1846)
PRO   Public Record Office
RW   *A Collection of All the Wills now Known to be Extant, of the Kings
       and Queens of England,* ed. J. G. Nichols (1780; reprint, 1969)
TRHS   *Transactions of the Royal Historical Society*
VES   *Vita Edwardi Secundi,* trans. N. Denholm-Young (London,
       1957)

NOTES

Chapter 1

1. Interested readers may consult Henrietta Leyser, *Medieval Women: A Social History of Women in England, 450–1500* (New York: St. Martin's Press, 1995), a broadly focused work not confined to noblewomen; Jennifer Ward, *Women of the English Nobility and Gentry, 1066–1500* (Manchester: Manchester University Press, 1995), has some specific references to Elizabeth de Burgh.

2. Consult Shulamith Shahar, *Childhood in the Middle Ages* (London: Routledge, 1990); Nicholas Orme, *From Childhood to Chivalry* (London: Methuen, 1984).

3. K. B. McFarlane, *The Nobility of Later Medieval England* (Oxford: Clarendon Press, 1973), p. 11.

4. GEC, 5:437 and 12:251 give September 16, 1295; 3:245 has 1292. For the place, Michael Altschul, *A Baronial Family in Medieval England: The Clares, 1217–1314* (Baltimore: Johns Hopkins Press, 1965), p. 155; an Irish inquisition taken after Elizabeth's brother's 1314 death stated she was born in England: *CIPM* 5, no. 538, p. 337. Authorities agree she was the last of four children; only the Tewkesbury annals call her the second: *MA,* 2:61–62.

5. Altschul, *Baronial Family,* pp. 34, 103–10.

6. The account of Joan's early life in Mary Ann Everett Green, *Lives of the Princesses of England* (London: Henry Colburn, 1850), 2:319–23, is corrected in detail by John C. Parsons, *The Court and Household of Eleanor of Castile in 1290.* Studies and Texts, 37 (Toronto: Pontifical Institute of Mediaeval Studies, 1977), p. 39n.

7. Altschul, *Baronial Family,* p. 149. Gilbert also swore to respect the rights of Joan's older sister, Eleanor, and any of her children, before those of Joan or her children by Gilbert.

8. Altschul, *Baronial Family,* pp. 148–50; Hilda Johnstone, *Edward of Caernarvon, 1284–1307* (Manchester: Manchester University Press, 1946), pp. 24–25; Green, *Princesses,* 2:331, 336–37; Michael Prestwich, *The Three Edwards* (London: Weidenfeld and Nicolson, 1980), p. 145.

9. The (assumed) January date discreetly puts the conception of Joan's first Monthermer child after their marriage. See John C. Parsons, *Medieval*

Queenship (New York: St. Martin's Press, 1993), specifically his essay "Mothers, Daughters, Marriage, Power: Some Plantagenet Evidence, 1150–1500," p. 76.

10. Michael M. Sheehan, "The Formation and Stability of Marriage in Fourteenth-Century England," *Medieval Studies* 33 (1971):229–30; Altschul, *Baronial Family*, pp. 233–34; Green, *Princesses*, 2:341–42, 345–46; *CCW*, 1:147. Before Edward heard of the marriage, he assigned Joan's children quarters in Bristol Castle, though Joan herself may not have resided there. The children had their own wardrobe from at least 1296. Ralph lost his title when Joan died in 1307; in any case, it would have passed to her son Gilbert at his majority.

11. Eleanor of Castile died in 1290; Edward I married Margaret of France in 1299.

12. E101/91/10.

13. Henry Murray Lane, *The Royal Daughters of England* (London: Constable, 1910), 1:182–84. Mary (b. 1297) married Earl Duncan of Fife: *CCW*, 1:256; Joan (b. 1299), a nun at Amesbury, is almost unknown to history; Thomas (b. October 4, 1301) and Edward (b.ca. April 11, 1304) had lands from King Edward II: *CChR*, 3:131–32. Elizabeth's ties to Edward de Monthermer are noted below. I am grateful to John C. Parsons for the Lane reference.

14. Clare A. Musgrave, "Household Administration in the Fourteenth Century with Special Reference to the Household of Elizabeth de Burgh, Lady of Clare" (M.A. thesis, University of London, 1923):3; the girls' wardrober had funds from the Clare's Usk bailiwick: Altschul, *Baronial Family*, p. 234. On Joan's travels, Janetta C. Sorley, *King's Daughters* (Cambridge: Cambridge University Press, 1937), p. 34.

15. *MA*, 2:334. Amesbury boarded several noble children in the early fourteenth century: Nicholas Orme, "The Education of the Courtier," in *English Court Culture in the Later Middle Ages*, ed. V. J. Scattergood and J. W. Sherborne (London: Gerald Duckworth, 1983), p. 201.

16. Francis Roth, *The English Austin Friars, 1249–1538* (New York: Augustinian Historical Institute, 1966), 1:618, quoting Osbern Bokenham or Bukenham, a fifteenth-century friar at Clare; *CAFC*, no. 189.

17. *Calendar of the Chancery Rolls, Various* (London: HMSO, 1912), p. 99; *CCR, 1318–1323*, p. 160; Green, *Princesses*, 2:358.

18. *CPR, 1301–1307*, p. 443; Natalie Fryde, *The Tyranny and Fall of Edward II, 1321–1326* (Cambridge: Cambridge University Press, 1979), p. 28.

19. Scott L. Waugh, *The Lordship of England: Royal Wardships and Marriages in English Society and Politics, 1217–1327* (Princeton: Princeton University Press, 1988), p. 102.

20. King Edward II's sexual preferences probably did not affect his relations with Elizabeth de Burgh. Historians suggest homosexual overtones to his fondness for three of the Clare sisters' husbands, including Elizabeth de Burgh's third husband, Roger Damory: T. B. Pugh, ed., *Glamorgan County*

History (Cardiff: University of Wales Press, 1971), 3:169. John Boswell, *Christianity, Social Tolerance and Homosexuality* (Chicago: University of Chicago Press, 1980), pp. 298–300, identifies Piers Gaveston and Hugh Despenser junior as the king's lovers; P. Chaplais, *Piers Gaveston: Edward II's Adoptive Brother* (Oxford: Clarendon Press, 1994) argues rather that Piers and Edward had an adoptive fraternal tie. Neither the king nor the three Clare husbands chose exclusively male partners; all fathered children by their wives.

21. *VES*, p. 2. I rely on Antonia Gransden, *Historical Writing in England,* vol. 2: *c. 1307 to the Early Sixteenth Century* (Ithaca: Cornell University Press, 1982), p. 37, that *VES* "reflects the views of an intelligent, sensible man who lived through the events of Edward II's reign."

22. F. M. Powicke and E. B. Fryde, eds., *Handbook of British Chronology,* 2nd ed. (London: Royal Historical Society, 1961), p. 422. For royal generosity, *CChR,* 3:110–11, 127, 129, 131; Frederick Devon, *Issues of the Exchequer* (London: John Murrary, 1837), pp. 119–20; William Dugdale, *The Baronage of England* (London, 1676), 1:42–43; J. S. Hamilton, *Piers Gaveston, Earl of Cornwall, 1307–1312* (Detroit: Wayne State University Press, 1988), p. 38.

23. *CPR, 1307–1313,* pp. 1, 21; *Calendar Justiciary Rolls, Ireland* (Dublin: Stationery Office, 1905), p. 41; Altschul, *Baronial Family,* p. 160; Sue Sheridan Walker, "Proof of Age of Feudal Heirs in Medieval England," *Medieval Studies* 35 (1973):308–9n.; J. R. S. Phillips, *Aymer de Valence, Earl of Pembroke, 1307–1324* (Oxford: Clarendon Press, 1972), pp. 26–28.

24. *CPR, 1307–1313,* p. 50; Altschul, *Baronial Family,* p. 46; Goddard Henry Orpen, *Ireland Under the Normans, 1216–1333* (Oxford: Clarendon Press, 1968), 4:149–50.

25. Robin Frame, *English Lordship in Ireland, 1318–1361* (Oxford: Clarendon Press, 1982), pp. 14–15. On the strategy of marrying siblings of two lineages: Waugh, *Lordship,* p. 38.

26. GEC, 12:177. *VES,* p. 6, has Gilbert's marriage on September 29; Orpen puts it after Elizabeth's. Green, *Princesses,* 2:436, has the king's sister, the nun Mary, taking a Clare sister to Gilbert's wedding on September 30, 1309. The year is wrong, but the sister was probably Elizabeth, en route to her wedding after a stay at Amesbury (cf. note 28 below). For the king's stay at Waltham, Charles H. Hartshorne, ed., *The Itinerary of King Edward the Second* (privately distributed, 1861), p. 3.

27. Manors at Antrim, Coleraine, Portrush, Portcaman (Bushmills), Drumtorsy, Dunsumery (Dunseverick), and Dundryff (Dundarave? near Bushmills), issues and profits of the river Bann and 'del Lyn', rents and profits in Twescard, and manors in Connacht and Munster: Goddard H. Orpen, "The Earldom of Ulster," pt. I, *Journal of the Royal Society of Antiquaries of Ireland* 43 (1913):44–45.

28. GEC, 12:177. If the journey noted in Green, *Princesses,* 2:436, was to her husband for consummation of vows exchanged a year earlier, she perhaps spent that year at Amesbury (cf. note 26 above).

29. John T. Gilbert, ed., *Chartularies of St. Mary's Abbey, Dublin* (London: Long-man, 1884), 2:342; Sorley, *Daughters,* p. 40, suggests he was born in England.

30. Aubrey Gwynn and R. Neville Hadcock, *Medieval Religious Houses: Ireland* (London: Longman, 1970), p. 296; J. C. Ward, "Fashions in Monastic En-dowment: The Foundations of the Clare Family, 1066–1314," *Journal of Ec-clesiastical History* 32 (1981):427–51; Edward Hutton, *The Franciscans in England, 1244–1538* (London: Constable and Co., 1926), p. 167; John A. Stow, *A Survey of London* (Oxford: Clarendon Press, 1971), 1:317; F. X. Martin, "The Augustinian Friaries of Pre-Reformation Ireland," *Augustini-ana* 6 (1956):356–57.

31. For a thorough discussion, Frame, *English Lordship* and James Lydon, ed., *England and Ireland in the Later Middle Ages* (Dublin: Irish Academic Press, 1981).

32. GEC, 12:177–78 is less concerned with John de Burgh than with his sib-lings' connections and Elizabeth's later marriages.

33. *Calendar Justiciary Rolls, Ireland,* 3:154, 157, 209, 271; *CCR, 1307–1313,* p. 85; T. E. McNeill, *Anglo-Norman Ulster: The History and Archaelogy of an Irish Barony, 1177–1400* (Edinburgh: John Donald, 1980), p. 68.

34. Orpen, "Earldom," pt. I, 45, thinks the period 1300-10 was peaceful; An-nette J. Otway-Ruthven, *A History of Medieval Ireland* (London: Ernest Benn, 1980), pp. 220–22, sees wars from about 1308 in which the Burghs upheld a native faction against one supported by the Clares. *Chartularies of St. Mary's Abbey,* 2:343 gives the year of John's death; Fryde, *Tyranny,* p. 34, states without citation that he was killed.

35. Frame, *English Lordship,* pp. 66–67.

36. Presumably the earl controlled Elizabeth's marriage until 1314 when, as an heiress, she became the king's tenant-in-chief. The earl perhaps preferred to leave her without a husband, who would have controlled her Irish jointure lands in areas important to the earl's lordship. After his 1315 problems, he may have changed his attitude, but by then the king controlled her marriage.

37. May McKisack, *The Fourteenth Century* (Oxford: Clarendon Press, 1959), p. 40, attributes the civil war later in Edward II's reign to greed over division of the Clare inheritance.

38. Henry S. Lucas, "The Great European Famine of 1315, 1316, and 1317," *Speculum* 5 (1930):345–46, 351; Ian Kershaw, "The Great Famine and Agrarian Crisis in England, 1315–1322," *Past and Present* 59 (1973):12–13.

39. *VES,* p. 61; Otway-Ruthven, *Medieval Ireland,* p. 225; Olive Armstrong, *Ed-ward Bruce's Invasion of Ireland* (London: John Murray, 1923), pp. 79–80; A. Martin Freeman, ed., *The Annals of Connacht (A.D. 1224–1544)* (Dublin: Dublin Institute for Advanced Studies, 1944), p. 241.

40. Armstrong, *Bruce's Invasion,* p. 86; Altschul, *Baronial Family,* p. 169; *Rotuli Parliamentorum* (London, 1783), 1:352.

41. *CPR, 1307–1313,* p. 492; Fryde, *Tyranny,* pp. 28, 30–31. In January 1310, Ed-ward II heard Hugh was abroad contrary to prohibition of such passage with-out royal license: *CCW,* 1:308, offers a rare early hint of Hugh's rashness.

42. *VES*, p. 6. Authorities realize contemporaries overly vilified Piers: Hilda Johnstone, "Isabella, the She-Wolf of France," *History* 21 (1936):209. He was made earl of Cornwall days after Edward became king, receiving all estates of Edward's cousin Edmund, late earl of Cornwall: *CPR, 1307–1313,* pp. 31, 43. In 1308 Piers was assigned lands in Aquitaine worth 3,000 marks sterling and, often jointly with Margaret, English lands as well: *CPR, 1307–1313,* p. 78 and *CChR,* 3:181.

43. *VES*, p. 6. *The Chronicle of Lanercost, 1272–1346,* trans. Sir Herbert Maxwell (Glasgow: James Maclehose and Sons, 1913), p. 187; *CPR, 1307–1313,* p. 83; Otway-Ruthven, *Medieval Ireland,* p. 219; for royal grants, e.g., *CChR,* 3:110, 111, 127, 129; *CPR, 1307–1313,* pp. 60, 79, 80, 106, 137.

44. Grants, privileges, and pardons at Gaveston's instance manifest his sway over the king: *CPR, 1307–1313,* pp. 180, 181, 187, 200, 205. *VES*, p. 8, says "his behaviour was worse than before."

45. *VES*, pp. 17, 20–21; John R. Maddicott, *Thomas of Lancaster, 1307–1322* (London: Oxford University Press, 1970), pp. 121–22; F. D. Blackley and G. Hermansen, eds., *The Household Book of Queen Isabella of England* (Edmonton: University of Alberta Press, 1971), p. 139.

46. Hamilton, *Gaveston,* p. 94; Maddicott, *Thomas,* pp. 123–24. For the surrender terms, Phillips, *Aymer,* pp. 33–35; Maddicott, *Thomas,* pp. 125–26; Hamilton, *Gaveston,* pp. 96–97. Dominicans undertook the grisly task of sewing Pier's head on his body before carrying it to Oxford: *VES*, p. 28.

47. *VES*, p. 30; *CCR, 1313–1318,* p. 139; Mark Buck, *Politics, Finance and the Church in the Reign of Edward II* (Cambridge: Cambridge University Press, 1983), p. 117n.

48. *CPR, 1313–1317,* pp. 578, 623–24.

49. *CCR, 1313–1318,* p. 87; Thomas Stapleton, "A Brief Summary of the Wardrobe Accounts of the 10th, 11th and 14th Years of King Edward the Second," *Archaeologia* 26 (1836):319–20; Hamilton, *Gaveston,* p. 101; *CPR, 1317–1321,* p. 43; *CIM,* 2:325–26. See note 99 below for contemporary uses of recognizances.

50. GEC, 12:250–51; Altschul, *Baronial Family,* p. 169; *CPR, 1307–1313,* p. 568; *CPR, 1313–1317,* p. 207.

51. John Bellamy, *Crime and Public Order in England in the Later Middle Ages* (London: Routledge and Kegan Paul, 1973), p. 58. Verdon evaded abduction charges by claiming Elizabeth walked to meet him outside the castle gate: *Rotuli Parliamentorum,* 1:352–53.

52. Sue Sheridan Walker, "Feudal Constraint and Free Consent in the Making of Marriages in Medieval England: Widows in the King's Gift," Canadian Historical Association, *Historical Papers* (1979):97–109.

53. *CCR, 1330–1333,* p. 53.

54. *CIPM,* 6: no. 54; 5: no. 187; 7: nos. 83, 170; A. J. Otway-Ruthven, "The Partition of the de Verdon Lands in Ireland in 1322," *Proceedings of the Royal Irish Academy* 66 (1967):401–59; A. Tomkinson, "Retinues at the Tournament of

Dunstaple, 1309," *EHR* 74 (1959):80. For his first marriage, *MA*, 5: 661–62; Lancaster had attended Maud's funeral: Maddicott, *Thomas*, pp. 51, 196. See also *CPR, 1307–1313*, p. 568; *Calendar Justiciary Rolls, Ireland*, pp. 237–39, 275, 278.

55. For William, see Musgrave, "Household," 6. On Theobald, see Kershaw, "Great Famine," 11. Croxden was founded by his ancestor Bertram de Verdon in 1178: Roy Midmer, *English Mediaeval Monasteries (1066–1540)* (Athens: University of Georgia Press, 1979), pp. 122–23.

56. For the Damory grants, *CCW*, 1:460; *CCR, 1313–1318*, p. 397; *CCR, 1318–1323*, p. 277. On the Montague grant, Waugh, *Lordship*, pp. 109–10 and *CCR, 1313–1318*, pp. 381–82. For Joan Verdon, GEC, 12:251; Stapleton, "Wardrobe Accounts," 337.

57. S.C.1/63/150.

58. *CCR, 1313–1318*, pp. 434, 443. The Richard de Burgo among her Irish attorneys may have been her former father-in-law; another appointee was Robert de Cheddeworth who remained in her service for years. For the December orders, *CCR, 1313–1318*, pp. 381–82. Waugh, *Lordship*, p. 69, illustrates royal power in such circumstances.

59. Hamilton Hall, "The Marshal Pedigree," *Journal of the Royal Society of Antiquaries* 43 (1913):16. There is one statement that Elizabeth married in February before the birth; for conflicting dates, *CPR, 1313–1317*, pp. 641, 644, 677.

60. *CIPM*, 7: no. 395. Nuns could not lawfully be godparents, but Mary had her own standards of conventual behavior: Eileen Power, *Medieval English Nunneries* (Cambridge: Cambridge University Press, 1922), p. 379; Michael Bennett, "Spiritual Kinship and Baptismal Name in Traditional European Society," in *Principalities, Powers and Estates*, ed. L. O. Frappell (Adelaide: Adelaide University Union Press, 1979), pp. 6, 8. Edward gave the more princely sum of £20 to the messenger who told him Elizabeth had borne Damory's daughter: Stapleton, "Wardrobe Accounts," 338.

61. E101/377/2 is the expense roll for this pilgrimage.

62. George A. Holmes, *The Estates of the Higher Nobility in Fourteenth-Century England* (Cambridge: Cambridge University Press, 1957), p. 74. Roger held Easton (Somerset) in 1316; it was awarded to him and Elizabeth when Gilbert's widow died in 1320, as it was in her dower: *Inquisitions and Assessment relating to Feudal Aids, 1284–1431* (London: HMSO, 1899–1908), 4:324; Altshul, *Baronial Family*, Appendix 2. For Roger's knighthood, H. S. Sweetman, ed., *Calendar of Documents relating to Ireland, 1302–1307* (London: HMSO, 1886), pp. 164, 169. On Richard, *CCR, 1307–1313*, pp. 365, 386, 387, 420. For Bannockburn: Phillips, *Aymer*, p. 193.

63. *CIPM*, 5: no. 538 summarizes inquests after Gilbert's death; PRO C47/9/23, C47/9/24 and C47/9/25 show each co-heir's purparty (partial summaries in Altschul, *Baronial Family*, pp. 304–5). A child born more than 11 months posthumously had no claims on the inheritance: *VES*, p. 62.

64. Pugh, *Glamorgan*, 3:167–68.

65. *CPR, 1313–17*, pp. 609, 622; Usk and Caerleon were in Gilbert's widow's dower, so seisin was delayed until she died in 1320: Altshul, *Baronial Family*, Appendix 2. On Verdon fees, *CCR, 1313–1318*, pp. 410, 413, 418–419, 420. The Verdon custody might erode quickly. Joan de Verdon was already wed in 1317, and could seek her share of the inheritance upon coming of age a few months later.

66. For Hallaton, *CPR, 1313–1317*, p. 677. This and other gifts were in payment of £100 Edward had promised: *CPR, 1313–1317*, p. 666 and *CPR, 1317–1321*, p. 388. The grant's phrasing and date compound problems in determining when Elizabeth and Roger wed. It is unlikely she was forced to marry before Isabella was born, though she may have agreed to do so by February 1317. The number of horses used on her pilgrimage increased in May, after a week spent with the king. Division of the Clare lands accelerated in May 1317, a course Edward might have delayed until Elizabeth married Damory. For Sandhall and Vauxhall, *CPR, 1313–1317*, pp. 666, 677. Edward had Damory's Gloucestershire lands seized in 1321; they were to be returned to Elizabeth in 1322: *CPR, 1321–1324*, p. 40; *CCR, 1318–1323*, pp. 603–4.

67. Phillips, *Aymer*, p. 134.

68. Maddicott, *Thomas*, pp. 197–98, summarizes the issues.

69. *CPR, 1313–1317*, pp. 577–79.

70. *CPR, 1313–1317*, p. 641; *CPR, 1317–1321*, p. 4.

71. *CCR, 1313–1318*, p. 477 (the Despensers did not bind each other). In 1334 Elizabeth was pardoned the £12,000 in recognizances that had escheated to the crown, after she claimed they "were made by compulsion": *CPR, 1330–1334*, p. 551. It is unclear how the Despensers could have coerced Damory in 1317, but Audley, in 1334, also said the recognizances were "obtained from him by force against his will": *CPR, 1330–1334*, p. 470.

72. Text of the November 1317 indenture in appendices to James Conway Davies, *The Baronial Opposition to Edward II* (Cambridge: Cambridge University Press, 1918), and Phillips, *Aymer*. See also Buck, *Politics, Finance*, p. 116; J. R. S. Phillips, "The Middle Party and the negotiating of the Treaty of Leake, August, 1318: A reinterpretation," *BIHR* 46 (1973):11–27. *CCR, 1313–1318*, pp. 577–78, shows Roger spoke for the king in Chancery in November 1317.

73. Phillips, "Middle Party," 21–22; *VES*, p. 80; Phillips, *Aymer*, pp. 119, 131.

74. Maddicott, *Thomas*, pp. 218–19; the text of the promise to Lancaster in Phillips, *Aymer*, pp. 321–22, with a note that the clause admitting complicity was struck out of the original; *VES*, pp. 87, 88.

75. Elizabeth M. Hallam, ed., *The Itinerary of Edward II and His Household, 1307–1328* (London: List and Index Society, 1984), p. 300. Hartshorne, *Itinerary*, has Edward dating documents from Clare on March 30. On the sermons, *CAFC*, nos. 158, 167. Indulgence sermons allowed penitents to avoid temporal penalties for confessed sins, but not the guilt itself. Sermons

advertised the indulgence's availability at a particular church and the number of days for which punishment would be remitted by attendance at (or
perhaps service to) that church. For the marriages, *CPR, 1317–1323,* pp.
125, 237. Roger sold Margery's to Lancaster's steward Robert de Holland,
the earl's junior partner: Maddicott, *Thomas,* pp. 56–57 and "Thomas of
Lancaster and Sir Robert Holland," *EHR* 86 (1971):450.

76. *CPR, 1317–1321,* p. 248; *CChR,* 2:400.

77. For the loans, *CCR, 1318–1323,* pp. 114, 202, 339; for Escrick: *CCR,
1323–1328,* p. 28. The couple acquired Kennington from John de
Merkyngfeld, canon of St Peter's, York: *CFR,* 5:27; *CChR,* 4:428. But in
July 1318 it was held by Anthony Pessagno of Genoa and his heirs for-
ever: *CCR, 1318–1323,* p. 2. Acquisition of Kennington may be linked
to money the king ordered Pessagno to deliver to Roger in summer
1319, though Merkyngfeld and another acknowledged in 1316 that they
owed Roger 200 marks: Davies, *Baronial Opposition,* p. 560; *CCR,
1313–1318,* p. 441.

78. E101/95/6; E101/506/23.

79. *CPR, 1317–1321,* pp. 418, 421; Hartshorne, *Itinerary,* p. 23; Phillips, *Aymer,*
p. 192.

80. *CPR, 1313–1317,* p. 306; Fryde, *Tyranny,* p. 48.

81. Fryde, *Tyranny,* p. 35.

82. Waugh, *Lordship,* p. 186, calls Damory an "official"; Buck, *Politics, Finance,*
pp. 132–33; for the last grant to Damory: *CPR, 1317–1321,* p. 519.

83. *VES,* p. 109; Pugh, *Glamorgan County,* 3:170–71.

84. E101/94/20.

85. There were perhaps skirmishes through third parties, e.g., Roger's effort to
secure Goldcliff Priory's patronage. William Rees, ed., *Calendar of Ancient
Petitions, Wales* (Cardiff: University of Wales Press, 1975), no. 2456n, links
this dispute to the Despenser-Damory rivalry after the Clare partition. J.
Conway Davies, "The Despenser War in Glamorgan," *TRHS,* 3rd series, 9
(1915):27–28, hints at Despenser's fraud and harshness against Damory and
Audley in his push to absorb all Clare lands in Wales. Despenser may have
had a plan of absorption, though its execution seems confined to later
years; he moved against Audley early on, but until 1321 it is hard to see
hostility toward Damory. An exception may be Llantrisant, a Despenser
castle assaulted in 1321 but which Elizabeth held in the 1330s: Altschul,
Baronial Family, p. 305, has it in her purparty; Davies, "Despenser War,"
24–25, has it in Eleanor's.

86. J. Goronwy Edwards, ed., *Calendar of Ancient Correspondence Concerning
Wales* (Cardiff: University Press Board, 1935), p. 219; Fryde, *Tyranny,* p. 43;
Maddicott, *Thomas,* p. 264.

87. *VES,* pp. 109, 110.

88. William Rees, *Caerphilly Castle,* rev. ed.(Caerphilly: Caerphilly Local History Society, 1974), pp. 59–60; Fryde, *Tyranny,* pp. 46, 74. The king probably saved face by giving Damory custody of Glamorgan in 1321: *Ancient*

Petitions, Wales, p. 153n.; *VES*, p. 111. *CCR, 1318–1323*, p. 464, says Damory "intruded" into Steeple Cleydon against the elder Despenser's enfeoffee, John de Haudlo. Elizabeth later challenged this account.

89. *VES*, pp. 113, 115; full text in *CCR, 1318–1323*, pp. 492–495.

90. *CFR*, 3:70; *CCR, 1318–1323*, pp. 402, 408.

91. *CPR, 1321–1324*, pp. 15–16; Davies, "Despenser War," 61n, says 103 received pardons on Damory's testimony, 45 on Audley's, 47 on Hereford's, and 60 on Mortimer of Wigmore's.

92. *CFR*, 3:79, 80; *CPR, 1321–1324*, p. 37. Fryde, *Tyranny*, p. 92, says Edward received £300 from the Damory and Badlesmere estates by February 17, 1322; *CFR*, 3:104–5, 99.

93. *CFR*, 3:100; *CCR, 1318–1323*, pp. 519, 425–26; *CFR*, 3:103; *CPR, 1321–1324*, p. 40. On the Scots, Joseph Bain, ed., *Calendar of Documents relating to Scotland* (Edinburgh: H. M. General Register House, 1888), 2:139–40; *CCR, 1318–1323*, pp. 525–26. *VES*, p. 121, claims the barons were "puffed-up by the Earl of Lancaster's protection. . . ."

94. Maddicott, *Thomas*, p. 305; *CCR, 1318–1323*, pp. 511–12; *VES*, pp. 118–19.

95. Probably Damory was wounded defending the river crossing at Burton-on-Trent: Phillips, *Aymer*, p. 223. Lists of those declared treasonous and those with whom the king took counsel are in *CCR, 1318–1323*, p. 522. For judgment and sentence, George Sayles, "The Formal Judgments on the Traitors of 1322," *Speculum* 16 (1941):58. Fryde, *Tyranny*, p. 62 says Edward buried Damory honorably.

96. Phillips, *Aymer*, pp. 146, 289; *VES*, p. 123; *CIM*, 2: nos. 468, 549.

97. Pugh, *Glamorgan*, 3:246; *CCR, 1318–1323*, p. 428. It uncertain how many children Elizabeth bore and how many were alive in 1322. William de Burgh, Isabella de Verdon, and Elizabeth Damory spent most of their childhood with Elizabeth. Later in life, she had masses said for "her daughter Margaret," but as she did not always distinguish daughters from granddaughters, this child's identity remains a mystery.

98. *Lanercost*, pp. 236–37; Fryde, *Tyranny*, p. 61, and passim for comprehensive discussion of 1322 and its aftermath.

99. Davies, *Baronial Opposition*, p. 36. Recognizances were an acknowledgment in Chancery of a debt and were commonly used in transactions between creditor and debtor. When a person made such a recognizance, he or she acknowledged that a monetary fine, perhaps loss of lands, or even imprisonment would result if the conditions were not met. Edward II used the device to keep the realm quiescent.

100. J. G. Bellamy, *The Law of Treason in England in the Middle Ages* (Cambridge: Cambridge University Press, 1970), p. 22n. Paula Dobrowolski, "Women and their Dower in the Long Thirteenth Century, 1265–1329," in *Thirteenth-Century England VI*, ed. Michael Prestwich, R. H. Britnell, and Robin Frame (Woodbridge: Boydell Press, 1997), pp. 157–64 has several examples to the contrary.

101. Fryde, *Tyranny*, p. 60.

102. Text (1321-early 1326) with discussion in G. A. Holmes, "A Protest Against the Despensers, 1326," *Speculum* 30 (1955):207–12.

103. *CchR*, 3:448.

104. The sheriff of Essex advanced £74 for her upkeep from the issues of his bailiwick; his executors finally recovered that sum from the Exchequer in May 1323: *CCR, 1318–1323*, p. 651.

105. *CPR, 1321–1324*, p. 176; *Ancient Petitions, Wales*, p. 391n.; Holmes, "Protest," 208n; *CPR, 1321–1324*, pp. 183, 191. (Despenser's spoilation of Gower had royal approval); *CCR, 1318–1323*, pp. 603–4.

106. Holmes, "Protest," 211; *CCR, 1318–1323*, p. 624.

107. For Scales and Horsele, *CPR, 1313–1317*, p. 641; *CPR, 1317–1321*, p. 4. On the Cheddeworths, E/101/506/23 and *CCR, 1313–1318*, p. 443 (undated; the editors suggest December 1316). Only two other names found in the early household accounts reappear after 1326, a London attorney who was not in the household and a butler/wine buyer: E101/506/23. The William de Brampton or Brompton of the early accounts may or may not be the William de Brampton who served Elizabeth, 1326–40.

108. Fryde, *Tyranny*, Appendix I, lists gifts and estimates their value; see also *CPR, 1321–1324*, pp. 294, 296.

109. Braose acknowledged in April 1324 he owed Hugh junior £10,000, a recognizance that placed enormous pressure on Braose to do Hugh's bidding: *CCR, 1323–1327*, p. 174. For Braose's conveyance to Despenser and Braose's heirs' later claims for compensation and recovery: *Ancient Petitions, Wales*, nos. 4549, 5449, 6641, 7975, 8107, 8631 and notes.

110. For the petitions, Holmes, "Protest," 210–12; Fryde, *Tyranny*, p. 116. Hugh could use more direct methods: Geoffrey de la Lee levied a fine to Hugh Despenser "in fear of death": *CIM*, 2:232. Bellamy, *Crime*, p. 176 cites the case of John Brumpton, imprisoned, stripped, and fastened to the ground by irons for three days until, fearing for his life, he enfeoffed Hugh with certain lands and tenements. The quote is *VES*, pp. 135–36.

111. *CChR*, 3:441–42, 463; *CPR, 1321–1324*, p. 79; *CCR, 1318–1323*, pp. 596, 628, 629 (where the remaining installments on a loan of £2,420 owed to Roger are to be paid to the king), 662; *CCR, 1323–1327*, pp. 28–29, 419–20; *CFR*, 2:261; *CIM*, 2: no. 509.

112. By May 1324 Elizabeth and another were able to extend a loan of £500: *CCR, 1323–1327*, p. 185.

113. *CCR, 1318–1323*, p. 440; *Calendar of the Memoranda Rolls (Exchequer), Michaelmas 1326-Michaelmas 1327* (London: HMSO, 1968), pp. 218, 311–12, 336; Natalie Fryde, ed., *List of Welsh Entries in the Memoranda Rolls, 1282–1343* (Cardiff: University of Wales Press, 1974), nos. 469, 891, and *CCR, 1330–1333*, pp. 139–40. For discussion of the Exchequer program of debt recovery in Edward II's later years, Buck, *Politics, Finance*, Chapter 8. For Joan's death, Hamilton, *Gaveston*, p. 101.

114. Prestwich, *Three Edwards,* p. 80; Paul C. Doherty, "Isabella, Queen of England, 1296–1330" (D. Phil. diss., Oxford, 1977), 139n.

115. John C. Parsons, "The Intercessionary Patronage of Queens Margaret and Isabella of France" in *Thirteenth-Century England VI,* ed. Michael Prestwich, R. H. Britnell, and Robin Frame (Woodbridge: Boydell Press, 1997), p. 155; J. Enoch Powell and Keith Wallis, *The House of Lords in the Middle Ages* (London: Weidenfeld and Nicolson, 1968), p. 297; Sophia Menache, "Isabella of France, Queen of England—A Reconsideration," *Journal of Medieval History* 10 (1984):110. *Lanercost,* p. 249, says Eleanor held Isabella's seal and was privy to her correspondence; T. F. Tout, *Chapters in the Administrative History of Medieval England* (Manchester: Manchester University Press, 1967), 5:241–42, disputes the story that Eleanor was forced on Queen Isabella.

116. *CChR,* 3:467, 469; *CCR, 1323–1327,* pp. 288–89; *CPR, 1324–1327,* p. 116; Fryde, *Tyranny,* pp. 113–15, details these and other Despenser crimes; cf. Dobrolowski, "Women and their Dower."

117. The wax-image incident led Hugh to write to the pope: *CPapR,* 2:461; on the bishops, Buck, *Politics, Finance,* passim, and Nigel Saul, "The Despensers and the Downfall of Edward II," *EHR* 99 (1984):1–33.

118. *VES,* pp. 138–40; on the domestic scene in 1325–26, Fryde, *Tyranny,* Chapter 11.

119. *CPapR,* 2:475; a papal suggestion that Hugh leave Edward went unheeded; *VES,* pp. 142–45.

120. *Lanercost,* pp. 250–51. Edward II perhaps tried to negotiate an alternative marriage for his son in 1325–26: *CCR, 1323–1327,* pp. 253–54, 344, 350–51, 417, 515–16, 547, 556–57, 576–77.

121. *CCR, 1323–1327,* pp. 471–72, 476, 479. 647.

122. For queens' political use of mediation and intercession, Parsons, "Intercessionary Patronage." Doherty, "Isabella," 168, notes that reliance on the Lancastrian faction was crucial to Isabella's coup. Menache, "Isabella of France," discusses contemporary attitudes toward her as reflected in the chronicles.

123. Overview in Saul, "Despensers and Downfall of Edward II," 1–33.

124. Buck, *Politics, Finance,* p. 145; *CPR, 1324–1327,* p. 30. For petitions and Irish attorneys, *CPR, 1321–1324,* pp. 274–75, 382; *CPR, 1324–1327,* pp. 347, 349. Verdon dower lands in Louth and Meath were leased at £90 yearly for nine years to her Verdon brother-in-law: Frame, *English Lordship,* pp. 62–63. See also Frame, p. 66; *CCR, 1323–1327,* p. 185 (the loan made jointly with Master Richard de Clare, parson of the church of Dunmow); *Suffolk in 1327, being a Subsidy Return,* Suffolk Green Books 9 (Woodbridge: George Booth, 1906), 2:204, 210; A. D. Mills, ed., *Dorset Lay Subsidy Rolls of 1332* (Dorchester: Dorset Record Society, 1971), pp. 91, 104, 112, 144.

125. Holmes, "Protest," 211–12; E101/91/23. A 1329 fee paid Eleanor and her new husband for the rental of Usk in earlier years underscores the

possibility of Elizabeth's control of Usk even before Despenser fell: E101/91/22.

126. *CCR, 1323–1327*, pp. 543–44; E101/506/23; Musgrave, "Household," 33n.; for those responsible for the recognizance: *CCR, 1323–1327*, pp. 537–38.

127. Holmes, "Protest," 210–12.

128. Joseph Hunter, "Journal of the Mission of Queen Isabella to the Court of France," *Archaeologia* 36 (1855):242–57.

129. E101/91/12; *CPR, 1321–1324*, p. 179.

130. Doherty, "Isabella," 80, suggests Isabella tried to save the elder Despenser's life; on Hugh junior, Fryde, *Tyranny*, pp. 192–93. See also *CCR, 1330–1333*, p. 175; *Lanercost*, pp. 253–54; Mansfield D. Forbes, ed., *Clare College, 1326–1926* (Cambridge: Cambridge University Press, 1928), 1:9n.

131. For Eleanor, *CPR, 1324–1327*, p. 620. For the other daughters, *CCR, 1323–1327*, p. 624; for Joan, Pugh, *Glamorgan*, 3:176 and *CCR, 1337–1339*, p. 501. *Calendar of Memoranda Rolls*, no. 437 has that house's costs of £39 16s. 7½d. in veiling the younger Eleanor. Margaret had been sent with a nurse and household to stay with a Thomas de Houk, but her parents failed to pay her bills: *CCR, 1327–1330*, pp. 47–48. GEC, 1:243; 2:130, adds a daughter Elizabeth (d. 1389), who married Maurice de Berkeley (1330–68); given the date of their marriage and Maurice's birth, she was probably born late in Hugh junior's ascendancy, and her given name may suggest an effort at rapprochement with Elizabeth de Burgh. See further, Chapter 3 below. On enclosures by Edward I and II, Michael Prestwich, *War, Politics and Finance under Edward I* (London: Faber and Faber, 1972), p. 280; Prestwich, *Edward I* (Berkeley: University of California Press, 1988), p. 203.

132. *CPR, 1324–1327*, p. 344; *Ancient Petitions, Wales*, pp. 59–60. It is unclear what penalties may have been imposed on Despenser's younger sons Edward, John and Gilbert.

133. *CCR, 1327–1330*, p. 1.

134. The hostile chronicler Geoffrey le Baker calls Isabella "Jezebel" and "she-lion." Menache discusses Isabella's treatment by historians, and with Johnstone remarks the nickname "she-wolf of France," used by later English authors. Modern scholars pick up the theme and the double-standard lives on in their works; Buck, e.g., ignores Edward II's infidelities and ends his *Politics, Finance*, as "Mortimer and his whore" invade England.

135. Fryde, *Tyranny*, pp. 200–206, discusses this topic.

136. E101/91/15; *CCR, 1327–1330*, p. 191 (in April he had told the escheator merely to stop demanding her homage: *CCR, 1327–1330*, p. 79).

137. The episode is covered in Doherty, "Isabella," and George A. Holmes, "The Rebellion of the Earl of Lancaster, 1328–9," *BIHR* 28 (1955):84–89.

138. Musgrave, "Household," 7. Isabella de Verdon proved her age in February 1332 and it is often assumed she married at this time, but *CPR, 1330–1334*, p. 152, indicates she married Henry Ferrers before July 8,

1331. The proof of age was meant to secure Isabella's Verdon purparty, which could not be assigned before she was 14. She could, however, have married earlier; her younger sister, Elizabeth Damory, married in 1328, aged nine or ten. If Ferrers was not yet the lady's son-in-law in 1328, he owed her 500 marks that May: *CCR, 1327–1330*, p. 379, and the Clare household paid to board his horses at the same time: E101/91/17. On the Verdon-Blount marriage, Robert Somerville, *History of the Duchy of Lancaster* (London: Chancellor and Council of the Duchy of Lancaster, 1953), p. 354; Blount and Ferrers witnessed the foundation charter of Lancaster's hospital at Leicester in 1330, a good indication of their position in the his ranks: *CPapR*, 2:41.

139. Menache, "Isabella," 108; Doherty, "Isabella," 68. For Usk, *CPR, 1327–1330*, p. 32.

140. *Ancient Petitions, Wales*, no. 4554; *CCR, 1327–1330*, p. 501.

141. The earl's control probably declined even before his death: Frame, *English Lordship*, p. 137. For the letters to Ireland, E101/91/12. On Cheddeworth, Frame, *English Lordship*, pp. 35–36; Thomas was with Elizabeth when she dictated her May 1326 protest. William's career is discussed in Chapter 3; for the aid, *Feudal Aids*, 6:555–57, a printed transcript based on PRO D.L.41/1/4.

142. Noble mothers often preferred to delay the consummation of daughters' marriages: Parsons, "Mothers, Daughters, Marriage, Power," 65–68.

143. *CPR, 1327–1330*, p. 282; *CCR, 1333–1337*, p. 509.

144. *CPR, 1327–1330*, p. 198. GEC, 4:45 agrees with the present citation, but 1:418–19 has 1326. For the pension, E101/91/17; it may have been initiated earlier, but accounts are missing. On Bardolf's commission, *Calendar of Memoranda Rolls*, no. 890; *CPR, 1327–1330*, p. 32.

145. *CPR, 1327–1330*, p. 426; *Calendar of Memoranda Rolls*, no. 668. In 1329–30, her income including arrears totaled £2939 15s. Many of her manors were leased at this time: Escrick, Kennington, Vauxhall, tenements in Babwell and St Edmunds, Pope's Hall, Mildenhall, and Kirkby Underknoll: E101/91/22.

146. Son of the William Montague who found favor with Edward II: Anthony Tuck, *Crown and Nobility, 1271–1461* (Totowa, NJ: Barnes and Noble, 1985), p. 102.

147. Rowena E. Archer, "Rich Old Ladies: The Problem of Late Medieval Dowagers," in *Property and Politics*, ed. Tony Pollard (New York: St. Martin's Press, 1984), p. 19; Forbes, *Clare College*, 1:12n says Elizabeth showed "perpetual mourning for the husband of her early youth, [John de Burgh]" in a seal bordered by drops resembling tears—an unlikely interpretation. A late fourteenth-century text in John R. H. Moorman, *The Grey Friars in Cambridge, 1225–1538* (Cambridge: Cambridge University Press, 1952), p. 83n, closely resembled Elizabeth's vow: "En la nomm du piere du fitz et de seint expirit Jeo Katherine Bernard femme nadgairs William Bernard face mon avowe a dieu a sa douce miere seinte marie et seint ffraunceys et toux

les seintz de paradys en vos mayns mon reverent piere en dieu Thomas par la grace de dieu Evesque de Ely que desore in avant serrai chaste de mon corps et seynte chastite garderay loialment et devoutement toux les jours de ma vie."

148. The complexities of fourteenth-century Irish politics are beyond the scope of this work. For details, Frame, *English Lordship* or Orpen, *Ireland Under the Normans*, vols. 3 and 4.

149. E101/91/23; PRO draft of Edward III's itinerary. See also Frame, *English Lordship*, p. 197; Orpen, *Ireland Under the Normans*, 4:234–35; GEC, 12:178; *CPR, 1330–1334*, p. 83; *CCR, 1330–1333*, p. 400; E101/91/24.

150. *CCR, 1330–1333*, pp. 532, 586; *Annals of Connacht*, pp. 271–73; Frame, *English Lordship*, pp. 36, 144–45; Orpen, *Ireland Under the Normans*, 4:246–49.

151. McFarlane, *Nobility*, pp. 69–70. The use had the added advantage of protecting lands from forfeiture for treason, and eliminated some hazards of wardship during minorities.

152. *CPR, 1330–1334*, p. 476. Sidney C. Ratcliff, ed., *Feet of Fines for Essex* (Colchester: Essex Archaelogical Society, 1929–49), 3:34, notes further that the "agreement was made by the precept of the king." For the second use, *CPR, 1334–1338*, pp. 384–85.

153. *CIPM*, 7: no. 537 (inquisitions taken after William's death).

154. *CPR, 1334–1338*, pp. 418–19.

155. *CPR, 1340–1343*, p. 187; *CPR, 1330–1334*, p. 490; *CPR, 1334–1338*, p. 31; Green, *Lives*, 3:177; E101/92/18.

156. Magnates knew their own genealogies and perhaps others' as well. The Ferrers and Bardolfs had noble and important ancestors, but that the Ferrers had held the comital title of Derby in the thirteenth century may have figured in Elizabeth's deliberations: *DNB*, 6:250–51. See also *CChR*, 4:426–27; *CPR, 1334–1338*, pp. 490–91; *CCR, 1337–1339*, pp. 261–62, 246.

157. *CPR, 1330–1334*, p. 209; *CFR*, 4:288–89; *CCR, 1339–1341*, pp. 209–10. E101/91/29 has one reference to Thomas de Cheddeworth active in Pembroke. The absence of accounts from the wardship is not exceptional; Irish income was often ignored in the household accounts as well.

158. *CPR, 1330–1334*, p. 551; *CPR, 1334–1338*, pp. 475–76; *CPR, 1338–1340*, p. 542; *CPR, 1340–1343*, p. 13; *CCR, 1333–1337*, pp. 426–27, 561, 580–81; *CCR, 1343–1346*, p. 174.

159. E.g., *CFR*, 5:11; *CCR, 1337–1339*, pp. 406, 528; *CCR, 1339–1341*, pp. 124, 258, 479; *CCR, 1341–1343*, p. 276; *CPR, 1343–1345*, p. 481.

160. *CCR, 1339–1341*, p. 12; *CPR, 1340–1343*, pp. 419–20, 547–48, 556; *CPR, 1334–1338*, p. 152; E101/92/23.

161. *CPR, 1343–1345*, pp. 187, 398; *CCR, 1343–1346*, p. 384, gives 1,000 acres. For the shire boundaries, *CIM*, 3:468.

162. *CCR, 1339–1341*, pp. 531–32. Elizabeth was again accused in 1348 of impeding collectors of customs at New Biggin: *CCR, 1346–1349*, p. 504.

163. Roy Martin Haines, *Archbishop John Stratford* (Toronto: Pontifical Institute of Mediaeval Studies, 1986), p. 273. Bishop Burghersh recruited foreign allies for the king's cause at the same time that he was accused of secreting wool; he visited Elizabeth in 1337, and she used his London house in 1341: E101/95/2; E101/92/13. For Ferrers, see GEC, 5:345. She was in frequent contact with the earl and countess of Northampton in the period: E101/92/9. Lancastrians' associations are noted above. The possibility exists that Elizabeth was aiding Henry Ferrers, who had a license to transport 20 sacks of wool from his Leicester manors. R. H. Hilton, "Medieval Agrarian History," *Victoria County History, Leicestershire*, ed. W. G. Hoskins (Oxford: Oxford University Press, 1954), 2:190–91, notes Henry had only one manor in Leicester, which probably did not produce enough wool to cover his license: *CCR, 1339–1341*, pp. 577–78. Elizabeth gave Beche a falcon in 1338: E101/92/9; E101/92/23; see also, Tout, *Chapters*, 3:121.

164. *Descriptive Catalogue of Ancient Deeds in the Public Record Office* (London: HMSO, 1890–1915), 3:142; 4:440; *CIM*, 2:349–50; C. G. Grimwood and S. A. Kay, *History of Sudbury, Suffolk* (Sudbury: Privately published, 1952), p. 94; *CPR, 1340–1343*, p. 531. For commissions, *CPR, 1343–1345*, p. 77; *CPR, 1348–1350*, p. 16; *CPR, 1334–1338*, p. 135; Nigel Saul, *Knights and Esquires: The Gloucestershire Gentry in the Fourteenth Century* (Oxford: Clarendon Press, 1981), pp. 178–79.

165. E101/92/23.

166. Banners are noted for Corpus Christi in E101/93/17; palms and rushes for Palm Sunday in E101/93/10; Easter decorations in E101/92/9; E101/458/4, E101/459/24, E101/459/25, and E101/459/26 detail purchases of materials and labor for her projects. For the architects Richard atte Cherche, Roger Stephen, William Carpenter, and John Cimenter: E101/459/25, E101/459/26; and John Harvey, *English Mediaeval Architects: A Biographical Dictionary down to 1550*, rev. ed. (Gloucester: Alan Sutton, 1987), pp. 52, 163, 283, 334. On her amusements, E101/95/7; E101/92/9.

167. David Knowles, *The Religious Orders in England* (Cambridge: Cambridge University Press, 1957), 2:7.

168. E101/92/24 and E101/92/28 cover 1344 with few gaps, giving some idea of Elizabeth's residence and travel patterns: Jan. 1–20, Bardfield, with a day trip to Thaxted; Jan. 21-Feb. 10, Clare, with a short trip to Hundon; Feb. 11-April 11, Anglesey, with a trip to Denny; April 13–18, travel to St Neots, Melchburn, Cambridge, Anglesey, Higham Ferrers; April 19-June 24, Clare, with trip to Rochford and Stoke; June 25-Aug. 8, Bardfield, with a day trip to Thaxted; Aug. 9–10, Clare; Aug. 11–22, Anglesey, Denny, Waterbeach; Aug. 23-Sept. 30, Clare, with trips to Standon, Hundon, and Dedham; Dec., Bardfield.

169. For 1338: E101/92/8; for 1340–42: E101/92/18, E101/92/22; for 1348–50: E101/93/2, E101/93/4.

170. 1328: E101/91/19; 1329: E101/91/21; 1331: E101/91/24, E101/91/25; 1332: E101/91/27; 1333: E101/95/10; 1334(3 visits): E101/92/2; 1337(2

visits): E101/92/4, E101/92/7, E101/95/2; 1339: E101/92/9; 1340: E101/92/12; 1341: E101/92/15; 1344(2 visits): E101/92/24; 1347(2 visits): E101/92/30.

171. *CPR, 1330–1334,* p. 477; *CPR, 1334–1338,* pp. 237, 245–46; *CPR, 1343–1345,* p. 3; *CPR, 1345–1348,* pp. 135–36; Forbes, *Clare College,* 1:58.

172. Sandra Raban, *Mortmain Legislation and the English Church, 1279–1500* (Cambridge: Cambridge University Press, 1982), p. 133 and passim; *CPR, 1334–1338,* p. 479.

173. *CPR, 1345–1348,* p. 255; *CPR, 1348–1350,* p. 7; *CPapR,* 3:252; *CPR, 1350–1354,* p. 71; A. R. Martin, *Franciscan Architecture in England* (Manchester: Manchester University Press, 1937), p. 125.

174. E101/95/8, E101/94/7; Harvey, *English Architects,* p. 124. Rames is an alternative spelling of Ramsey and the one used in the Clare accounts: Harvey, pp. 240–41. On Alan, Nikolaus Pevsner and Priscilla Metcalf, *The Cathedrals of England* (New York: Viking, 1985), 1:117–19. Harvey, *English Architects,* p. 312, opts for the masons' superior talents; E101/92/11, E101/92/13. Alan visited Elizabeth in 1346–47, just as his former craftsmen did: E101/95/8. For the masons' visits, E101/92/30.

175. E101/94/7. Lady Berkeley was perhaps Katherine, widow of Maurice Berkeley, but more likely Elizabeth Berkeley, who was Elizabeth de Burgh's niece. Lady Monthermer probably was Margaret, widow of Elizabeth's half-brother Thomas de Monthermer. Lady Bluet was Eleanor, whose second husband was John Bluet; she had been granted an annuity by John Bardolf as Eleanor Monpynzoun, her first husband's surname. Lady Zouche was Eleanor, widow of Alan la Zouche, son of Eleanor Despenser's second husband: *CIPM,* 9: nos. 46, 67. *Familia* generally refers to a noble's household personnel. In the Clare accounts those persons named as belonging to Elizabeth's *familia* seem to be friends, family, or important household officials rather than gardeners or grooms, suggesting a degree of fondness on the lady's part.

176. There is no agreement on the date; most put it between late July and September. See J. F. D. Shrewsbury, *A History of the Bubonic Plague in the British Isles* (Cambridge: Cambridge University Press, 1970), pp. 37–39, 66 (fig. 7) and Robert S. Gottfried, *The Black Death* (New York: Free Press, 1983), p. 58. Contemporary chroniclers disagreed on the point of entry, but most modern authorities opt for Weymouth (Melcombe Regis).

177. E101/93/2; Shrewsbury, *Bubonic Plague,* p. 67.

178. E101/91/14. These men included Robert Fleming, John Gough, Nicholas Damory, John de la Lee, and "others of the *familia.*" William Rees, "The Black Death in Wales," in *Essays in Medieval History,* ed. R. W. Southern (London: Macmillan, 1968), pp. 181–82, notes that Usk, Llantrisant, Trelleck, and Monmouth were affected by the pestilence, which hit hardest in the spring of 1349 in Abergavenny, less than ten miles northwest of Usk.

179. E101/94/17; E101/93/2.

180. A rare example is Reginald de Ewer, who had a gift of 10s. for his soul in 1339–40: E101/92/11; another is John Hostel (or Ostelar), in whose name alms were given to the paupers for his soul in 1342: E101/91/13.

181. For John, E101/93/2; E101/93/6. On William, E101/95/2; E101/92/11; E101/92/12; E101/92/23; E101/93/2.

182. E101/93/2; E101/93/4; E101/94/17. For gifts to the king, E101/94/17; E101/93/2.

183. W. W. Capes, *Charters and Records of Hereford Cathedral* (Hereford: Wilson and Phillips, 1908), pp. 48–9. This manor is near Bullingham, a southern suburb of Hereford, today called Bullinghope.

184. *CPR, 1348–1350,* p. 411, for William; E101/93/9 for Philippa; and E101/93/4 and E101/93/9 for Elizabeth.

185. *CPR, 1330–1334,* p. 476. *RW,* p. 34, notes seed corn, farm animals, and carts young Elizabeth would receive, including those from Bardfield and the Welsh estates.

186. E101/93/6; E101/93/4.

187. *MA,* 2:55.

188. Eleanor paid for the windows, but died before their installation, which would have been completed by 1350, about the time Hugh Despenser junior's effigy was erected. Completion of either project might merit a celebration, though the effigy could have stirred dark memories. Elizabeth's friend, Hugh Despenser III's widow, held the advowson after his death. She married, as her third husband, possibly in the spring of 1350, Guy de Brian, a man occasionally found in Elizabeth's service and *familia.* Medieval sources are rarely informative about dates for second or third weddings, but the ceremony logically could have occurred at the abbey. Brian built his own tomb there during his lifetime.

189. *CIPM,* 9: no. 205. Roger Damory's nephew once held the manor, but in financial distress, he pledged his Oxford lands for loans: James A. Blomfield, *History of the Deanery of Bicester* (London: Parker and Co., 1882), 2:10–11. While the manor does not figure in Blomfield's list of sales by young Richard Damory in the 1340s or 1350s, Bletchingdon probably had been acquired by Hugh de Plescy, as Elizabeth held two parts of the vill from him: *Feudal Aids,* 4:181.

190. William was not yet of age in 1350: Blomfield, *Bicester,* 1:5–6. On the Damorys, Blomfield, *Bicester,* 2:7.

191. Midmer, *Monasteries,* p. 108; E101/93/4.

192. Musgrave, "Household," 21, 67; *BRUC,* p. 548; Gottfried, *Black Death,* pp. 65–66.

193. E101/93/4; E101/95/9.

194. E101/93/12; E101/91/12; E101/92/4; E101/92/5; E101/95/2; E101/92/9; E101/92/11; E101/94/7. See also Harvey, *English Architects,* p. 107. For two of Felsted's construction contracts, L. F. Salzman, *Building in England down to 1540* (Oxford: Clarendon Press, 1952), pp. 433–34 and 436–37. The Minoress' 1488 rental accounts mention a "great house"

within the close, possibly Elizabeth's: Edward M. Tomlinson, *A History of the Minories, London* (London: Smith, Elder, 1907), p. 58. A 1374 document describes the area: Gerald A. Hodgett, ed., *The Cartulary of Holy Trinity, Aldgate* (London: London Record Society, 1971), no. 957; Martha Carlin's sketch of the location appears in Jennifer C. Ward, "Elizabeth de Burgh, Lady of Clare (d. 1360)," in *Medieval London Widows, 1300–1500,* ed. Caroline M. Barron and Anne F. Sutton (London: Hambledon Press, 1994), p. 39.

195. E101/95/7; E101/93/17.

196. E101/93/17; E101/93/18; E101/93/20; E101/94/1.

197. E101/93/17; E101/93/20. It is unclear where the butchering was done.

198. E101/93/20; E101/95/7; E101/93/18.

199. E101/93/17; E101/95/9.

200. E101/95/9. Perhaps the game was for Mary de St Pol at Denny or Elizabeth's daughter-in-law Matilda at Campsey, but nuns at either convent would have shared in the gift.

201. *CPR, 1354–1358,* pp. 419, 442.

202. *CCR, 1354–1360,* p. 189; *CPR, 1354–1358,* p. 412; *CPR, 1358–1361,* p. 85; E101/94/1; E101/94/2.

203. *CPR, 1354–1358,* p. 655; *CPR, 1358–61,* p. 269.

204. For Elizabeth Brian, E101/94/2 and *CIPM,* 10:414–20; on Isabella, E101/94/2 and F. D. Blackley, "Isabella of France, Queen of England, 1308–1358, and the Late Medieval Cult of the Dead," *Canadian Journal of History,* 15 (1980):28–30.

205. E101/93/20; E101/94/1. Joan, Isabella's daughter, was resident with her at Hertford in 1358. For Bredon: *BRUO,* 1:257–58, and Charles H. Talbot, *Medicine In Medieval England* (New York: American Elsevier, 1967), pp. 198–200.

206. E101/94/2.

207. *RW,* p. 34, ostensibly signed and witnessed at Clare, September 25, 1355, though E101/93/17 has Elizabeth in London on that date. No other year fits this account, so presumably she engaged in a small fiction because place and day were symbolically important to her. The Minories was dissolved in the sixteenth century and the premises opened to a newer piety's iconoclasm.

Chapter 2

1. Clare A. Musgrave, "Household Administration in the Fourteenth Century with Special Reference to the Household of Elizabeth de Burgh, Lady of Clare" (M.A. thesis, University of London, 1923):42, thought Elizabeth deliberately tried to keep her true worth a secret; Christopher Dyer, *Standards of Living in the Later Middle Ages* (Cambridge: Cambridge University Press, 1989), p. 29. There are no true modern equivalents for

fourteenth-century English money, but the denominations used in the accounts are: £ (pound), mark (2/3s of a pound), shilling (*s.*), penny (*d.*), half-penny (*ob.*), and quarter of a penny (*q.*).

2. George A. Holmes, *The Estates of the Higher Nobility in Fourteenth-Century England* (Cambridge: Cambridge University Press, 1957), has excellent summaries of crops and profits of her manors where such data are available. E101/93/8, a useful document for information on income and purchases, has been translated in part by Jennifer C. Ward, *Women of Nobility and Gentry, 1066–1500* (Manchester: Manchester University Press, 1995), pp. 162–79.

3. *CIPM,* 12: no. 319; Gladys A. Thornton, *History of Clare, Suffolk* (Cambridge: W. Heffer and Sons, 1928), pp. 33–34, 100–101, 176, and "A Study in the History of Clare, Suffolk, with special reference to its development as a Borough," *TRHS,* 4th series, 11 (1928):90, 92–94. The town court possessed gallows and a pillory; Elizabeth's records mention fabrication of a cucking stool: E101/458/4.

4. R. H. Britnell, *Growth and Decline in Colchester, 1300–1525* (Cambridge: Cambridge University Press, 1986), pp. 21–22; E101/92/9; E101/459/26; E101/94/2; E101/92/17; E101/93/8; Thornton, *History of Clare,* pp. 78, 103. The town of Clare was small, with about 400 to 500 residents in the fourteenth century.

5. Thornton, *History of Clare,* pp. 34, 71, 173; Holmes, *Estates,* p. 153; Teresa McLean, *Medieval English Gardens* (New York: Viking Press, 1981), p. 233; E101/91/25; E101/92/2.

6. E101/458/4; E101/459/24; E101/92/27; E101/93/16; Holmes, *Estates,* pp. 147–48, 155; charcoal production at Bardfield and Hundon had to be supplemented by outside purchases: *CIPM,* 10: no. 637.

7. E101/92/13; E101/93/8; E101/92/27; E101/93/17; E101/94/1; E101/95/9.

8. E101/93/8; E101/93/19; E101/92/9; E101/459/24; *CIPM,* 10: no. 637.

9. E101/93/6; E101/93/8; E101/92/11; E101/92/14; E101/94/2.

10. *CIPM,* 10: no. 637; C. G. Grimwood and S. A. Kay, *A History of Sudbury, Suffolk* (Sudbury: privately published, 1952), pp. 85–86; Helen Suggett, "The Use of French in England in the Later Middle Ages," in *Essays in Medieval History,* ed. R. W. Southern (London: Macmillan, 1968), p. 221; M. S. Giuseppi, "Some Fourteenth-Century Accounts of Ironworks at Tudeley, Kent," *Archaeologia* 64 (1913):145–64. Elizabeth preferred Spanish iron for domestic use rather than that of Southfrith.

11. E101/92/11; E101/92/7; E101/92/3; E101/92/9; E101/94/2; Desmond Hawkins, *Cranborne Chase* (London: Victor Gollancz, 1980), p. 35, reckons that Cranborne chase consisted of 250,000 acres, partly wooded and partly in arable or pasture; Holmes, *Estates,* pp. 109–11, 143, 145, 148; *Dorset Inquisitiones Post-Mortem, 1216–1485* (Shelborne: Sautell, 1916), 1:195–96, gives the following evaluation of the annual worth of her Dorset lands at the time of her death: Cranborne, £70; Tarrant Gunville, £15; Pimperne,

£20 5s.; Steeple, £17 1s. 8d.; borough of Wareham, £16 3d. ob.; Wyke, £30 2s.; Portland, £33 15s. 6d.; borough of Weymouth, £14 15s. 6d. This represents a good income, but one considerably less than she realized on these estates in 1338–39.

12. E101/91/23; E101/93/4; for Brandon and Newbold: E101/92/4; E101/92/7; E101/92/13; E101/92/27; E101/93/19. Newbold rarely figured in the household accounts. The birth there of William Ferrers in 1333 suggests Elizabeth may have left the management and profits to Henry and Isabella Ferrers for some of the period of the accounts. For Lutterworth: E101/93/19; Farnham: E101/92/27; E101/94/2; Hallaton, E101/92/11; E101/92/13; *CPR, 1338–1340,* p. 477; Bletchingdon, E101/93/19; E101/94/2; Holmes, *Estates,* pp. 144, 146–47.

13. Holmes, *Estates,* p. 102, has a map of the lordship; for the differences between Welsh and English holdings and tenants: William Rees, *South Wales and the March, 1284–1415: A Social and Agrarian Study* (London: Oxford University Press, 1924). His examples often come from Elizabeth's manors, although not necessarily during her tenure as lady.

14. R. R. Davies, *Lordship and Society in the March of Wales, 1282–1400* (Oxford: Clarendon Press, 1978), pp. 188, 181.

15. E101/92/7; E101/92/3; E101/93/6; E101/93/10; E101/94/2; E101/92/7; E101/92/9. Other nobles with estates in Wales and England also brought in cattle: H. P. R. Finberg, "An Early Reference to the Welsh Cattle Trade," *Agricultural History Review,* 2 (1954):12–14; Rees, *South Wales,* pp. 110–11, 198.

16. Davies, *Lordship,* pp. 114, 118, 121, 194; Holmes, *Estates,* pp. 143–44; E101/94/2(1358–59) shows six such convoys; fewer trips were recorded in other years.

17. Elizabeth's clerks tended to use the titles interchangeably, even for the same individual in different years.

18. Michael Altschul, *A Baronial Family in Medieval England: The Clares, 1217–1314* (Baltimore: Johns Hopkins Press, 1965), pp. 293–94; Robin Frame, *English Lordship in Ireland, 1310–1361* (Oxford: Clarendon Press, 1982) p. 64, where he includes a tabulation of Elizabeth's Irish income.

19. E101/91/18; Frame, *English Lordship,* pp. 64–65, 186. The affair was also essential to the Poers, who had fled Ireland to the more comfortable environment of Edward III's England and Elizabeth's hospitality: *ibid.,* pp. 179–80; Kevin Down, "Colonial Society and Economy in the High Middle Ages," in *A New History of Ireland,* ed. A. Cosgrove (Oxford: Clarendon Press, 1987), pp. 449, 462.

20. Frame, *English Lordship,* p. 63; E101/91/13, which probably dates from 1342; Annette J. Otway-Ruthven, "The Partition of the Verdon Lands in Ireland in 1332," *Proceedings of the Royal Irish Academy* 66 (1968)C: 409, notes that her Verdon dower lands are never enumerated satisfactorily; 437–41 has an extant rental of 1350–51 and a document describing her dower lands in Kells.

21. T. E. McNeill, *Anglo-Norman Ulster: The History and Archaelogy of an Irish Barony, 1177–1400* (Edinburgh: John Donald, 1980), Appendix 3; Frame, *English Lordship,* p. 63; Down, "Colonial Society," pp. 462, 467; Irish receipts rarely appeared in the household accounts: E101/93/8 and E101/93/10 are exceptions.

22. Frame, *English Lordship,* pp. 69–71, 116–17, 312; Ralph owed Elizabeth money, setting up some sense of obligation: E101/93/8; E101/95/8; E101/93/18; E101/93/12.

23. Frame, *English Lordship,* pp. 63–64, notes Sir Edmund de Burgh the Scot paid the lady rents until 1357–58; *CIPM,* 12: no. 332, notes that Lionel collected £200 from Connacht when he came to Ireland after 1361 in a military capacity, but the lands were worthless after his departure.

24. *Inquisitions and Assessments relating to Feudal Aids, 1284–1431* (London: HMSO, 1908), 6:555–57 for the collection in Suffolk; E101/93/19; E101/93/8.

25. Some of Elizabeth's advowsons are listed in *CIPM,* 10: no. 637; others may be recorded in bishop's registers when a presentation was made, such as *The Registers of Roger Martival, Bishop of Salisbury, 1315–1330,* ed. Kathleen Edwards, Canterbury and York Society, 50 (Oxford: Oxford University Press), 1:96, 105, 277, 302, 339, 372; E101/92/19; E101/92/27; E101/459/24.

26. Nikolaus Pevsner, *Suffolk,* Buildings of England Series (Harmondsworth: Penguin, 1961), p. 150; Thornton, *History of Clare,* pp. 79–80; Mansfield D. Forbes, ed., *Clare College, 1326–1926,* 1:22–23, 32, notes the keep's internal diameter was 52 feet; McLean, *English Gardens,* p. 115.

27. E101/458/4; E101/459/24; *CIPM,* 10: no. 637.

28. J. K. Knight, "Usk Castle and its Affinities," in *Ancient Monuments and their Interpretation: Essays presented to A. J. Taylor,* ed. M. R. Apted, R. Gilyard-Beer, and A. D. Saunders (Chichester: Phillimore, 1977), pp. 147–48; E101/92/13; E101/92/14; E101/91/13; E101/92/18; E101/92/22; E101/94/7; E101/93/2; E101/93/4.

29. Davies, *Lordship,* p. 44; Musgrave, "Household," 64, states Philip represented her in parliament; food distributions are only recorded during visits, but officials may have practiced charity in her name in other years, as they did at Clare.

30. Kate Mertes, *The English Noble Household, 1250–1600* (Oxford: Basil Blackwell, 1988), Appendix A, notes Elizabeth's household numbered about 100, more than any contemporary lay lord.

31. Musgrave, "Household," has devoted her thesis to Elizabeth's household organization. I shall concentrate on activities rather than structure.

32. E101/93/4; E101/91/25; E101/92/5; Clare had at least three ovens; Bardfield one large and two small ones: E101/92/3; E101/93/4; E101/92/7; E101/92/9.

33. Rishton also had some brewery duties; E101/94/4; E101/95/2; E101/92/13; E101/91/12; E101/92/7; E101/92/27; E101/92/9.

34. R. H. Britnell, "*Advantagium Mercatoris*: A Custom in Medieval English Trade," *Nottingham Medieval Studies* 24 (1980):37–41; E101/91/17; E101/92/12; Dyer, *Standards,* p. 58, notes the normal brewing ratio produced 50 to 96 gallons from a quarter of malt.

35. H. A. Monckton, *A History of English Ale and Beer* (London: Bodley Head, 1966), for malting and brewing procedures; Dyer, *Standards,* pp. 192–93; *RW,* p. 27; E101/93/4. Usk may have been deficient in facilities for malt-making. Once, malt was made in Tewkesbury and then carted to Usk, perhaps because of an inconvenient water supply, where some water had to be hauled by cart or buckets attached to a yoke: E101/92/13; E101/92/14.

36. E101/91/25.

37. Ellen Wedemeyer Moore, *The Fairs of Medieval England* (Toronto: Pontifical Institute of Mediaeval Studies, 1985), p. 117; E101/92/27 offers good examples of God's penny, but with varying numbers of pennies involved; E101/93/8; E101/91/25; E101/91/17 notes wine consumption for 1328–29: 33 *dolia,* one pipe, 14½ pitchers. A *dolium* contained 252 gallons; E101/95/2 states that a pipe has 110 gallons.

38. E101/92/23; *RW,* pp. 24–25, 27–28; prayers offered for Reginald's soul in E101/92/11.

39. E101/95/2; E101/93/20; E101/92/1; E101/92/13; E101/92/14; E101/91/25; E101/459/24; grapes bought for verjuice: E101/93/2; E101/93/4; Andre Simon, *A Concise Encyclopaedia of Gastronomy* (New York: Harcourt, Brace, 1952), p. 699.

40. Cattle drives in E101/92/7, E101/92/11; sheep: E101/93/17, E101/93/18; pigs: E101/92/24, E101/92/27; cattle larder: E101/91/14, E101/93/2, E101/93/9, E101/95/9; guarding stock: E101/92/22, E101/92/11, E101/91/14, E101/93/2; for women working temporarily in the larder: E101/93/9, E101/93/18, E101/93/20, E101/95/2, E101/95/7.

41. The rationale for the poultry supplying small animals must have been size, but since the poultry was subsidiary to the kitchen, it is not an important distinction. Gifts of kid: E101/92/7; ten kids for Whitsuntide dinner: E101/91/14; 1348–49 inventory with 28 swans: E101/93/2; E101/92/11; E101/92/12; E101/94/7.

42. Mark Bailey, *A Marginal Economy? East Anglian Breckland in the Later Middle Ages* (Cambridge: Cambridge University Press, 1989), pp. 129–35; Elspeth M. Veale, *The English Fur Trade in the Later Middle Ages* (Oxford: Clarendon Press, 1966), p. 213; Ernest Callard, *The Manor of Freckenham* (London: Bodley Head, 1924), p. 59. Freckenham supplied 559 rabbits in 1350–51, with the bailiff receiving a credit of 2*d.* for each rabbit. The household then sold 576 rabbit skins for 36*s.* 11*d. q:* E101/93/8.

43. E101/92/27 shows Southwold manor supplying two lasts of red herring worth £6; E101/93/4 for lamprey rent.

44. The Clare pond was stocked with bream for Henry Percy's amusement. He probably fished with a rod rather than a net: E101/91/25; trough for hold-

ing pike and for eel storage: E101/92/12; pike kept in Bardfield pond: E101/95/2.

45. Annie Grant, "Animal Resources," in *The Countryside in Medieval England,* ed. Grenville Astill and Annie Grant (Oxford: Basil Blackwell, 1988), p. 171; E101/94/9 for pickled salmon; salmon being prepared for shipment: E101/91/18; baking, flouring, and spicing of lampreys at Gloucester: E101/92/3; E101/95/2; E101/92/12; E101/93/4.

46. Grant, "Resources," pp. 172–73, on stockfish: E101/93/4; E101/95/7; E101/93/6.

47. Porpoise: E101/93/20; whale: E101/91/25 and E101/92/4; baked congers and turbot: E101/95/7. The 1340–41 account in E101/92/14 notes purchases for the year: 10 lasts of red herring, 1 barrel of white herring, 1,000 pilchars, 1,000 stockfish, 60 shellfish, 1,300 mackerel, 582 cod, 129 salmon, 185 pike, 56 lampreys, 3 barrels of sturgeon, 12 whales (or pieces of whale), 180 congers, 6,000 eels, plus 134 and 1/2 sticks of eels. A last contains 10,000 to 20,000 herring.

48. E101/93/13; E101/95/2; on June 5, 1350, 600 whelks were served but only 7 crabs: E101/93/4, E101/93/2; Grant, "Resources," p. 173.

49. The 1350–51 inventory roll shows 153 "beasts of the chase": E101/93/8; for a buck being received as "food rent": E101/95/2; E101/92/7; E101/92/3. After salting, hunters packaged the venison in canvas or barrels and arranged for carts for the trip to Clare. The household also needed salt for pickling, seasoning, and fish preservation. In 1339–40, the household purchased 75 quarters of salt, with a quarter usually containing eight bushels: E101/92/11.

50. E101/92/13; E101/94/2. The accounts do not mention fox fur for household or livery purposes; one year Elizabeth gave the Clare friars 24 fox pelts: E101/92/7.

51. E101/92/9; E101/92/13; E101/92/14; E101/95/2; E101/93/8.

52. E101/93/9; E101/92/14; E101/95/2. Larks also could be roasted or cooked on a lark spit; spoonbills are a type of heron; fieldfare are small thrush-like birds sometimes substituted for larks in pasties: Simon, *Gastronomy,* pp. 601, 561, 575.

53. E101/92/24; E101/93/20; E101/95/7; E101/92/30.

54. E101/459/24; E101/91/17; E101/92/27; E101/93/12; for an orchard garden at her London residence: E101/93/19.

55. E101/92/27; E101/92/2. Some spices were concocted into medicinals. The saucery used 200 gallons of vinegar in 1344–45.

56. E101/92/27 has a typical list of confections purchased. F. Godefroy, *Lexique de L'Ancien Français* (Paris: Librairie Honoré Champion, 1967), p. 312, identifies madrian as a sort of fruit, while R. E. Latham, *Revised Medieval Latin Word List* (London: British Academy, 1980), p. 285, opts for ginger.

57. E101/95/2; E101/92/27; 40 pounds of Cyprus sugar was purchased in 1320: E101/94/9; in 1339–40, £105 7s. 5d. q. was the cost for spices, wax, and canvas, with £10 8s. 3d. for confections: E101/92/11.

58. E101/93/10; E101/93/9; E101/92/24; E101/93/4; E101/93/12; E101/92/22; E101/93/19; E101/95/2; E101/93/2; E101/94/20; E101/92/2.

59. For locks: E101/95/2, E101/92/12, E101/92/13, E101/92/24, E101/91/14, E101/93/2, E101/93/4; for cooperage: E101/95/2, E101/92/9, E101/92/13, E101/92/24; for mending: E101/93/2; E101/93/4.

60. E101/94/2; E101/93/10; E101/459/24; for a year's purchase of 118,000 peat turves and 3,650 sedge sheaves: E101/92/27; sedge was utilized for thatching as well as for fuel: Bailey, *Marginal Economy*, p. 164; For coal purchases: E101/93/10, E101/95/2; Dyer, *Standards*, p. 73, suggests its primary use was at the forge or in burning lime; E101/94/2.

61. *RW*, p. 25. Torches were also made for the Monthermer wake.

62. E101/92/27; E101/95/2; E101/92/13; E101/91/12; E101/91/25; E101/92/12. Purchase of wicks at 2*d. ob. q.* per pound: E101/94/1; in 1326 the household paid 2*d.*, slightly higher than the 1½*d.* norm that Dyer reports in *Standards*, p. 74. Elizabeth bought 340 pounds of Lubeck wax in 1344–45, with three pounds of red wax probably intended for sealing wax.

63. E101/92/9; E101/92/13; E101/92/24; E101/93/4; E101/92/2; E101/92/12; E101/92/30; E101/92/4; E101/93/2.

64. E101/92/13 for examples at London and Usk.

65. E101/93/9 for Clare; E101/93/2 for cleaning the well at Usk; E101/92/13 for yokes.

66. E101/93/17; E101/93/18; E101/91/24; E101/91/27; E101/92/4. Until the advent of commercial sanitary napkins and tampons, women rinsed out cloths they used to catch the menstrual flow. Elizabeth's laundress would have performed this task.

67. E101/93/4; E101/93/20; E101/93/12 for tubs and soap; E101/93/20, E101/95/9 for potash; E101/92/9; E101/92/24 for soap-making.

68. E101/92/9; E101/92/12; E101/92/13; E101/92/7; E101/92/30. Master W. Medic~ attended the Damory household in 1320–21, with no mention of the purpose of his stay; Master Simon Bredon was part of the lady's *familia* in the late 1350s: E101/93/20; E101/94/1.

69. E101/93/10; E101/95/2. John Ypotecar left Elizabeth's service in 1337 with a retirement gift of 6*s.* 8*d.*, succeeded by William Ypotecar, employed from 1338–49: E101/92/4; E101/95/2; for medicines or medicinals: E101/93/10; E101/94/20; E101/93/12.

70. E101/92/12; E101/93/4; E101/94/20; E101/93/20; E101/92/9; E101/92/24.

71. E101/93/8; horses boarding at Brandon, Newbold, and Lutterworth: E101/92/7.

72. E101/94/7 and E101/95/8 are good examples of marshalsea accounts; E101/93/8 mentions that a man and a page cared for three destriers at Usk, and that ten destriers and colts were sent to board at Brandon.

73. E101/92/11; E101/92/20; E101/92/29; E101/93/2; E101/92/2; E101/92/4; E101/92/12; E101/95/2; E101/93/8 for the eight murrain deaths in 1350–51, examples of named horses, hide purchases, and sale of old cartwheels.

74. See above for the 1350 move from Wales to Clare; Elizabeth also hired carts and horses when her own stock was inadequate: E101/92/24.

75. For a breakdown: E101/92/9. If only household horses were shod, average consumption would be a set of new horseshoes for each horse each month: E101/94/2; E101/93/8 noted eight barrels of Swedish iron left over from the previous year and the purchase of 2,367 pounds of Spanish iron in the current year; in December, 1350, cloutcovers, linch-pins or axles, hurters, and cloutnails were purchased.

76. E101/91/29; E101/95/2; E101/93/8; Marjorie Nice Boyer, "Mediaeval Suspended Carriages," *Speculum* 34 (1959):359–66; *RW,* pp. 28, 35.

77. The staff manufactured 38,989 horse breads of mixtel and peas in 1350–51, supplemented by 3,880 breads from the pantry: E101/93/8; for guides in the Walsingham area, at Malling and at Acle: E101/92/4; E101/92/12; E101/92/30.

78. In 1330–31, annual messenger costs were £39 4s. 8d. q.: E101/91/24; for Tottenham: E101/93/18; E101/94/7; E101/93/20; E101/95/9; E101/93/8; E101/92/12; E101/94/2.

79. E101/93/9. For example, on November 29, 1350, the marshalsea was charged with wages for 2 valets, 20 grooms (*garcons*), and 4 pages. Some worked in other departments.

80. E101/91/12; E101/92/5; E101/92/7; E101/92/8; E101/92/9; E101/92/12; E101/92/17; E101/92/18; E101/92/29; E101/92/30; E101/93/4; E101/93/13; E101/93/17; E101/93/18; E101/94/1; E101/94/2; E101/95/7; E101/92/23; for Margery's staff work: E101/92/19; E101/93/10; Musgrave, "Household," 62–63.

81. *CPR, 1334–1338,* p. 490; E101/92/9; E101/92/11; E101/93/8; *RW,* pp. 24, 41. His daughter Elizabeth Torel also received a bequest.

82. Matthew received 2d. a day in wages: E101/91/12; Henry is mentioned as receiving livery in E101/92/9; E101/92/23; E101/92/13. In 1352 Queen Philippa had a personal illuminator, Master Robert, who might have been Elizabeth's former servant: Jonathan J. G. Alexander, *Medieval Illuminators and Their Methods of Work* (New Haven: Yale University Press, 1992), p. 27. *RW,* p. 28; E101/93/17 notes Corpus Christi banners; Paul Binski, *Painters* (Toronto: University of Toronto Press, 1991), p. 31, says green, Elizabeth's favorite color, was also that of many contemporaries, who saw it as "health-giving and fertile."

83. E101/91/30 is the sole surviving account for this department. Markeby received a legacy from John de Chichester, a leading London goldsmith, so probably Markeby worked in London at least in later years: T. F. Reddaway, *The Early History of the Goldsmiths' Company, 1327–1509* (London: Edward Arnold, 1975), p. 292.

84. E101/92/2; E101/92/3; E101/92/13; E101/92/14; E101/91/25; John Cherry, *Goldsmiths* (Toronto: University of Toronto Press, 1992), p. 55; Marian Campbell, "Gold, Silver and Precious Stones," in *English Medieval Industries,* ed. John Blair and Nigel Ramsay (London: Hambledon Press, 1991), pp. 140–41.

85. Robert Aurifaber and Robert de Tewkesbury may be the same person, indifferently labeled by the household clerks. E101/92/9 for Thomas's errand; E101/92/3 and E101/92/4 for Robert's; Thomas's horses appear in marshalsea accounts of 1346–47 and 1347–48: E101/95/8, E101/94/7.

86. For Freynch: E101/92/11 and Reddaway, *Goldsmiths,* pp. 27–29; for Burton: E101/93/5 and A. H. Thomas, ed., *Calendar of Plea and Memoranda Rolls (London), 1323–1364* (Cambridge: Cambridge University Press, 1926), pp. 242–43; purchases made from Mundene and Northampton appear in E101/93/12. For Elizabeth's interest in gold work and other arts: Frances A. Underhill, "Elizabeth de Burgh: Connoisseur and Patron," in *The Cultural Patronage of Medieval Women,* ed. June Hall McCash (Athens: University of Georgia Press, 1996).

87. *RW,* pp. 25–26, 30–32. The vestments were complete outfits with several items traditional for clerical dress; Hereford Cathedral, Dean and Chapter Archives, #4625.

88. E101/93/12; E101/92/23. Cheiner is identified as an embroiderer in A. G. I. Christie, *English Medieval Embroidery* (Oxford: Clarendon Press, 1938), p. 36.

89. E101/92/9; E101/94/2 and E101/93/8 for shearing costs; E101/93/10 mentions Margery Mareschal sewing for boys in Elizabeth's care. In 1331–32, the lady's livery costs were £94 14s. 7d. ob., including furs: E101/91/27; in 1358–59 cloth costs totaled £216 11s. 5d., with furs costing £85 18s.: E101/94/2.

90. This livery account is in E101/94/2. Recipients of the russet are not mentioned but costs are under livery expenditures. Some russet might have been for paupers.

91. E101/93/8; E101/93/12; E101/92/12; she gave shoes to drovers at least once: E101/94/9. Francis Grew and Margrethe de Neergaard, *Shoes and Patens,* Medieval Finds from Excavations in London 2 (London: Museum of London, 1988), p. 120, note shoe prices averaged 5d. to 6d. a pair in the fourteenth century.

92. Musgrave, "Household," 96–97.

93. Some lay members are discussed in a later chapter. Clerics on Elizabeth's council include: John de London, keeper of the wardrobe, subsequently clerk of the chamber (1325–27); Alan de Medefeld, keeper of the wardrobe (1326–32); John de Lenne, keeper of the wardrobe (see below); Robert de Stalynton, clerk of the chamber (see below); William d'Oxwich, clerk of the chamber, whose early schooling at King's Bench was paid for by Elizabeth (1331–52); William de Manton, eventually clerk of the combined wardrobe and chamber; in the household from 1337 to 1359. After Eliza-

beth's death he joined Lionel's staff and after 1361, he became keeper of the king's Wardrobe. By 1364 he was also dean of Lichfield: *Handbook of British Chronology*, p. 78; John Le Neve, *Fasti Ecclesiae Anglicanae* (London: Institute for Historical Research, 1962), 10:6. For more complete details on the lady's council, see Musgrave, "Household."

Chapter 3

1. See *CIM*, 3:246–47, for lady of Weymouth, a designation never appearing in her accounts; *CCR, 1327–1330*, p. 191, uses this title in 1327.
2. Mansfield D. Forbes, ed., *Clare College, 1326–1926* (Cambridge: Cambridge University Press, 1928), 1:12–13.
3. *CAFC*, no. 162. An earlier indulgence sermon coincided with a visit of Edward II to Elizabeth and Roger Damory, where the initiative might have been the king's.
4. Francis Roth, *The English Austin Friars, 1249–1538* (New York: Augustinian Historical Institute, 1961), 1:618; *CAFC*, no. 189.
5. Richard Morris, "Tewkesbury Abbey: The Despenser Mausoleum," *Transactions of the Bristol and Gloucestershire Archaeological Society* 93 (1974):143 and 145, posits that Hugh Despenser was responsible for the remodeling scheme of Tewkesbury Abbey, allowing Eleanor and her son Hugh credit for modifications necessary to include space for Eleanor's second husband, William la Zouche, and the execution of the windows. Hugh Despenser junior's purpose was said to be inclusion of himself in the ranks of the Clares. This interpretation does not impinge on my argument for Eleanor's memorialization of her ancestors, but adds the thought that her husband shared in this venture. Later in the century Guy de Brian, who had married Hugh Despenser III's widow, wanted burial at Tewkesbury Abbey.
6. Hugh became earl of Gloucester only in 1337: Anthony Tuck, *Crown and Nobility, 1271–1461* (Totowa, N.J.: Barnes and Noble, 1985), p. 330; he then adopted the Clare heraldic arms: Forbes, *Clare College,* 1:9n.
7. Medieval noblewomen were persistently conscious of their natal families: John C. Parsons, "'Never was a body buried in England with such solemnity and honour': The Burials and Posthumous Commemorations of English Queens to 1500," in *Queens and Queenship in Medieval Europe,* ed. Anne J. Duggan (Woodbridge: Boydell Press, 1997), pp. 328–29, and note 35.
8. Clare A. Musgrave, "Household Administration in the Fourteenth Century, with Special Reference to the Household of Elizabeth de Burgh, Lady of Clare" (M.A. thesis, University of London, 1923):3; Michael Altschul, *A Baronial Family in Medieval England, The Clares, 1217–1314* (Baltimore: Johns Hopkins Press, 1965), pp. 233–34, notes accounts for the girls' expenses originated from the Usk lordship where they shared services of a dependent wardrober with their Monthermer siblings.

9. F. D. Blackley and G. Hermansen, eds., *Household Book of Queen Isabella, for the Fifth Regnal Year of Edward II* (Edmonton: University of Alberta Press, 1971), pp. xiii–xiv; T. B. Pugh, ed., *Glamorgan County History* (Cardiff: University of Wales Press, 1971), 3:174, describes Eleanor as "deeply involved in Hugh Despenser's schemes."

10. *CCR, 1323–1327,* pp. 62, 553, 590; *CCR, 1330–1333,* p. 182. *CPR, 1324–1327,* pp. 339–40 describes many of the treasures.

11. *CCR, 1327–1330,* pp. 275–76, 283, 590; *CPR, 1327–1330,* p. 433; William Rees, *Caerphilly Castle,* rev. ed. (Caerphilly: Caerphilly Local History Society, 1974), p. 91; Pugh, *Glamorgan,* 3:175 says £5,000 was repaid to gain possession, but the remaining amount was never paid; *CPR, 1330–1334,* p. 292; GEC, 12:959; J. Robert Wright, *The Church and the English Crown, 1305–1334* (Toronto: Pontifical Institute of Mediaeval Studies, 1980), pp. 331–32; *CPapR,* 2:394.

12. GEC, 12:959; E101/91/22; E101/91/23; E101/91/24.

13. *CPR, 1334–1338,* pp. 283, 298.

14. Elizabeth and Hugh Audley also exchanged letters and he visited her at least once, in June 1339: E101/92/9; E101/92/11; E101/92/13; Elizabeth's prayers for Margaret's soul are in E101/93/12.

15. *CCR, 1333–1337,* pp. 580–81. The clerks may have ignored Eleanor and Margaret before 1337 because they held no title more exalted than lady.

16. Elizabeth's half-sister Isabella married Maurice Berkeley about 1316, so some contact was possible before her death in 1337: GEC, 2:128–29.

17. E101/91/18; E101/92/7; E101/92/12; E101/92/11; Master Martin, fetched from London, was a surgeon who later joined Edward III overseas: Charles H. Talbot and E. A. Hammond, *The Medical Practitioners in Medieval England* (London: Wellcome Historical Medical Library, 1965), p. 410.

18. John Weever, *Ancient Funerall Monuments* (1631; reprint, Norwood, NJ: Walter J. Johnson, 1979), p. 740. *CAFC,* no. 162: Bishop Paschal's 1347 indulgence sermons included Monthermer as well as Joan.

19. Janetta Sorley, *King's Daughters* (Cambridge: Cambridge University Press, 1937), p. 54, claims Thomas de Monthermer used Elizabeth's castle as his home, and that Edward de Monthermer, "feeble in mind or body or both," lived with Elizabeth for 18 years.

20. *CCR, 1327–1330,* p. 352; GEC, 4: 272–73; Tuck, *Crown and Nobility,* p. 104; Pugh, *Glamorgan,* 3:176.

21. E101/92/9; E101/92/12; E101/92/11; E101/92/13, E101/94/7; GEC, 4:272–73; *CPapR,* 3:141; *CCR, 1327–1330,* p. 352; Tuck, *Crown and Nobility,* p. 104; Pugh, *Glamorgan,* 3:176.

22. E101/95/8; his mother's visit: E101/94/7; GEC, 4:274–75 identifies Edward as the grandson of Henry Ferrers; *CIPM,* 10: no. 333, makes his grandfather William Ferrers, a much more compelling case on biological grounds, for if GEC is correct both Edward's mother, Anne, and grandmother Isabella de Verdon gave birth at the age of nine or ten.

23. E101/95/8.

24. E101/93/2; E101/93/4.

25. Pugh, *Glamorgan,* 3:175; *CCR, 1327–1330,* pp. 47–48; GEC, 2:130. This was the grandson of the Maurice who married Isabella, half-sister of Elizabeth.

26. For Gilbertine nuns' profession: Rose Graham, *S. Gilbert of Sempringham and the Gilbertines* (London: Elliot Stock, 1901), p. 102; *CCR, 1323–1327,* p. 624; *CCR, 1337–1339,* p. 501. The problem with this last entry, dated October 6, 1338, is that it refers to Joan and Eleanor, daughters of "Hugh Despenser the Elder." Hugh Despenser III had been rehabilitated by 1338, so perhaps the "elder" refers to his father, not his grandfather, who was designated "the elder" in the 1320s.

27. E101/92/5; E101/92/7; E101/93/12; *CPR, 1343–1345,* p. 158; *CCR, 1349–1354,* p. 285.

28. *CPapR,* 3:164 gives Richard's version of parental compulsion to marital intercourse, which resulted in the birth of a son, conveniently forgetting the births of two daughters; GEC, 1:242–44.

29. GEC, 2:130; E101/92/7; she appeared in E101/92/12; E101/92/13; E101/92/14; E101/92/15.

30. E101/92/29; *DNB,* 18:865.

31. E101/94/2; *CPapR,* 3:137.

32. See Shulamith Shahar, *Childhood in the Middle Ages* (London: Routledge, 1990), pp. 156–57, for the injunction to honor one's parents. Elizabeth founded a chantry for Gilbert de Clare, either her father or brother.

33. GEC, 12:178, claims that William came to England in 1322 or 1323. The earl of Ulster came to England in 1317 via Wales, affording him opportunity to deliver William to his mother. GEC has confused this William de Burgh with William Liath de Burgh, the earl of Ulster's cousin, who received royal summons to England in 1322 and 1323: Robin Frame, *English Lordship in Ireland, 1318–1361* (Oxford: Clarendon Press, 1982), p. 136; *CCR, 1313–1318,* pp. 560, 579; Kenneth Fowler, *The King's Lieutenant: Henry of Grosmont, First Duke of Lancaster, 1310–1361* (New York: Barnes and Noble, 1969), p. 27, suggests that William spent time in Earl Henry of Lancaster's household.

34. *CCR, 1327–1330,* p. 185; *CFR,* 4:14; *CPapR,* 2:257; E101/91/17; E101/91/18; Frame, *English Lordship,* p. 184; Ranald Nicholson, "A Sequel to Edward Bruce's Invasion of Ireland," *Scottish Historical Review* 42 (1963):33–34.

35. E101/91/18; E101/91/12; E101/91/17; Frame, *English Lordship,* p. 181, lists Hugh de Burgh among this group; a Hugh de Burgh served in the lady's household in 1326 and for some years after, eventually going to Ireland as chief baron of the Exchequer in Dublin; Arnold le Poer was seneschal of Kilkenny, part of which was included in Elizabeth's Clare inheritance: *ibid.,* p. 178.

36. *CCR, 1327–1330,* p. 196; PRO draft itinerary of Edward III; E101/91/18 is William's roll, outlining his activities over several months;

Juliet Vale, *Edward III and Chivalry: Chivalric Society and its Context, 1270–1350* (Woodbridge: Boydell Press, 1982), Appendix 12; Juliet R.V. Barker, *The Tournament in England, 1100–1400* (Woodbridge, Suffolk: Boydell Press, 1986), pp. 115–16.

37. GEC, 12:178 states that the ceremony occurred on May 22, 1328 in London; but the earl's household roll has a heading on one membrane: "Expenses of the Earl of Ulster made knight at Evesham on 24 June, year 2": E101/91/18. Pike galantyn was served at his post-dubbing feast: the recipe is in Constance B. Hieatt and Sharon Butler, *Pleyn Delit: Medieval Cookery for Modern Cooks* (Toronto: University of Toronto Press, 1976), no. 55. The 31 pike for William's affair cost £6 12s.

38. Nicholson, "Sequel," 38; Bruce's wife had died a few years earlier.

39. E101/91/21; *RW*, p. 34.

40. *CCR, 1333–1337,* pp. 70, 248–49; *CCR, 1337–1339,* pp. 170, 369. These calendars also provide examples of the crown's responses to Matilda's requests for respite from royal financial demands and of royal provision for her; *CPR, 1330–1334,* p. 490; *CPR, 1338–1340,* p. 305; Scott L. Waugh, *The Lordship of England: Royal Wardships and Marriages in English Society and Politics, 1217–1327* (Princeton: Princeton University Press, 1988), pp. 108–109, 196–97.

41. E101/92/2; E101/92/9; E101/92/13; E101/92/11; *DNB*, 11:214–15. The marriage date is uncertain as noted by B. C. Hardy, *Philippa of Hainault and Her Times* (London: John Long, 1910), pp. 133–35, but must have occurred before 1355, when Lionel's and Elizabeth's daughter, Philippa, was born.

42. Some Irish chroniclers saw Matilda as the true power behind Ralph's activities: Robin Frame, "The Justiciarship of Ralph Ufford: Warfare and Politics in Fourteenth-Century Ireland," *Studia Hibernica* 13 (1973):10.

43. E101/92/28; E101/94/7. Elizabeth's rolls consistently acknowledged little Elizabeth's title as countess, but never refer to Lionel as earl of Ulster.

44. *CCR, 1346–1349,* p. 214; Eileen Power, *Medieval English Nunneries, c. 1275 to 1535* (Cambridge: Cambridge University Press, 1922), p. 113.

45. E101/94/7; E101/94/3; E101/93/4; E01/93/9; E101/93/17; E101/93/18; E101/93/20. Elizabeth's sister or sisters are a problem. *CPR, 1338–1340,* p. 445, mentions a Margaret, daughter of William, earl of Ulster. H. T. Knox, "Occupation of Connaught by the Anglo-Normans after A. D. 1237," *Journal of the Royal Society of Antiquaries of Ireland,* Part 2, 12:406, states that Margaret and a twin sister, Isabella, were born to William and Matilda after his death. Presumably these girls died in childhood. The Margaret who visited Clare in 1350 is certainly Margaret Ufford. Geoffrey Chaucer served in the household of Countess Elizabeth in the late 1350s, so it is very possible that he accompanied her on these visits to her grandmother, the lady of Clare.

46. E101/93/12. Philippa was married by July 1359, when she was about four: Frederick Devon, *Issues of the Exchequer* (London: John Murray, 1837) pp. 170, 172. The lady of Clare was in London that month, so possibly she at-

tended this celebration, though she seemed to avoid weddings as well as funerals: E101/95/9.

47. E101/91/15; E101/91/25. Elizabeth was purchasing cloth for Isabella in 1330–31, but this did not demand co-residency. GEC, 5:348 and *CIPM,* 9: no. 379 disagree over the date of William's birth, but he seems to be the second child of the marriage.

48. GEC, 5:345–46; E101/92/2; E101/92/11; E101/91/13 for her gifts; E101/92/3; E101/92/7 for Henry's; E101/92/13. Just where this London residence was is unclear, though it cannot have been the home she built later near the Minories.

49. For example, *CCR, 1333–1337,* p. 678; *CFR,* 5:55; *CPR, 1334–1338,* pp. 384–85, 472, 553, 560; *CPR, 1338–1340,* p. 110; *CChR,* 4:399, 443.

50. E101/92/7 mentions contact made with Isabella, probably in 1337; E101/92/8; E101/92/11 (the undated entry is under the cost of oats for 1339–40); E101/92/13; E101/92/14; E101/458/4; E101/459/26; E101/92/29; E101/95/8; E101/92/2; E101/92/12; E101/94/7; *CCR, 1341–1343,* p. 460.

51. Susan Groag Bell, "Medieval Women Book Owners: Arbiters of Lay Piety and Ambassadors of Culture," in *Women and Power in the Middle Ages,* ed. Mary Erler and Maryanne Kowaleski (Athens: University of Georgia Press, 1988), p. 179, notes that mothers' gifts of books to daughters showed an interest in their futures through selection of important devotional teaching aids.

52. E101/92/13; E101/92/14.

53. Henry acknowledged a debt of 5,000 marks to the earl of Warwick in April 1340, probably associated with Philippa's marriage: *CCR, 1339–1341,* p. 462. Elizabeth was married to David de Strabolgi after the king granted Henry his marriage, worth 1,000 marks in August 1342: *CPR, 1340–1343,* pp. 500–501.

54. Nicholas H. Nicolas, *Testamenta Vetusta* (London: Nichols and Son, 1826), 1:63–64. Almost certainly the little girls were placed in the convent to avoid their inheritance of the Beauchamp estates as the only heirs of their father, who would have succeeded to the earldom.

55. The manors were Saham and Neketon: *CIPM,* 10, no. 590; E101/93/20; Nicholas, *Testamenta Vetusta,* 1:76.

56. E101/93/10; E101/93/12.

57. GEC, 14:308; James E. Doyle, *The Official Baronage of England* (London: Longmans, Green, 1886), 1:94; *CPR, 1340–1343,* p. 417; Sir James Balfour Paul, ed., *The Scots Peerage* (Edinburgh: David Douglas, 1904), 1:432–33. Some of David de Strabolgi's lands were in Ireland and therefore less than profitable; his English inheritance was burdened by his mother's dower interests, and she only predeceased him by two years. E101/92/28; E101/95/8; E101/93/12. Buge is fine lambskin, often imported.

58. *CCR, 1354–1360,* p. 130; *Scot's Peerage,* 1:432–33; E101/93/20.

59. *RW,* pp. 36–37; Nicholas, *Testamenta Vetusta,* 1:76; *CCR, 1360–1364,* pp. 253–54, 384; GEC, 1:308. Before the earl of Athol died in 1369, the

couple had two daughters, Elizabeth and Philippa. Later the countess
married John Maleweyn, a merchant, sometime before her death in
1375: Weever, *Funerall Monuments,* p. 275.

60. William was born at Newbold Verdon, part of Elizabeth's Verdon dower:
GEC, 5:348; E101/92/2; E101/92/12; E101/92/24; E101/95/8;
E101/94/7.

61. E101/92/24 (May 1344); E101/92/28 (January 1345); E101/95/8 (August
and September 1347); E101/93/4 (May 1352); E101/92/27; E101/93/4.

62. *CCR, 1354–1360,* pp. 9–10, 214, 411, 493, 504; *CCR, 1360–1364,* pp.
60, 122, 147; GEC, 5:348–49; E101/93/8.

63. E101/93/20; Nicholas, *Testamenta Vetusta,* 1:76; *RW,* p. 36. William married
twice: Margaret Ufford and then Margaret, daughter of Henry Percy. His
brother-in-law was Bishop Thomas Percy of Norwich. Not only did
William have decent landholdings and knights' fees, but he allied himself
with leading noble families.

64. The titular sheriff was Earl Henry of Lancaster: *LS,* p. 72; *CPR,
1338–1340,* pp. 184, 217, 229, 235; GEC, 12:252; E101/92/24;
E101/93/19.

65. *CPR, 1327–1330,* p. 32; *CPapR,* 3:614; E101/95/8; E101/94/7.

66. *CPR, 1330–1334,* p. 135; *CPR, 1338–1340,* p. 182; GEC, 12:252.

67. E101/91/27; E101/92/3. The boy may have been a brother of Nicholas
Damory. GEC, 4:48, note C, describes Nicholas as a probable first cousin
of Sir Richard Damory, son of Richard Damory, who was Roger's brother.

68. He seems to have possessed no Welsh or Irish manors: *CIPM,* 7: no. 243.
GEC, 1:418, lists the service laconically, without the usual mention of im-
portant battles; J. Enoch Powell and Keith Wallis, *The House of Lords in the
Middle Ages* (London: Weidenfeld and Nicolson, 1968), pp. 348–49.

69. *CPR, 1338–1340,* p. 148; *CCR, 1360–1364,* p. 108. For oyer and ter-
miner examples: *CPR, 1334–1338,* p. 448; *CPR, 1343–1345,* p. 400;
CPR, 1345–1348, p. 388. For examples of justice of peace and laborers:
Bertha H. Putnam, *The Enforcement of the Statutes of Labourers, 1349–1359*
(New York: Columbia University Press, 1908). For the survey of ditches:
CCR, 1354–1360, pp. 260–61, 274–75.

70. E101/92/2; E101/95/2; E101/92/4; E101/92/9; E101/92/4;
E101/92/12; E101/92/28; E101/92/29; E101/93/4; E101/93/9;
E101/93/10; E101/93/13; E101/94/1.

71. *RW,* pp. 34–36; Marjorie Nice Boyer, "Mediaeval Suspended Carriages,"
Speculum 34 (1959):359–66 for a description of these chariots. She left no
bequest for her grandson William Bardolf, born in 1349.

72. Sorley, *Daughters,* p. 54, claims the organ belonged to John.

73. E101/93/12; E101/93/10; E101/92/4; E101/92/12; E101/92/13;
E101/92/28; E101/92/29; E101/93/4; E101/93/9; E101/93/13;
E101/94/1; E101/92/11; Sorley, *Daughters,* p. 54, claims that after Isabella
Ferrers's death, the Bardolfs "lived with the Lady or she with them, some-
times at Bardfield but mostly at Clare"; GEC, 1:419; *CPapR,* 1:232 for the

Bardolfs' indult for a portable altar. After the deaths of his mother-in-law and wife, John traveled to Assisi where he died and was buried.

74. Placing some people in the family category and others in the friendship classification is quite arbitrary and perhaps a bit misleading.

75. Colin Morris, *Discovery of the Individual* (New York: Harper and Row, 1973), pp. 106–7.

76. E101/94/20 records a visit of Queen Isabella and the countess of Pembroke to Elizabeth at Kennington. The roll is undated, but the date must be 1320, given that October 9 is a Thursday and the lord of the manor is mentioned. The problem is that Aymer did not marry Mary until 1321; his first wife died in September 1320, so there should not have been a countess of Pembroke in October: J. R. S. Phillips, *Aymer de Valence, Earl of Pembroke, 1307–1324: Baronial Politics in the Reign of Edward II* (Oxford: Clarendon Press, 1972), p. 6; E101/91/16; E101/91/19; E101/91/21; E101/91/25.

77. Elizabeth first bought for Mary in 1331: E101/91/24; other cloth gifts of identical material given to the countess are in E101/92/9; E101/92/13; E101/92/11; E101/93/8; E101/94/1; E101/94/2; Mary gave Elizabeth cloth (not necessarily identical to her own outfit): E101/93/12. I am not suggesting a sexual dimension, but rather suspension of the normal, hierarchical pattern of livery connotations.

78. Mary received grants of exemption from confiscation imposed on aliens in England during the Hundred Years' War. She must have been quite astute and clever to maintain friendships on both sides of the Channel and to avoid hostility during the conflict. No visits in London show in Elizabeth's accounts, which was normal as no travel expenses were involved. She may have been to Mary's residence of Cheshunt in 1355: E101/93/18; Mary's visits to Elizabeth are found in E101/91/25; E101/92/2; E101/93/2; E101/93/4; her messages or letters to Elizabeth are in E101/93/12; E101/94/7; E101/95/8; Elizabeth sent couriers and letters to Mary, which are found in E101/92/9; E101/92/11; E101/92/13; E101/92/14; E101/93/10; E101/94/1; E101/94/2.

79. *CPR, 1327–1330,* p. 166; Hilary Jenkinson, "Mary de Sancto Paulo, Foundress of Pembroke College, Cambridge," *Archaeologia* 66 (1914–15):414. Mary lost her Welsh lands after the earl's death and none show in her post-mortem inquisitions. Frame calls kinship with the king, an "imponderable but real advantage": *English Lordship,* p. 186. David predeceased Mary, so the properties went to his daughters, Elizabeth and Philippa, both of whom married into the Percy family: *CIPM,* 14: no. 339.

80. Jenkinson, "Mary de Sancto Paulo," 425–26, 432–35; "Inventory of Church Goods, *temp* Edward III," *Norfolk Record Society* 19 (1974), part 2: facing 186 and 187, has illustrations of her seals and a paten. Mary had three breviaries, one of which Jenkinson thought to be extant.

81. Elizabeth's trips to Denny are found in E101/92/3; E101/92/7; E101/92/24 and E101/92/30; trips to Waterbeach in E101/92/9 and

E101/92/13; trips that included both locations in E101/92/24 and E101/92/28. Jenkinson, "Mary de Sancto Paulo," 420n, suggests Mary's contact with the Minoresses of Lourcine-lez-Saint-Marcel of Paris.

82. Meetings between 1345 and 1348, the year of Mary's charter, are found in E101/92/28; E101/92/30; E101/95/8; E101/94/7; E101/93/2; Jenkinson, "Mary de Sancto Paulo," 422–24; *CPR, 1343–1345,* p. 568; James B. Mullinger, *The University of Cambridge* (Cambridge: University of Cambridge Press, 1873), 1:236–39.

83. Jenkinson comments on Mary's lack of female friends of her station, but his interpretation depends heavily on her will of 1377 when her dearest friends were dead; J. Hunter, "Journal of the Mission of Queen Isabella to the Court of France and of Her Long Residence in That Country," *Archaeologia* 36 (1855), 250–52; Edward A. Bond, "Notices of the Last Days of Isabella, Queen of Edward the Second, drawn from an Account of the Expenses of her Household," *Archaeologia,* 35 (1854), 462.

84. See F. Royston Fairbank, "The Last Earl of Warenne and Surrey," *Yorkshire Archaeological Journal,* 19 (1907):193–264, for detailed coverage of John and Joan; Mary Ann Everett Green, *Lives of the Princesses of England from the Norman Conquest* (London: Henry Colburn, 1850), 2:316; *CPapR,* 3:116 and 1:287; *CPR, 1345–1348,* p. 226, where Joan is described as "staying beyond the seas in the King's service"; her safe-conduct to visit shrines is in *CPR, 1348–1350,* p. 514.

85. E101/93/4; E101/92/7; E101/94/2; *CPapR,* 3:431; see E101/93/20 for a visit to Elizabeth in London.

86. E101/95/8; *CPapR,* 1:287; *RW,* p. 37.

87. Probably both were born in 1295. For Isabella's birthday: F. D. Blackley, "Isabella of France, Queen of England 1308–1358, and the Late Medieval Cult of the Dead," *Canadian Journal of History* 15 (1980), 23n.

88. E101/92/7; E101/92/9; letters from Elizabeth are in E101/92/7; E101/92/9; E101/92/11; E101/92/13; E101/93/12. Elizabeth visited a queen at Bury St Edmunds in 1340, probably Philippa rather than Isabella: E101/92/14. Bond, "Notices," 468; Blackley, "Isabella: Cult of the Dead," 24n.

89. *CPR, 1313–1317,* pp. 131, 201; Blackley, "Isabella: Cult of the Dead," 42; Bond, "Notices," 454. Isabella donated money or goods, but apparently made no foundations. She celebrated obits for her father, mother, husband, and son, John of Eltham. Obits were considerably cheaper than chantries. Isabella's alms bill for her last year was £298 18s. 7d. ob. on overall expenditures exceeding £9,000: Bond, "Notices," 469.

90. Isabella's last account shows £1,399 spent on jewels: Bond, "Notices," 469; for an inventory of books: Vale, *Edward III and Chivalry,* Appendix 10.

91. When Isabella was a reigning queen, she often gave life settlements to former staff, especially to females; Elizabeth provided for poor women in her will and supported a female anchoress. The case is weakest for Joan, but documentation for her is meager. In an intriguing article, "Rich Old

Ladies: The Problem of Late Medieval Dowagers," in *Property and Politics,* ed. Tony Pollard (New York: St Martin's Press, 1984), Rowena Archer demonstrates that wealthy widows often controlled family assets to the detriment of heirs. She implicitly assumes this to be a problem, while recognizing that no information on contemporary opinion of the issue survives. None of the heirs of these four friends suffered from the late falling-in of the widows' estates. Isabella, Joan, and perhaps Elizabeth deserved some compensation for the pain and injury of their marriages. Quite arguably, Mary and Elizabeth directed their resources to nobler ends than did their heirs after their deaths.

92. E101/91/25; E101/92/13; Elizabeth visited the old earl at Higham Ferrers the year before his death: E101/92/24; E101/92/28; young Henry appeared in William de Burgh's expense roll, as he accompanied his brother-in-law to tourneys: E101/91/18; Kenneth Fowler, *The King's Lieutenant: Henry of Grosmont, First Duke of Lancaster, 1310–1361* (New York: Barnes and Noble, 1967), p. 15.

93. Fowler, *King's Lieutenant,* pp. 70, 92, 99, 100, 106–117; E101/92/30; E101/95/8; E101/93/4; E101/93/9; E101/93/8; E101/93/12; E101/93/18; *Le livre de seyntz medicines,* ed. E. J. F. Arnould (Oxford: Anglo-Norman Text Society, 1940).

94. Fowler, *King's Lieutenant,* pp. 26, 194. The crusading ideal was alive in the period: Maurice Keen, "Chaucer's Knight, the English Aristocracy, and the Crusades," in *English Court Culture in the Later Middle Ages,* ed. V. J. Scattergood and J. W. Sherburne (London: Gerald Duckworth, 1983), pp. 45–61, especially pp. 57–60.

95. E101/92/11; E101/92/28; E101/94/7; E101/93/4; E101/93/9; E101/93/17.

96. No visitor was more assiduous than the prince in his calls on Elizabeth: E101/93/20: December 1, 1357, January 23–25, 1358, February 28-March 1, 1358, March 5–7 1358, May 17, 1358, July 16, 1358, August 2, 1358, August 15, 1358; E101/95/9: December 28–30, 1358, May 23, 1359, May 31, 1359, June 4, 1359, June 28, 1359, July 21, 1359, July 28, 1359, August 3, 14, 15, 18, 20, 21, 25, 1359; E101/94/2; John Harvey, *The Black Prince and His Age* (Totowa, N.J.: Rowman and Littlefield, 1976), p. 87, notes that hawking was the prince's favorite recreation.

97. E101/93/20; E101/94/7; E101/93/4; E101/95/9; Harvey, *Black Prince,* p. 162; *RW,* p. 37; *Register of the Black Prince* (London: HMSO, 1933), 4:90, 209, 253, 294–95, 307, 385.

98. Harvey, *Black Prince,* pp. 59, 102. Joan married Thomas Holand, then Earl William of Salisbury, without any legal termination of her first union. The second marriage was annulled and Joan continued as Holand's wife until his death in December 1360. The countess of Kent visited Elizabeth in October 1355, but the accounts mention no other occasions: E101/93/18.

99. Queen Philippa's daughter Isabella visited once; two royal children accompanied their mother on one visit: E101/93/4; E101/93/9;

E101/93/12 for the harper. Elizabeth visited Woodstock in April 1334: E101/92/2; she traveled to Bury St Edmunds to see the queen in December 1340: E101/92/14; the queen visited Elizabeth in London on September 26, 1355: E101/93/17. The last two instances probably concern Philippa, but could be Queen Isabella.

100. E101/91/23; E101/92/7; E101/92/12; E101/93/2; E101/93/4; E101/93/20; PRO Draft of Edward III's itinerary; Vale, *Edward III*, p. 53; *RW*, p. 37; *CCR, 1346–1349*, p. 587; *CCR, 1349–1354*, p. 197; *CPR, 1348–1358*, p. 255.

101. James E. Doyle, *The Official Baronage of England* (London: Longmans, Green, 1886), 2:163–65. John married twice: Alice Fitzalan and later Margaret Basset. The latter union encountered problems, perhaps caused by the discovery that they were related. They ceased to live together by 1331: *CPapR*, 2:49. E101/91/30; E101/92/2; E101/92/3; E101/93/12; E101/92/4; George A. Holmes, *The Estates of the Higher Nobility in Fourteenth-Century England* (Cambridge: Cambridge University Press, 1957), pp. 20–21, suggests that "both suffered from a life-long infirmity."

102. Elizabeth's visits: E101/92/24, E101/92/30; the earl's visits: E101/94/7, E101/95/8; transport and gifts: E101/93/6, E101/93/12; the earl's will: Nicholas, *Testamenta Vetusta*, 1:66–68.

103. E101/92/9; E101/92/13; E101/95/8; E101/92/13; E101/93/12; E101/93/4; E101/95/7; E101/92/24; E101/93/18; E101/93/20; GEC, 9:667. The earl's affection for Elizabeth surfaced earlier in a chantry foundation where prayers were to be offered for his family and Elizabeth de Burgh, lady of Clare: ibid, 6:469n.

104. The earl's visits: E101/92/12; E101/95/8; E101/93/4; E101/93/9; the countess's visits: E101/92/12; E101/92/30; E101/95/8; E101/93/9; E101/93/20; Elizabeth's visit: E101/92/12.

105. E101/92/9; E101/92/11; E101/94/7; E101/92/13; E101/93/2; E101/93/9; E101/93/20; E101/95/8; E101/94/7.

106. E101/93/2; E101/93/12; E101/95/8; E101/93/8; E101/93/9; E101/93/20; E101/94/7; E101/95/8; E101/93/10; Roy Midmer, *English Mediaeval Monasteries 1066–1540* (Athens, Ga.: University of Georgia Press, 1979), p. 319.

107. E101/92/23; E101/92/30; E101/95/8; E101/91/25; E101/93/12; E101/93/20; E101/94/2; letters to a Sir Percy were sent to York in 1350–51: E101/93/8; E101/93/10.

108. See E101/92/11; E101/92/12; E101/93/4; E101/93/9; E101/94/7; E101/95/8 for Thomas; E101/92/9; E101/92/12; E101/92/28; E101/94/7; E101/95/8; E101/93/4 for Lady FitzWauter.

109. The arrears was for 20s.: E101/91/12; *RW*, p. 30.

110. E101/507/8; E101/91/27; E101/95/10; E101/95/2; E101/92/9; E101/91/29; E101/92/27; E101/92/11; E101/92/8; E101/92/7.

111. Suzanne was on the 1343 livery list and received Elizabeth's best outfit in her will: E101/92/23; *RW*, p. 24.

Chapter 4

1. George A. Holmes, *The Estates of the Higher Nobility in Fourteenth-Century England* (Cambridge: Cambridge University Press, 1957), p. 59.

2. J. F. Maddicott, *Law and Lordship: Royal Justices as Retainers in Thirteenth- and Fourteenth-Century England, Past and Present* Supplement 4 (Oxford: Past and Present Society, 1978), for a detailed analysis of the practice of retaining royal justices.

3. Maddicott, *Law and Lordship*, p. 23; J. G. Bellamy, *Bastard Feudalism and the Law* (Portland, Ore.: Areopagitica Press, 1989), pp. 52–53; *CCR, 1327–1330*, pp. 185–86, 219.

4. *CCR, 1327–1330*, pp. 185–86, 219; E101/91/12; E101/94/12; *CPR, 1324–1327*, pp. 347, 349, 351; *CPR, 1327–1330*, pp. 150, 207; *CPR, 1330–1334*, p. 171; Maddicott, *Law and Lordship*, p. 22; Edward Foss, *The Judges of England* (London: Longman, Brown and Longmans, 1851), 3:510.

5. Maddicott, *Law and Lordship*, pp. 23, 30; Elisabeth G. Kimball, *A Cambridgeshire Gaol Delivery Roll, 1332–1334* (Cambridge: Cambridge Antiquarian Records Society, 1978), p. 7; *CCW,* 1:582; Foss, *Judges,* 3:503; *CFR, 1337–1347*, pp. 372, 500; E101/91/22; *CIPM,* 8: no. 519.

6. Maddicott, *Law and Lordship*, pp. 30, 43–44; *CPR, 1324–1327*, p. 137; *CPR, 1330–1334*, p. 138; *Year Books, 17 Edward III* (Rolls Series), pp. 202–3; E101/92/23. Elizabeth's 1343 livery list is a well-preserved account for the most part, but the knight classification is only partially legible, in contrast with most of the remainder of the document.

7. *CPR, 1354–1358*, p. 655; E101/93/20; Bertha H. Putnam, *The Place in History of William Shareshull* (1950; reprint, Holmes Beach, Fla.: William W. Gaunt, 1986), pp. 98–99; Foss, *Judges,* 3:504–6.

8. *DNB,* 3:1262; E101/93/10; E101/93/12; E101/93/20. Cavendish was murdered during the 1381 uprising.

9. *DNB,* 19:801; E101/92/13; E101/92/23; E101/94/2; *CFR, 1337–1347*, p. 520; *CPR, 1350–1354*, p. 510. Thorpe became chancellor of England after Elizabeth's death.

10. E101/93/12; *CCR, 1346–1349*, p. 20; *CCR, 1349–1354*, p. 76; Maddicott, *Law and Lordship*, p. 48; Foss, *Judges,* 3:450.

11. Authorities differ in their assessment of Shareshull. Putnam is fairly adulatory in her book; Foss, *Judges,* 3:505 comments that he was "more a political and parliamentary judge than a man of the law."

12. E101/92/23; E101/92/11; Foss, *Judges,* 3:485–86.

13. May McKisack, *The Fourteenth Century, 1307–1399* (Oxford: Clarendon Press, 1959), p. 152; E101/95/2; E101/92/13.

14. Richard Magrath, "Sir Robert Parving, Knight of the Shire for Cumberland and Chancellor of England," *Transactions of the Cumberland and Westmoreland Antiquarian and Archaelogical Society,* new series 19 (1919):64; Foss, *Judges,* 3:476; E101/92/11; E101/92/13; E101/93/12.

15. For Wallore: Maddicott, *Law and Lordship,* p. 56; Foss, *Judges,* 3:541. For St Pol: Bertie Wilkinson, *The Chancery under Edward III* (Manchester: Manchester University Press, 1929), pp. 156, 207; Foss, *Judges* 3:487–88; T. F. Tout, *Chapters in the Administrative History of Mediaeval England* (Manchester: Manchester University Press, reprint, 1967), 3:159n. For Stowe: John Le Neve, *Fasti Ecclesiae Anglicanae, 1300–1541* (London: University of London, Institute for Historical Research, 1962), 5:13; Tout, *Chapters,* 3:125n; *CCR, 1349–1354,* p. 219; *CPapR,* 2:305, 375; *CPR, 1334–1338,* pp. 32, 45; *Inquisitions and Assessment relating to Feudal Aids, 1284–1431* (London: HMSO: 1899–1908), 2:162; Foss, *Judges,* 3:514; E101/92/2. For Everdon: Tout, *Chapters,* 3:125n; *CPR, 1321–1324,* p. 429; Foss, *Judges,* 3:427; E101/91/25.

16. Tout, *Chapters,* 6:37, 43, 46; E101/92/23; E101/93/4. Both women suffered under the Despenser regime. Lady Talbot (then Elizabeth Comyn) spent over a year in prison before she succumbed to Despenser pressure to grant father and son valuable manors and castles: William Rees, ed., *Calendar of Ancient Petitions relating to Wales* (Cardiff: University of Wales Press, 1975), no. 8132 and note.

17. Unless otherwise noted, references to livery are from E101/92/23.

18. Wake: *CPR, 1324–1327,* pp. 216–17; *CPR, 1327–1330,* p. 90; *CPR, 1338–1340,* pp. 63, 481. Cary earlier had several forest and Welsh keeperships and was constable of Corfe castle: *CFR, 1327–1337,* pp. 220, 368; *CFR, 1337–1347,* p. 245.

19. *CIPM,* 11: no. 573.

20. Bere: *LS,* p. 60; Horsele: *Feudal Aids,* 4:348; Colpeper: E101/92/11; *CIPM,* 7: no. 62.

21. Middleton: E101/93/12; *LE,* p. 89; *CCR 1349–1354,* pp. 36, 51. Coggeshall: E101/93/10; *LS,* p. 44.

22. John's son William was also a sheriff there, held land from the lady and attended parliament: Philip Morant, *History and Antiquities of the County of Essex* (1768; reprint, East Ardsley: EP Publishing, 1978), 1: xii; *LS,* pp. 43–44; *CIPM,* 8: nos. 681, 682; E101/92/3.

23. *CPR, 1334–1338,* pp. 137–39; *CFR, 1337–1347,* pp. 51, 432, 434, 445; E101/92/9 for 1338–39, E101/94/2 for 1358–59.

24. *Feudal Aids,* 3:25, 483, 5:43, 69; *CCR, 1354–1360,* p. 202; *LS,* p. 12; *LE,* p. 15; E101/95/2; E101/92/12; E101/92/4.

25. *CPR, 1340–1343,* pp. 221–22; Morant, *Essex,* 1:xii; *CCR, 1349–1354,* p. 314; E101/92/13, E101/92/11; *CIPM,* 8: no. 375.

26. E101/91/12; E101/92/11; *CIPM,* 8: no. 571; Morant, *Essex,* l:xii; *CCR, 1349–1354,* p. 314.

27. *Feudal Aids,* 2:163; R. E. C. Kirk and E. F. Kirk, eds., *Feet of fines for Essex* (Colchester: Essex Archaelogical Society, 1899–1949), 3: no. 462; *CChR,* 5:77; *CIPM,* 8: no. 571.

28. E101/95/2; E101/92/4; E101/92/9; E101/92/11.

29. E101/92/3; E101/92/9; E101/92/11; E101/91/12; Tout, *Chapters,* 2:336n., 346.

30. E101/91/12; E101/92/10; *CFR, 1327–1337*, pp. 142, 504; *CPR, 1327–1330*, p. 282; *CPR, 1330–1334*, p. 296; *CPR, 1340–1343*, p. 10; Morant, *Essex*, 1:xii; *CCR, 1330–1333*, p. 342.

31. *CCR, 1343–1346*, pp. 229, 552; Clare A. Musgrave, "Household Administration in the Fourteenth Century with Special Reference to the Household of Elizabeth de Burgh, Lady of Clare" (M. A. thesis, University of London, 1923):34; Bertha H. Putnam, *The Enforcement of the Statutes of Labourers, 1349–1359* (New York: Columbia University Press, 1908), p. 58; Gladys A. Thornton, *A History of Clare, Suffolk* (Cambridge: W. Heffer and Sons, 1928), p. 172; E101/92/10; E101/92/14; E101/92/22; E101/92/20, E101/93/12; *CIPM*, 10: no. 613.

32. Musgrave, "Household," 56–57; *CIPM*, 9: no. 113; *Calendar of Memoranda Rolls (Exchequer), Michaelmas 1326-Michaelmas 1327* (London: HMSO, 1968), no. 2271; E101/92/23; E101/92/9; Kimball, *Gaol Delivery*, p. 15; *CPR, 1343–1345*, p. 422; *CPR, 1334–1338*, p. 136; *CCR, 1337–1339*, p. 127; *LE*, p. 15; *LS*, p. 12.

33. Albert C. Chibnall, *Richard Badew and the University of Cambridge, 1315–40* (Cambridge: Cambridge University Press, 1963), pp. 38, 40–41; *CPR, 1348–1350*, p. 96.

34. E101/92/10; E101/93/10; E101/93/8; E101/92/27; E101/92/14; E101/92/24; E101/94/2; E101/93/19; *RW*, pp. 26, 41; *CCR, 1349–1354*, p. 208; *CCR, 1354–1360*, pp. 612, 614; *LE*, p. 15.

35. E101/92/4; E101/92/9; E101/95/2; E101/93/8; E101/93/12; *CIPM*, 10: pp. 5, 315; Putnam, *Statutes of Labourers*, p. 133.

36. *LE*, p. 43; *LS*, p. 43; E101/93/1; E101/93/12; E101/94/2; *RW*, pp. 27, 41.

37. There were a few other married staff, such as Robert Mareschal and Colmet de Morley in the higher offices and the gardener at the bottom. Mareschal also held some landed property.

38. Warren O. Ault, ed., *Court Rolls of the Abbey of Ramsey and of the Honor of Clare* (New Haven: Yale University Press, 1928), p. xxvii; for example, peas and beans were purchased in 1358–59 from the rector of Stansfels' farmer, the bailiff of Samford, Margaret de Herstede, the Clare market, the rector of Oxening, and Sir Peter de Ereswell: E101/94/2. One of her ladies, Elizabeth Torel, daughter of Robert Mareschal, received gifts and legacies: E101/93/10; *RW*, p. 24.

39. G. H. Martin, "The Borough and Merchant Community of Ipswich, 1317–1422" (D. Phil diss., Oxford University, 1955):186; E101/93/12. Simon Thebaud eventually became Simon Sudbury, archbishop of Canterbury.

40. E101/93/8; E101/95/2; E101/92/9; E101/459/26.

41. E101/459/24; E101/93/12; the schoolmaster was John Chaplain who may also have had household duties: Thornton, *History of Clare*, p. 139; Antonia Gransden, "The Reply of a Fourteenth-Century Abbot of Bury St Edmunds to a Man's Petition to be a Recluse," *EHR* 75 (1960):464, confirms the anchorhold; *RW*, pp. 32–33.

42. E101/93/12.

43. Bourne, E101/94/7; Chikewell, E101/95/8; Culpho, E101/92/7; Clement, E101/93/10; Evesham, E101/95/8.

44. Roy Martin Haines, *Archbishop John Stratford* (Toronto: Pontifical Institute of Mediaeval Studies, 1986), p. 501; E101/92/24; E101/95/2; E101/92/13.

45. Gravesend: E101/91/25; E101/92/2; his horses were cared for on two other occasions, when he may have met Elizabeth: E101/91/25; E101/95/2. Stratford: E101/95/8; E101/92/11; E101/93/6; the marshalsea paid expenses for the bishop's horses another time: E101/92/24.

46. John Aberth, "Crime and Justice Under Edward III: The case of Thomas de Lisle," *EHR* 107 (1992):283–84, 291; E101/95/8; E101/92/13; E101/92/11; E101/93/6.

47. E101/92/3; E101/95/8; E101/93/20. For Bateman's career, see A. Hamilton Thompson, "William Bateman, Bishop of Norwich, 1344–1355," *Norfolk and Norwich Archaeological Society Transactions* 25 (1935):102–37.

48. E101/91/18; E101/93/6.

49. E101/92/9; E101/92/12; E101/93/12; Roy Midmer, *English Mediaeval Monasteries (1066–1540)* (Athens, Ga.: University of Georgia Press, 1979), p. 310; *MA,* 6:393, dates the fire in 1351; *RW,* p. 32.

50. K. W. Barnardiston, *Clare Priory* (Cambridge: W. Heffer and Sons, 1962), pp. 18–19; *CAFC,* nos. 161, 162, (the friary was still receiving grain in 1350–51); E101/93/8; E101/91/17; E101/91/24; E101/93/12; E101/95/2; *RW,* p. 33.

51. *CFR, 1337–1347,* pp. 32–33; Christopher Harper-Bill and Richard Mortimer, eds., *Stoke by Clare Cartulary.* Suffolk Record Society (Woodbridge: Boydell Press, 1982), 3:2, 7–8.

52. E101/95/2; E101/93/18; E101/93/8; E101/93/12; *Stoke Cartulary,* 3:17; *RW,* p. 32.

53. Origins of the house are obscure, but the Clare family usually is credited with part of its foundation; E101/91/19; E101/95/8; E101/92/2; E101/92/4.

54. E101/92/3; E101/92/4; E101/92/23; E101/92/8; E101/92/9; E101/92/11; E101/92/13; E101/92/27; E101/92/28. Arderne was a secular priest with residential privileges, but not a member of the convent. Lady Bardolf stopped often on journeys to and from her mother: E101/93/9; E101/93/13; other visits from family members: E101/94/1; E101/95/7.

55. Some abbots and priors corresponded with Elizabeth or enjoyed her hospitality. For example, Bury St Edmunds' prior stopped with a retinue in the Christmas season of 1336; Elizabeth wrote Bury's Abbot William of Bernham several times between 1339 and 1341; the prior of Thetford rated a gift of 40s. soon after his installation; the Augustinian priors Simon de Wyverton and Thomas Clare of Walsingham corresponded with Elizabeth and the latter sent her a gift of fish: E101/95/2; E101/92/11; E101/92/13; E101/93/12; E101/94/2; *CPapR,* 1:523.

56. Horses of the following clerics are found in 1347: the abbots of Colchester, Tilty, Walden, and Dereham; the priors of Barnwell, Coxford, Kersey, Sheringham, Chicksands, Stoke by Clare, Anglesey, Walsingham, and Ely: E101/95/8; E101/93/6. Kersey and Sheringham fit this category: Midmer, *Monasteries,* pp. 179, 284.

57. The prior of Walsingham held part of a knight's fee in Little Walsingham from Elizabeth; she held lands in Lakenheath from the prior of Ely and the abbot of Bury St Edmunds: *Feudal Aids,* 3:548; Michael Altschul, *A Baronial Family in Medieval England: The Clares, 1217–1314* (Baltimore: Johns Hopkins Press, 1965), p. 208.

Chapter 5

1. E101/377/2.

2. E101/92/12 for the 1340 trip; E101/95/7 for 1353.

3. E101/92/2; E101/92/4; E101/92/8; E101/92/9; E101/95/8; the 1347 pilgrimage is in E101/92/30. The only relic mentioned in her will is a fragment of the True Cross.

4. *RW,* pp. 37, 31.

5. Henry of Lancaster successfully petitioned the pope for his chapel clerks to receive offerings made there though church law required them to be directed to the local church: *CPapR,* 1:78; John A. Moorman, *Church Life in England in the XIIIth Century* (Cambridge: Cambridge University Press, 1946), p. 16. The offerings at Clare and Bardfield in the 1351–52 accounting period totaled over 85s.: E101/93/12.

6. E101/92/23; Ann K. Warren, *Anchorites and their Patrons in Medieval England* (Berkeley: University of California Press, 1985), pp. 96–98, for rites formalizing transition to the anchorite profession.

7. E101/92/23; E101/93/12; E101/93/8. Anne probably became an anchoress before 1346, because that year her hackney called at Clare, presumably to collect the Christmas livery: E101/95/8; E101/93/9 has Elizabeth in Radwinter in 1351, but does not mention the purpose of her visit.

8. E101/93/17; E101/93/20; E101/93/12; E101/94/2; E101/94/1; *RW,* p. 24; Rotha Mary Clay, *The Hermits and Anchorites of England* (London: Methuen, 1914), pp. 214–15.

9. E101/91/19; E101/93/12; E101/458/4. The roofing materials cost 5s. 4d.

10. Miri Rubin, *Charity and Community in Medieval Cambridge* (Cambridge: Cambridge University Press, 1987), pp. 84, 89; Ralph B. Pugh, *Imprisonment in Medieval England* (London: Cambridge University Press, 1968), pp. 315–37; E101/93/12 mentions many charitable initiatives, but is rather unique in content, so it is impossible to know if certain acts were isolated or typical of other years with less informative documentation.

11. Paupers fed at Clare and Hundon while the lady was in Wales in E101/93/4; E101/93/18 shows the paupers in Clare and Bardfield fed

while she was in London. For an early example of her feeding schedule: E101/91/17; E101/92/11 and E101/95/7 mention almoners.

12. In 1327–28, 18½ quarters of grain were baked into bread and 6,760 herrings were given out for two feedings: E101/91/17; in 1336–37 the paupers got 2,804 loaves and 4,280 white herrings on All Souls', and 3,598 loaves and 6,090 herring on St Gregory's day: E101/95/2; for Maundy Thursday: E101/92/30; E101/93/12; for her birthday: E101/93/13; E101/95/7. The almonry used baskets for the distributions; the household purchased dishes reserved for the poor: E101/92/2; E101/93/2; E101/93/4; E101/92/22; E101/92/24; E101/92/30; E101/95/2; E101/93/19.

13. She donated 15*d.* to the earl's group in 1351–52, anticipating the sum would provide them with fish for a day: E101/93/12; for cloth expenditures: E101/92/3, E101/92/13, E101/92/11. One entry in 1338–39 mentions livery for pages and paupers, hinting at a distinctive outfitting for a group of poor: E101/92/9; in E101/459/26, she hired paupers to collect stones for a daily stipend of 1*d.*, more likely for a small group.

14. E101/95/2; wine stored poorly in the fourteenth century so perhaps the household was clearing out its stocks of wine near the end of their shelf life. This somewhat uncharitable assumption is strengthened by the absence of the cheaper ale in all but one of the surviving documents. For wine distributions: E101/91/25; E101/92/2; E101/92/24; E101/92/12; E101/92/22; E101/93/17; for ale: E101/92/24.

15. E101/93/20; E101/95/9. Precise comparisons are difficult because of shifting household bookkeeping practices and a format change in alms. In 1331–32 the major distributions to the paupers cost £12 16*s.* 9*d. ob.*: E101/91/27; in 1357–58, major distributions cost only £1 18*s.* 2*d.*, but the total cost of feeding paupers was £50 16*s.*: E101/93/20.

16. E101/93/12; E101/92/12; E101/91/13; *RW,* p. 23; Joel T. Rosenthal, *The Purchase of Paradise: Gift Giving and the Aristocracy, 1307–1485* (London: Routledge & Kegan Paul, 1972), pp. 104–7.

17. *RW,* pp. 40–41; Rubin, *Charity,* pp. 152, 182–83.

18. *CPR, 1317–1321,* p. 42.

19. *CPR, 1327–1330,* pp. 61, 243; *CPR, 1330–34,* pp. 39, 101, 159; Seiriol Evans, *The Medieval Estate of the Cathedral and Priory of Ely* (Ely: Dean and Chapter of Ely, 1973), p. 11; Sandra Raban, *Mortmain Legislation and the English Church, 1279–1500* (Cambridge: Cambridge University Press, 1982), pp. 94–101.

20. *CPR, 1330–1334,* pp. 39, 477; *MA,* 6:395–96; Edward Hailstone, Jr., *The History and Antiquities of the Parish of Bottisham and the Priory of Angleseye in Cambridgeshire* (Cambridge: Cambridge Antiquarian Society, 1873), pp. 261–62; W. J. Harrison, *Notes on the Masters, Fellows, Scholars and Fellows of Clare College, Cambridge* (Cambridge: Printed for the College, 1953), pp. 22–23. The lady also founded a chantry at the Premonstratensian house at Dereham for the soul of Gilbert de Clare: *CPR, 1334–1338,* pp. 252–53.

21. The canons' letter is found in "Petition of the Prior and Canons of Walsingham," ed. James Lee-Warner, *Archaelogical Journal* 26 (1869):169–73.

22. Charles Green and A. B. Whittingham, "Excavations at Walsingham Priory, Norfolk, 1961," *Archaelogical Journal* 125 (1968):271, 273, ascribing later additions to the Augustinian church as flowing from Elizabeth's testamentary provisions; *CPR, 1345–1348,* pp. 255; *CPR, 1350–1355,* p. 71; *CPapR,* 3:252; A. R. Martin, *Franciscan Architecture in England* (Manchester: Manchester University Press, 1937), p. 125.

23. My figures are drawn from Roy Midmer, *English Mediaeval Monasteries (1066–1540)* (Athens, Ga.: University of Georgia Press, 1979).

24. *CPR, 1334–1338,* p. 237; *BRUC,* pp. 548, 580; Christopher Harper-Bill and Richard Mortimer, eds., *Stoke By Clare Cartulary* (Woodbridge: Boydell Press, 1982), 3:20; Clare A. Musgrave, "Household Administration in the Fourteenth Century with Special Reference to the Household of Elizabeth de Burgh, Lady of Clare"; Albert C. Chibnall, *Richard Badew and the University of Cambridge, 1315–40* (Cambridge: Cambridge University Press, 1963), pp. 36–41. J. R. Wardale, *Clare College* (London: F. E. Robinson, 1899), p. 31, suggests Badew approached the lady. Since he was accused by Warin de Bassingbourne of robbery and assault, it seems unlikely that Elizabeth would have been open to Badew's appeal: Chibnall, *Badew,* p. 38.

25. E101/91/17; E101/91/27; E101/91/24; E101/92/4; E101/92/13; costs of transporting the boys also appears in E101/95/2 for 1336–37.

26. *CPR, 1345–1348,* pp. 135–36. Chibnall, *Badew,* p. 41, notes that King's Hall, a royal foundation for 32 scholars, had endowments of £103. Clare Hall was to have about half that number of scholars. Elizabeth's statutes of 1359 suggest that revenues were less than £60. Section 8 says that when the "revenues of the said house shall chance to be increased to the annual value of twenty pounds sterling . . .": James Heywood, *Early Cambridge University and College Statutes* (London: Henry G. Bohn, 1855), p. 128.

27. *CPapR,* 3:269; *CPR, 1350–1354,* p. 510. The commissioners included men well-known to her: the prior of Anglesey, Robert Thorpe, John Dengayne, and Thomas de Friskeneye. Friskeneye held a master's degree from Oxford; the lady sent for him in 1353: E101/95/7. Probably Elizabeth restored the existing hall and added some new buildings sometime in the 1350s. In her 1359 statutes for the college, the hall or house is mentioned, as well as a separate building for ten poor boys: Heywood, *Statutes,* p. 137.

28. Astrik L. Gabriel, *Garlandia: Studies in the History of the Mediaeval University* (Notre Dame, Ind.: The Mediaeval Institute, 1969), p. 219; the preamble is in Heywood, *Statutes,* pp. 113–14; James B. Mullinger, *The University of Cambridge from the Earliest Times to the Royal Injunctions of 1535* (Cambridge: Cambridge University Press, 1873), 1:250–52; *Documents relating to the University and Colleges of Cambridge* (London, 1852), pp. 121–22.

29. Heywood, *Statutes,* pp. 137, 141.

30. Heywood, *Statutes,* pp. 138–41.

31. Rowbury: Mark Buck, *Politics, Finance and the Church in the Reign of Edward II: Walter Stapeldon, Treasurer of England* (Cambridge: Cambridge University Press, 1983), p. 100; James F. Baldwin, *The King's Council in England during the Middle Ages* (Oxford: Clarendon Press, 1913), p. 80; T. F. Tout, *The Place of Edward II in English History,* 2nd rev. ed., ed. Hilda Johnstone (1936; reprint, Westport, Conn.: Greenwood, 1976) p. 330; Graham Pollard, "Mediaeval Chests at Cambridge," *BIHR* 17 (1939–40):120–21. Salmon: *DNB,* 17:694; T. F. Tout, *Chapters in the Administrative History of England* (Reprint, Manchester: Manchester University Press, 1967), 2:214; Kathleen Edwards, "Bishops and Learning in the Reign of Edward II," *Church Quarterly Review,* 138 (1944):84; Kathleen Edwards, "The Social Origins and Provenance of the English Bishops during the Reign of Edward II," *TRHS,* 5th series, 9 (1959):65. Cobham: *DNB,* 4:613–14; Edwards, "Bishops and Learning," 59, 62, 81.

32. *DNB,* 17:694 and above.

33. Waldo E. L. Smith, *Episcopal Appointments and Patronage in the Reign of Edward II* (Chicago: American Society of Church History, 1938), p. 81; Edwards, "Social Origins," 57; *CAFC,* nos. 158, 167; Ernest Harold Pearce, *Thomas Cobham, Bishop of Worcester, 1317–1321* (London: Society for Promoting Christian Knowledge, 1923), pp. 254–56.

34. Heywood, *Statutes,* pp. 131, 138–141; "in ecclesia parochiale dicta Domus" in the original Latin: *Documents: Cambridge,* 2:141; *RW,* p. 30; Aubrey Attwater, *Pembroke College* (Cambridge: Cambridge University Press, 1936), p. 8.

35. James Westphal Thompson, *The Medieval Library* (New York: Hafner, 1967), p. 645; E101/92/27; E101/93/8; E101/93/12; (Robert the Illuminator was on her staff for several years: E101/92/9; E101/92/13); *RW,* p. 31. The Bible could have been in Latin or in French, for French translations were available in the fourteenth century: G. W. H. Lampe, ed., *Cambridge History of the Bible* (Cambridge: Cambridge University Press, 1969), 2:448, 451; M. T. Clanchy, *From Memory to Written Record: England, 1066–1307* (Cambridge: Harvard University Press, 1979), p. 196.

36. Possibly Master Richard de Clare encouraged her interest. He served her brother, Gilbert, as chancellor of Cardiff and was an executor of Gilbert's will. Richard was more noted for royal service than learning, but early in the fourteenth century he was pursuing studies: Michael Altschul, *A Baronial Family in Medieval England: The Clares, 1217–1314* (Baltimore: Johns Hopkins Press, 1965), pp. 239–40; *CPapR,* 2:12. Richard de Clare's benefices included one at Dunmow near Clare; he visited Elizabeth in 1326: E101/91/12.

37. Blithe: E101/92/8; E101/92/9; E101/92/23; *BRUC,* p. 68. Boys: E101/92/13; E101/91/13; E101/92/23; E101/92/27; E101/92/28; *BRUC,* p. 85. Stalyngton: *BRUC,* p. 548; E101/92/2; E101/92/19; E101/92/27; E101/92/3; E101/92/29; E101/92/23; E101/93/4; E101/93/12.

38. E101/92/5; E101/92/23; E101/95/7; E101/93/6; E101/94/1; *RW,* pp. 25, 41; *CFR,* 7:151–52; 9:392. He was also rector of Kedington in Suffolk: *BRUC,* p. 363.

39. *BRUC,* p. 415; Harrison, *Notes,* pp. 22–23; Wardale, *Clare College,* pp. 13–14.

40. Edwards, "Bishops and Learning" and J. R. L. Highfield, "The English Hierarchy in the Reign of Edward III," *TRHS* 6 (1956):115–38 for an overview.

41. Gravesend also studied at Oxford and left books to Merton College: Edwards, "Bishops and Learning," 62, 85. For Stratford: Highfield, "English Hierarchy," 130. Gravesend's visits to Elizabeth in February and November 1331 and in April and August 1334: E101/91/25; E101/92/2; Stratford's visits in E101/95/8. Burghersh was sometimes called the third founder of Oriel: Edwards, "Bishops and Learning," 62, 64–65, 76; E101/95/2.

42. A. Hamilton Thompson, "William Bateman, Bishop of Norwich, 1344–1355," *Norfolk and Norwich Archaelogical Society Transactions* 25 (1935):127; Walter E. Hook, *Lives of the Archbishops of Canterbury* (London: Richard Bentley, 1865), 4:245–46; E101/93/12; John Le Neve, *Fasti Ecclesiae Anglicanae, 1300–1541* (London: University of London, Institute for Historical Research, 1962), 1:95; 2:34; 3:19, for his early collection of offices.

43. Le Neve, *Fasti,* 11:21; David Walker, "The Medieval Bishops of Llandaff," *Morgannwg* 6 (1962):128–29; *DNB,* 15:434; E101/95/8; E101/93/12; E101/93/20; *CAFC,* no. 162.

44. E101/94/7; E101/95/8; E101/92/9; E101/94/7.

45. Hook, *Lives,* 4:87, 94, 96; E101/92/7. Gordon Leff, "Thomas Bradwardine's 'De Causa Dei,'" *Journal of Ecclesiastical History,* 7 (1956):21–29 and David Knowles, *The Religious Orders in England* (Cambridge: Cambridge University Press, 1957), 2:74–89, for surveys of his work and influence.

46. E101/91/12; E101/92/9; E101/92/11; E101/92/13; Le Neve, *Fasti,* 5:13; 2:288; *CPapR,* 1:209, 252; *CCR, 1349–1354,* p. 488; *CIPM,* 10: no. 638.

47. E101/93/19; *BRUC,* p. 336; Wardale, *Clare,* p. 14. The property in question, Borden's Hostel, was still owned by Clare Hall in the fifteenth century, so perhaps the sale never was completed: Damian Riehl Leader, *A History of the University of Cambridge* (Cambridge: Cambridge University Press, 1988), p. 259. R. W. Hunt, "Medieval Inventories of Clare College Library," *Transactions of the Cambridge Bibliographic Society* 1 (1950):116, lists Spaldyng's donations. He was a fellow of the Hall and may have played some role in enlisting Elizabeth's support, for she arranged for his pension of 100s. at Anglesey priory in the late 1350s: Harrison, *Notes: Clare College,* pp. 22–23; Hailstone, *Angleseye,* p. 261.

48. Heywood, *Statutes,* p. 143.

49. E101/94/2; E101/92/7; E101/93/12; E101/93/8; E101/93/10; E101/93/18; E101/94/2; *BRUC,* pp. 562, 563.

50. E101/92/9; E101/459/26; E101/95/8; John H. R. Moorman, *The Grey Friars in Cambridge, 1225–1538,* The Birbeck Lectures, 1948–49 (Cambridge: Cambridge University Press, 1952), p. 176; Bede Jarrett, *The English Dominicans,* revised and abridged by Walter Gumbley (London: Oates and Washbourne, 1937), pp. 78, 178; Jeremy Catto and Ralph Evans, eds., *The History of University of Oxford* (Oxford: Clarendon Press, 1992), 2:21; *BRUO,* 1:613–14, 2:780.

51. Leader, *Cambridge,* p. 170; Andrew G. Little, *Franciscan Papers, Lists, and Documents* (Manchester: Manchester University Press, 1943), p. 143

52. E101/91/12; E101/91/25; Little, *Franciscan Papers,* p. 195; Moorman, *Grey Friars,* pp. 95–96; *BRUO,* 1:477; Knowles, *Religious Orders,* 1:247; *DNB,* 4:988–89. For other friars summoned to the lady: E101/92/9; E101/92/4.

53. E101/93/12; E101/92/11; Moorman, *Grey Friars,* pp. 199–200; *RW,* p. 33.

54. Leader, *Cambridge,* p. 178, notes that the Franciscans followed Augustine, Bonaventure, and Scotus; the Dominicans favored Thomism and the Augustinians worked in the tradition of Giles of Rome. William A. Pantin, *The English Church in the Fourteenth Century* (Cambridge: Cambridge University Press, 1955), p. 205, reminds us that Chaucer mentioned Bradwardine's ideas on free will and predestination in the "Nonne Preestes Tale."

55. Leader, *Cambridge,* p. 86; Mullinger, *Cambridge,* 1:249n.; Heywood, *Statutes,* p. 114.

Chapter 6

1. She prosecuted lawsuits for 16 years against John Botelar and Robert Breton, who had taken her lands in 1322: *CCR, 1318–1323,* p. 603; *CCW,* 1:527; E101/92/9; Scott L. Waugh, "For King, Country and Patron: The Despensers and Local Administration, 1321–1322," *Journal of British Studies* 22 (1983):34.

2. For Blithe: *CPR, 1361–1364,* p. 397; for Plessys: *Calendar of Wills proved and enrolled in the Court of Husting, London, 1258–1688* (London: City of London, 1890), 2:48–49.

3. E101/92/2.

4. Mansfield D. Forbes, ed., *Clare College 1326–1926* (Cambridge: Cambridge University Press, 1928), 1:13.

5. James B. Mullinger, *The University of Cambridge from the Earliest Times to the Royal Injunctions of 1535* (Cambridge: Cambridge University Press, 1873), 1:314.

SELECT BIBLIOGRAPHY

Manuscript Sources

Hereford Cathedral:
    Dean and Chapter Archives, #4625
London, Public Record Office:
    E101 Exchequer, King's Remembrancer: Various Accounts
    S.C.1 Special Collections: Ancient Correspondence
    Itinerary of Edward III (Draft in progress)

Printed Sources

Primary

Annals of Connacht. Edited by A. Martin Freeman. Dublin: Institute for Advanced Studies, 1944.

Calendar of Ancient Correspondence concerning Wales. Edited by J. Goronwy Edwards. Board of Celtic Studies History and Law Series, 2. Cardiff: University Press Board, 1935.

Calendar of Ancient Petitions relating to Wales. Edited by William Rees. Board of Celtic Studies History and Law Series, 28. Cardiff: University of Wales Press, 1975.

Calendar of Chancery Rolls, Various, 1277–1326. London: HMSO, 1912.

Calendar of Chancery Warrants, 1244–1326. Vol. 1. London: HMSO, 1927.

Calendar of the Charter Rolls. Vols. 4 and 5. 1898 and 1920. Reprint. Nendeln: Kraus, 1972.

Calendar of the Close Rolls. Edward II, 4 vols.; Edward III, 14 vols. London: HMSO, 1892–1913.

Calendar of Documents relating to Ireland, 1171–1307. Edited by H. S. Sweetman. 5 vols. London: HMSO, 1875–1886.

Calendar of Documents relating to Scotland. Edited by Joseph Bain. Edinburgh: H. M. General Register House, 1888.

Calendar of Entries in the Papal Registers relating to Great Britain and Ireland. Edited by W. H. Bliss. 3 vols. London: HMSO, 1895–1897.

Calendar of the Feet of Fines for Suffolk. Edited by Walter Rye. Ipswich: Suffolk Institute of Archaeology, 1900.

Calendar of the Fine Rolls. Vols. 3–7. London: HMSO, 1912–1923.

Calendar of Inquisitions Miscellaneous (Chancery). Vols. 2 and 3. London: HMSO, 1916 and 1937.

Calendar of Inquisitions Post Mortem. Vols. 4–11. London: HMSO, 1908–1935.

Calendar of the Justiciary Rolls of Ireland: I to VII Years of Edward II. Dublin: Stationery Office, 1905.

Calendar of Memoranda Rolls (Exchequer), Michaelmas 1326-Michaelmas 1327. London: HMSO, 1968.

Calendar of the Patent Rolls. Edward II, 5 vols.; Edward III, 16 vols. London: HMSO, 1893–1916.

Calendar of Plea and Memoranda Rolls (London), 1323–1364. Edited by A. H. Thomas. Cambridge: Cambridge University Press, 1926.

Calendar of Wills proved and enrolled in the Court of Husting, London, 1258–1688. Edited by Reginald R. Sharpe. Vol. 2. London: City of London, 1890.

Cambridgeshire Gaol Delivery Roll, 1332–1334. Edited by Elisabeth G. Kimball. Cambridge: Cambridge Antiquarian Records Society, 1978.

Cartulary of the Augustinian Friars of Clare. Edited by Christopher Harper-Bill. Suffolk Records Society Publications, 9. Woodbridge: Boydell Press, 1991.

Cartulary of Holy Trinity, Aldgate. Edited by Gerald A. Hodgett. London: London Record Society, 1971.

Charters and Records of Hereford Cathedral. Edited by W. W. Capes. Hereford: Wilson and Phillips, 1908.

Chartularies of St. Mary's Abbey, Dublin. Edited by John T. Gilbert. 2 vols. London: Longman, 1884.

Chronicle of Lanercost, 1272–1346. Translated by Sir Herbert Maxwell. Glasgow: James Maclehose and Sons, 1913.

A Collection of All the Wills now Known to be Extant, of the Kings and Queens of England. Edited by J. G. Nichols. 1780. Reprint. New York: AMS Press, 1969.

Court Rolls of the Abbey of Ramsey and of the Honor of Clare. Edited by Warren O. Ault. New Haven: Yale University Press, 1928.

Descriptive Catalogue of Ancient Deeds in the Public Record Office. Vols. 3 and 4. London: HMSO, 1890–1915.

Devon, Frederick. *Issues of the Exchequer.* London: John Murray, 1837.

Documents relating to the University and Colleges of Cambridge. Vol. 2. London, 1852.

Dorset Inquisitiones Post-Mortem, 1216–1485. Vol. 1. Shelborne: Sautell, 1916.

Dorset Lay Subsidy Roll of 1332. Edited by A. D. Mills. Dorchester: Dorset Record Society, 1971.

Dugdale, sir William. *Monasticon Anglicanum.* Edited by John Caley, Sir Henry Ellis, and The Rev. Bulkeley Bandinel. 6 vols. in 8 books. London: James Bohn, 1846.

Feet of Fines for Essex. Edited by R. E. C. Kirk and E. F. Kirk. 3 vols. Colchester: Essex Archaelogical Society, 1899–1949.

Giuseppi, M. S. "Some Fourteenth-Century Accounts of Ironworks at Tudeley, Kent." *Archaeologia* 64(1913), 145–64.

Heywood, James. *Early Cambridge University and College Statutes.* London: Henry G. Bohn, 1855.

Holmes, George A. "A Protest Against the Despensers, 1326." *Speculum* 30(1955), 207–12.

Household Book of Queen Isabella of England, for the Fifth Regnal Year of Edward II. Edited by F. D. Blackley and G. Hermansen. Edmonton: University of Alberta Press, 1971.

Hunt, R. W. "Medieval Inventories of Clare College Library." *Transactions of the Cambridge Bibliographic Society* 1(1950), 105–25.

Hunter, J. "Journal of the Mission of Queen Isabella to the Court of France and of Her Long Residence in That Country." *Archaeologia* 36(1855), 242–57.

Inquisitions and Assessments relating to Feudal Aids, 1284–1431. 6 vols. London: HMSO, 1899–1908.

"Inventory of Church Goods *temp* Edward III." *Norfolk Record Society* 19(1947), parts 1 and 2.

The Itinerary of Edward II and His Household, 1307–1328. Edited by Elizabeth M. Hallam. List and Index Society, 211. London: List and Index Society, 1984.

The Itinerary of King Edward the Second. Edited by Charles H. Hartshorne. Private distribution, 1861.

Lee-Warner, James, ed. "Petition of the Prior and Canons of Walsingham." *Archaeological Journal* 26(1869), 169–73.

Le livre de seyntz medicines; the unpublished devotional treatise of Henry of Lancaster. Edited by E. J. F. Arnould. Anglo-Norman Texts, 2. Oxford: Basil Blackwell, 1940.

List of Escheators for England and Wales. List and Index Society, 72. London: HMSO, 1971.

List of Sheriffs for England and Wales. List and Index Society, 9. London: HMSO, 1898.

List of Welsh Entries in the Memoranda Rolls, 1282–1343. Edited by Natalie Fryde. Cardiff: University of Wales Press, 1974.

Ministers Accounts. "Possessions of the Contrariants." Lists and Indexes 5, part 1. New York: Kraus, 1963.

Register of Edward the Black Prince. Parts 1–4. London: HMSO, 1930–33.

Registers of Roger Martival, Bishop of Salisbury, 1315–1330. Vol. 1. Canterbury and York Society, 50. Edited by Kathleen Edwards. Oxford University Press, 1959.

Ross, C. D. "The Household Accounts of Elizabeth Berkeley, Countess of Warwick, 1420–1." *Transactions of the Bristol and Gloucestershire Archaelogical Society* 70–71(1951–52), 81–105.

Rotuli Parliamentorum. London, 1783.

Sayles, George. "The Formal Judgments on the Traitors of 1322." *Speculum* 16(1941), 57–63.

Stapleton, Thomas. "A Brief Summary of the Wardrobe Accounts of the 10th, 11th and 14th Years of King Edward the Second." *Archaeologia* 26(1836), 318–45.

Stoke By Clare Cartulary. Edited by Christopher Harper-Bill and Richard Mortimer. 3 vols. Suffolk Record Society. Woodbridge: Boydell Press, 1982.

Stow, John. *A Survey of London.* Notes by Charles L. Kingsford. Vol. 1. Oxford: Clarendon Press, 1971.

Suffolk in 1327, being a Subsidy Return. Suffolk Green Books 9, Vol. 2. Woodbridge: George Booth, 1906.

Vita Edwardi Secundi. Translated by N. Denholm-Young. London: Thomas Nelson and Sons, 1957.

Ward, Jennifer. *Women of the English Nobility and Gentry, 1066–1500.* Manchester: Manchester University Press, 1995.

Weever, John. *Ancient Funerall Monuments.* 1631. Reprint. Norwood, N.J.: Walter J. Johnson, 1979.

Year Books of the Reign of King Edward the Third. Rolls Series.

Unpublished Theses and Manuscripts

Doherty, Paul C. "Isabella, Queen of England, 1296–1330." D.Phil. diss., Oxford University, 1977.

Martin, G. H. "The Borough and the Merchant Community of Ipswich, 1317–1422." D.Phil. diss., Oxford University, 1955.

Musgrave, Clare A. "Household Administration in the Fourteenth Century with Special Reference to the Household of Elizabeth de Burgh, Lady of Clare." M. A. thesis, University of London, 1923.

Secondary Works

Aberth, John. "Crime and Justice under Edward III: The Case of Thomas de Lisle." *EHR* 107(1992), 283–301.

Alexander, Jonathan J. G. *Medieval Illuminators and Their Methods of Work.* New Haven: Yale University Press, 1992.

Altschul, Michael. *A Baronial Family in Medieval England: The Clares, 1217–1314.* Baltimore: Johns Hopkins Press, 1965.

Archer, Rowena E. "Rich Old Ladies: The Problem of Late Medieval Dowagers." In *Property and Politics,* edited by Tony Pollard. New York: St. Martin's Press, 1984.

Aries, Philippe. *Centuries of Childhood.* Translated by Robert Baldick. New York: Vintage, 1962.

Armstrong, Olive. *Edward Bruce's Invasion of Ireland.* London: John Murray, 1923.

Attwater, Aubrey. *Pembroke College.* Cambridge: Cambridge University Press, 1936.

Bailey, Mark. *A Marginal Economy? East Anglian Breckland in the Later Middle Ages.* Cambridge: Cambridge University Press, 1989.

Baldwin, James F. *The King's Council in England during the Middle Ages.* Oxford: Clarendon Press, 1913.

Barnardiston, K. W. *Clare Priory.* Cambridge: W. Heffner and Sons, 1962.

Barker, Juliet R. V. *The Tournament in England, 1100–1400.* Woodbridge: Boydell Press, 1986.

Bell, Susan Groag. "Medieval Women Book Owners: Arbiters of Lay Piety and Ambassadors of Culture." In *Women and Power in the Middle Ages,* edited by Mary Erler and Maryanne Kowaleski. Athens, Ga.: University of Georgia Press, 1988.

Bellamy, J. G. *The Law of Treason in England in the Later Middle Ages.* Cambridge: Cambridge University Press, 1970.

———. *Crime and Public Order in England in the Later Middle Ages.* Toronto: University of Toronto Press, 1973.

———. *Bastard Feudalism and the Law.* Portland, Ore.: Areopagitica Press, 1989.

Bennett, Michael. "Spiritual Kinship and Baptismal Name in Traditional European Society." In *Principalities, Powers and Estates,* edited by L. O. Frappell. Adelaide: Adelaide University Union Press, 1979.

Binski, Paul. *Painters.* Toronto: University of Toronto Press, 1991.

Blackley, F. D. "Isabella of France, Queen of England 1308–1358, and the Late Medieval Cult of the Dead." *Canadian Journal of History* 15(1980), 23–47.

———. "The Tomb of Isabella of France, Wife of Edward II of England." *International Society for the Study of Church Monuments Bulletin* 8(1984), 161–64.

Blomfield, James A. *A History of the Deanery of Bicester.* 2 vols. London: Parker, 1882.

Bond, Edward A. "Notices of the Last Days of Isabella, Queen of Edward the Second, drawn from an Account of the Expenses of her Household." *Archaeologia* 35(1854), 453–69.

Boswell, John. *Christianity, Social Tolerance and Homosexuality.* Chicago: University of Chicago Press, 1980.

Bourdillon, A. F. C. *The Order of Minoresses in England.* Manchester: Manchester University Press, 1926.

Boyer, Marjorie Nice. "Mediaeval Suspended Carriages." *Speculum* 34(1959), 359–66.

Britnell, R. H. "*Advantagium Mercatoris:* A Custom in Medieval English Trade." *Nottingham Medieval Studies* 24(1980), 37–50.

———. *Growth and Decline in Colchester, 1300–1525.* Cambridge: Cambridge University Press, 1986.

Brown, R. Allen, H. M. Colvin and A. J. Taylor. *The History of the King's Work.* Vols. 1 and 2. London: HMSO, 1963.

Buck, Mark. *Politics, Finance and the Church in the Reign of Edward II: Walter Stapeldon, Treasurer of England.* Cambridge: Cambridge University Press, 1983.

Callard, Ernest. *The Manor of Freckenham.* London: Bodley Head, 1924.

The Cambridge History of the Bible. Vol. 2. Edited by W. H. Lampe. Cambridge: Cambridge University Press, 1969.

Campbell, Marian. "Gold, Silver and Precious Stones." In *English Medieval Industries,* edited by John Blair and Nigel Ramsay. London: Hambledon Press, 1991.

Catto Jeremy and Ralph Evans, eds. *The History of the University of Oxford.* Vol. 2, *Late Medieval Oxford.* Oxford: Clarendon Press, 1992.

Chaplais, Pierre. *Piers Gaveston: Edward II's Adoptive Brother.* Oxford: Clarendon Press, 1994.

Cheney, C. R. *Handbook of Dates for Students of English History.* London: Royal Historical Society, 1970.

Cherry, John. *Goldsmiths.* Toronto: University of Toronto Press, 1992.

Chibnall, Albert C. *Richard Badew and the University of Cambridge, 1315–40.* Cambridge: Cambridge University Press, 1963.

Christie, A. G. I. *English Medieval Embroidery.* Oxford: Clarendon Press, 1938.

Clanchy, M. T. *From Memory to Written Record: England, 1066–1307.* Cambridge, Mass.: Harvard University Press, 1979.

Clay, Rotha Mary. *The Hermits and Anchorites of England.* London: Methuen, 1914.

Cokayne, G. E. *The Complete Peerage,* new ed. Revised and edited by V. Gibbs *et al.* 13 vols. London: St. Catherine's Press, 1910–57.

Davies, James Conway. "The Despenser War in Glamorgan." *TRHS,* 3rd series, 9 (1915), 21–64.

———. *The Baronial Opposition to Edward II: Its Character and Policy.* Cambridge: Cambridge University Press, 1918.

Davies, R. R. *Lordship and Society in the March of Wales, 1282–1400.* Oxford: Clarendon Press, 1978.

———. *Conquest, Coexistence and Change: Wales: 1063–1415.* Oxford: Clarendon Press, 1987.

Dictionary of National Biography. Edited by Sir Leslie Stephen and Sir Sidney Lee. 22 vols. 1885–1901. Reprint. London: Oxford University Press, 1949–1950.

Dobrowolski, Paula. "Women and their Dower in the Long Thirteenth Century, 1265–1329." In *Thirteenth-Century England VI,* edited by Michael Prestwich, R. H. Britnell, and Robin Frame. Woodbridge: Boydell Press, 1997.

Down, Kevin. "Colonial Society and Economy in the High Middle Ages." In *A New History of Ireland,* edited by A. Cosgrove. Oxford: Clarendon Press, 1987.

Doyle, James E. *The Official Baronage of England.* 3 vols. London: Longmans, Green, 1886.

Dugdale, Sir William. *The Baronage of England.* Vols. 1 and 2. London, 1676.

Dyer, Christopher. *Standards of Living in the Later Middle Ages.* Cambridge: Cambridge University Press, 1989.

Edwards, Kathleen. "Bishops and Learning in the Reign of Edward II." *Church Quarterly Review* 138(1944), 57–86.

———. "The Social Origins and Provenance of the English Bishops during the Reign of Edward II." *TRHS,* 5th ser., 9 (1959), 51–79.

———. *The English Secular Cathedrals in the Middle Ages,* 2nd ed. Manchester: Manchester University Press, 1967.

Ekwall, Eilert. *Concise Dictionary of English Place-Names,* 4th ed. Oxford: Clarendon Press, 1960.

Emden, A. B. *A Biographical Register of the University of Oxford to A. D. 1500.* 3 vols. Oxford: Clarendon Press, 1957–59.

———. *A Biographical Register of the University of Cambridge to 1500.* Cambridge: Cambridge University Press, 1963.

Evans, Seiriol. *The Medieval Estate of the Cathedral Priory of Ely.* Ely: Dean and Chapter of Ely, 1973.

Fairbank, F. Royston. "The Last Earl of Warenne and Surrey." *Yorkshire Archaeological Journal* 19(1907), 193–264.

Finberg, H. P. R. "An Early Reference to the Welsh Cattle Trade." *Agricultural History Review* 2(1954), 12–14.

Forbes, Mansfield D., ed. *Clare College, 1326–1926.* Vols. 1 and 2. Cambridge: Cambridge University Press, 1928.

Foss, Edward. *The Judges of England.* Vol. 3. London: Longman, Brown and Longmans, 1851.

Fowler, Kenneth. *The King's Lieutenant: Henry of Grosmont, First Duke of Lancaster, 1310–1361.* New York: Barnes and Noble, 1967.

Frame, Robin. "The Justiciarship of Ralph Ufford: Warfare and Politics in Fourteenth-Century Ireland." *Studia Hibernica* 13(1973), 7–47.

———. *English Lordship in Ireland, 1318–1361.* Oxford: Clarendon Press, 1982.

Fryde, Natalie. *The Tyranny and Fall of Edward II, 1321–1326.* Cambridge: Cambridge University Press, 1979.

Gabriel, Astrik L. *Garlandia: Studies in the History of the Mediaeval University.* Notre Dame, Ind.: The Mediaeval Institute, 1969.

Gask, G. E. "The Medical Staff of King Edward the Third." In *Sidelights on the History of Medicine,* edited by Sir Zachary Cope. London: Butterworth, 1957.

Given-Wilson, Chris. *The English Nobility in the Late Middle Ages: The Fourteenth-Century Political Community.* London: Routledge & Kegan Paul, 1987.

Glamorgan County History. Vol. 3, *The Middle Ages,* edited by T. B. Pugh. Cardiff: University of Wales Press, 1971.

Godefroy, Frédéric. *Lexique de l'Ancien Français.* Paris: Libraire Honoré Champion, 1967.

Gottfried, Robert S. *The Black Death.* New York: Collier Macmillan, 1983.

Graham, Rose. *S. Gilbert of Sempringham and the Gilbertines.* London: Elliot Stock, 1901.

Gransden, Antonia. "The Reply of a Fourteenth-Century Abbot of Bury St Edmunds to a Man's Petition to be a Recluse." *EHR* 75(1960), 464–67.

———. *Historical Writings in England.* Vol. 2, *c. 1307 to the Early Sixteenth Century.* Ithaca: Cornell University Press, 1982.

Grant, Annie. "Animal Resources." In *The Countryside in Medieval England,* edited by Grenville Astill and Annie Grant. Oxford: Basil Blackwell, 1988.

Green, Charles and A. B. Whittingham. "Excavations at Walsingham Priory, Norfolk, 1961." *Archaelogical Journal* 125(1968), 255–90.

Green, Mary Ann Everett. *Lives of the Princesses of England from the Norman Conquest.* Vols. 2 and 3. London: Henry Colburn, 1850.

Grew, Francis and Margrethe de Neergaard. *Shoes and Patens.* Medieval Finds from Excavations in London 2. London: Museum of London, 1988.

Grimwood, C. G. and S. A. Kay. *A History of Sudbury, Suffolk.* Sudbury: privately published, 1952.

Gwynn, Aubrey and R. Neville Hadcock. *Medieval Religious Houses: Ireland.* London: Longman, 1970.

Hailstone, Edward, Jr. *The History and Antiquities of the Parish of Bottisham and the Priory of Angleseye in Cambridgeshire.* Cambridge: Cambridge Antiquarian Society, 1873.

Haines, Roy Martin. *Archbishop John Stratford.* Toronto: Pontifical Institute of Mediaeval Studies, 1986.

Hall, Hamilton. "The Marshal Pedigree." *Journal of the Royal Society of Antiquaries* 43(1913), 1–29.

Hamilton, J. S. *Piers Gaveston, Earl of Cornwall, 1307–1312.* Detroit: Wayne State University Press, 1988.

Handbook of British Chronology. Edited by Sir F. M. Powicke and E. B. Fryde. 2nd ed. London: Royal Historical Society, 1961.

Hardy, B. C. *Philippa of Hainault and Her Times.* London: John Long, 1910.

Harrison, W. J. *Notes on the Masters, Fellows, Scholars and Exhibitions of Clare College, Cambridge.* Cambridge: Printed for the College, 1953.

Harvey, John. *The Black Prince and His Age.* Totowa, N.J.: Rowman and Littlefield, 1976.

———. *English Mediaeval Architects: A Biographical Dictionary down to 1550.* Rev. ed. Gloucester: Alan Sutton, 1987.

Hawkins, Desmond. *Cranborne Chase.* London: Victor Gollancz, 1980.

Hieatt, Constance B. and Sharon Butler. *Pleyn Delit: Medieval Cookery for Modern Cooks.* Toronto: University of Toronto Press, 1976.

Highfield, J. R. L. "The English Hierarchy in the Reign of Edward III." *TRHS* 6(1956), 115–38.

Hilton, R. H. "Medieval Agrarian History." In *Victoria County History, Leicestershire,* Vol. 2, edited by W. G. Hoskins. Oxford: Oxford University Press, 1954.

Holmes, George A. "The Rebellion of the Earl of Lancaster, 1328–9." *BIHR* 28(1955), 84–89.

———. *The Estates of the Higher Nobility in Fourteenth-Century England.* Cambridge: Cambridge University Press, 1957.

Hook, Walter E. *Lives of the Archbishops of Canterbury.* Vols. 3 and 4. London: Richard Bentley, 1865.

Hutton, Edward. *The Franciscans in England, 1224–1538.* London: Constable, 1926.

Jacobs, E. F. "Founders and Foundations in the Later Middle Ages." *BIHR* 35(1962), 29–46.

Jarrett, Bede. *The English Dominicans.* Revised and abridged by Walter Gumbley. London: Oates and Washbourne, 1937.

Jenkinson, Hilary. "Mary de Sancto Paulo, Foundress of Pembroke College, Cambridge." *Archaeologia* 66(1914–15), 401–46.

Johnstone, Hilda. "Isabella, the She-Wolf of France." *History* 21(1936), 208–18.

———. *Edward of Carnarvon, 1284–1307.* Manchester: Manchester University Press, 1946.

Keen, Maurice. "Chaucer's Knight, the English Aristocracy and the Crusade." In *English Court Culture in the Later Middle Ages,* edited by V. J. Scattergood and J. W. Sherborne. London: Gerald Duckworth, 1983.

Kershaw, Ian. "The Great Famine and Agrarian Crisis in England, 1315–1322." *Past and Present* 59(1973), 3–50.

Knight, J. K. "Usk Castle and its Affinities." In *Ancient Monuments and their Interpretation: Essays presented to A. J. Taylor,* edited by M. R. Apted, R. Gilyard-Beer, and A. D. Saunders. Chichester: Phillimore, 1977.

Knowles, David. *The Religious Orders in England.* 2 vols. Cambridge: Cambridge University Press, 1957.

Knox, Hubert T. "The Occupation of Connaught by the Anglo-Normans after A. D. 1237." *Journal of the Royal Society of Antiquaries of Ireland* 12(1902), 132–38, 393–406; 13(1903), 58–74, 179–89, 284–94.

Lane, Henry Murray. *The Royal Daughters of England.* Vol. 1. London: Constable & Co., 1910.

Latham, R. E. *Revised Medieval Word-List.* London: The British Academy, 1980.

Leader, Damian Riehl. *A History of the University of Cambridge.* Vol. 1. Cambridge: Cambridge University Press, 1988.

Leff, Gordon. "Thomas Bradwardine's *De Causa Dei.*" *Journal of Ecclesiastical History* 7(1956), 21–29.

LeNeve, John. *Fasti Ecclesiae Anglicanae, 1300–1541.* 11 vols. London: University of London, Institute for Historical Research, 1962.

Leyser, Henrietta. *Medieval Women: A Social History of Women in England, 450–1500.* New York: St. Martin's Press, 1995.

Linnard, William. *Welsh Woods and Forests: History and Utilization.* Cardiff: National Museum of Wales, 1982.

Little, Andrew G. *Franciscan Papers, Lists, and Documents.* Manchester: Manchester University Press, 1943.

Lucas, Angela. *Women in the Middle Ages: Religion, Marriage and Letters.* New York: St. Martin's Press, 1983.

Lucas, Henry S. "The Great European Famine of 1315, 1316 and 1317." *Speculum* 5(1930), 343–77.

Lydon, James, ed. *England and Ireland in the Later Middle Ages.* Dublin: Irish Academic Press, 1981.

Maddicott, J. R. *Thomas of Lancaster, 1307–1322: A Study in the Reign of Edward II.* London: Oxford University Press, 1970.

———. "Thomas of Lancaster and Sir Robert Holland: A Study in Noble Patronage." *EHR* 86(1971), 449–72.

———. *Law and Lordship: Royal Justices as Retainers in Thirteenth- and Fourteenth-Century England. Past and Present* Supplement 4. Oxford: Past and Present Society, 1978.

Magrath, Richard. "Sir Robert Parving, Knight of the Shire for Cumberland and Chancellor of England." *Transactions of the Cumberland and Westmoreland Antiquarian and Archaelogical Society,* new series 19(1919), 30–91.

Martin, A. R. *Franciscan Architecture in England.* Manchester: Manchester University Press, 1937.

Martin, F. X. "The Augustinian Friaries of Pre-Reformation Ireland." *Augustiniana* 6(1956), 347–84.

McFarlane, K. B. *The Nobility of Later Medieval England.* The Ford Lectures for 1953 and Related Studies. Oxford: Claredon Press, 1973.

McKisack, May. *The Fourteenth Century, 1307–1399.* Oxford: Clarendon Press, 1959.

McLean, Teresa. *Medieval English Gardens.* New York: Viking Press, 1981.

McNamara, JoAnn and Suzanne F. Wemple. "Sanctity and Power: The Dual Pursuit of Medieval Women." In *Becoming Visible: Women in European History,* edited by Renate Bridenthal and Claudia Koonz. Boston: Houghton Mifflin, 1977.

McNeill, T. E. *Anglo-Norman Ulster: The History and Archaelogy of an Irish Barony, 1177–1400.* Edinburgh: John Donald, 1980.

Menache, Sophia. "Isabella of France, Queen of England—A Reconsideration." *Journal of Medieval History* 10(1984), 107–24.

Mertes, Kate. *The English Noble Household, 1250–1600.* Oxford: Basil Blackwell, 1988.

Midmer, Roy. *English Mediaeval Monasteries (1066–1540).* Athens, Ga.: University of Georgia Press, 1979.

Monckton, H. A. *A History of English Ale and Beer.* London: The Bodley Head, 1966.

Moore, Ellen Wedemeyer. *The Fairs of Medieval England.* Toronto: Pontifical Institute of Mediaeval Studies, 1985.

Moorman, John H. R. *Church Life in England in the XIIIth Century.* Cambridge: Cambridge University Press, 1946.

———. *The Grey Friars in Cambridge, 1225–1538.* The Birbeck Lectures, 1948–49. Cambridge: Cambridge University Press, 1952.

Morant, Philip. *History and Antiquities of the County of Essex.* 2 vols. 1768. Reprint, East Ardsley: EP Publishing, 1978.

Morris, Colin. *Discovery of the Individual.* New York: Harper and Row, 1973.

Morris, Richard. "Tewkesbury Abbey: The Despenser Mausoleum." *Transactions of the Bristol and Gloucestershire Archaeological Society* 93(1974), 142–55.

Mullinger, James B. *The University of Cambridge from the Earliest Times to the Royal Injunctions of 1535.* Vol. 1. Cambridge: Cambridge University Press, 1873.

Newton, Stella Mary. *Fashion in the Age of the Black Prince.* Totowa, N.J.: Rowman and Littlefield, 1980.

Nicolas, Nicholas H. *Testamenta Vetusta.* Vol. 1. London: Nichols and Son, 1826.

Nicholson, Ranald. "A Sequel to Edward Bruce's Invasion of Ireland." *Scottish Historical Review* 42(1963), 30–40.

Orme, Nicholas. *Education in the West of England, 1066–1548.* Exeter: University of Exeter, 1976.

———. "The Education of the Courtier." In *English Court Culture in the Later Middle Ages,* edited by V. J. Scattergood and J. W. Sherborne. London: Gerald Duckworth, 1983.

———. *From Childhood to Chivalry.* London, Methuen, 1984.

Orpen, Goddard H. "The Earldom of Ulster." *Journal of the Royal Society of the Antiquaries of Ireland* 43(1913), 30–46, 133–43; 44(1914), 51–66; 45(1915), 123–42; 50(1920), 167–77; 51(1921), 68–76.

———. *Ireland Under the Normans, 1216–1333.* 4 vols. Oxford: Clarendon Press, 1920.

Otway-Ruthven, Annette J. "The Partition of the Verdon Lands in Ireland in 1332." *Proceedings of the Royal Irish Academy* 66(1968)C, 401–44.

————. *A History of Medieval Ireland*. London: Ernest Benn, 1980.

Pantin, William A. *The English Church in the Fourteenth Century*. Cambridge: Cambridge University Press, 1955.

Parsons, John Carmi. *The Court and Household of Eleanor of Castile, 1290*. Studies and Texts, 37. Toronto: Pontifical Institute of Mediaeval Studies, 1977.

————. "Mothers, Daughters, Marriage, Power: Some Plantagenet Evidence, 1150–1500." In *Medieval Queenship,* edited by John Carmi Parsons. New York: St. Martin's Press, 1993.

————. "The Intercessionary Patronage of Queens Margaret and Isabella of France." In *Thirteenth-Century England VI,* edited by Michael Prestwich, R. H. Britnell, and Robin Frame. Woodbridge: Boydell Press, 1997.

————. "'Never was a body buried in England with such solemnity and honour': The Burial and Posthumous Commemorations of English Queens to 1500." In *Queens and Queenship in Medieval Europe,* edited by Anne J. Duggan. Woodbridge: Boydell Press, 1997.

Paul, Sir James Balfour, ed. *The Scots Peerage*. Vol. 1. Edinburgh: David Douglas, 1904.

Pearce, Ernest Harold. *Thomas de Cobham, Bishop of Worcester, 1317–1321*. London: Society for Promoting Christian Knowledge, 1923.

Pevsner, Nikolaus. *Suffolk*. Buildings of England Series. Harmondsworth: Penguin, 1961.

Pevsner, Nikolaus and Priscilla Metcalf. *The Cathedrals of England*. Vol. 1. New York: Viking, 1985.

Phillips, J. R. S. *Aymer de Valence, Earl of Pembroke, 1307–1324: Baronial Politics in the Reign of Edward II*. Oxford: Clarendon Press, 1972.

————. "The 'Middle Party' and the Negotiating of the Treaty of Leake, August, 1318: A Reinterpretation." *BIHR* 46(1973), 11–27.

Pollard, Graham. "Mediaeval Loan Chests of Cambridge." *BIHR* 17(1939–40), 113–129.

Powell, J. Enoch and Keith Wallis. *The House of Lords in the Middle Ages*. London: Weidenfeld and Nicolson, 1968.

Power, Eileen. *Medieval English Nunneries, c. 1275 to 1535*. Cambridge: Cambridge University Press, 1922.

Prestwich, Michael. *War, Politics and Finance under Edward I*. London: Faber and Faber, 1972.

————. *The Three Edwards*. London: Weidenfeld and Nicolson, 1980.

————. *Edward I*. Berkeley: University of California Press, 1988.

Pugh, Ralph B. *Imprisonment in Medieval England*. London: Cambridge University Press, 1968.

Putnam, Bertha H. *The Enforcement of the Statutes of Labourers, 1349–1359*. New York: Columbia University Press, 1908.

————. *The Place in History of William Shareshull*. 1950. Reprint, Holmes Beach, Fla.: William W. Gaunt and Sons, 1986.

Raban, Sandra. *Mortmain Legislation and the English Church, 1279–1500*. Cambridge: Cambridge University Press, 1982.

Reddaway, T. F. *The Early History of the Goldsmiths' Company, 1327–1509*. London: Edward Arnold, 1975.

Rees, William. *South Wales and the March, 1284–1415: A Social and Agrarian Study*. London: Oxford University Press, 1924.

———. "The Black Death in Wales." In *Essays in Medieval History*, edited by R. W. Southern. London: Macmillan, 1968.

———. *Caerphilly Castle*. Rev. ed. Caerphilly: Caerphilly Local History Society, 1974.

Rosenthal, Joel T. "The Universities and the English Nobility." *History of Education Quarterly* 9(1969), 415–37.

———. *The Purchase of Paradise: Gift Giving and the Aristocracy, 1307–1485*. London: Routledge & Kegan Paul, 1972.

Roth, Francis. *The English Austin Friars, 1249–1538*. 2 vols. New York: Augustinian Historical Institute, 1961–66.

Rubin, Miri. *Charity and Community in Medieval Cambridge*. Cambridge: Cambridge University Press, 1987.

Salzman, L. F. *Building in England down to 1540*. Oxford: Clarendon Press, 1952.

Saul, Nigel. *Knights and Esquires: The Gloucestershire Gentry in the Fourteenth Century*. Oxford: Clarendon Press, 1981.

———. "The Despensers and the Downfall of Edward II." *EHR* 99(1984), 1–33.

Shahar, Shulamith. *Childhood in the Middle Ages*. London: Routledge, 1990.

Sheehan, Michael M. "The Formation and Stability of Marriage in Fourteenth-Century England." *Medieval Studies* 33(1971), 228–63.

Shrewbury, J. F. D. *A History of the Bubonic Plague in the British Isles*. Cambridge: Cambridge University Press, 1970.

Simon, Andre. *A Concise Encyclopaedia of Gastronomy*. New York: Harcourt, Brace, 1952.

Smith, Waldo E. L. *Episcopal Appointments and Patronage in the Reign of Edward II*. Chicago: American Society of Church History, 1938.

Somerville, Robert. *History of the Duchy of Lancaster*. Vol. 1. London: Chancellor and Council of the Duchy of Lancaster, 1953.

Sorley, Janetta C. *King's Daughters*. Cambridge: Cambridge University Press, 1937.

Suggett, Helen. "The Use of French in England in the Later Middle Ages." In *Essays in Medieval History*, edited by R. W. Southern. London: Macmillan, 1968.

Talbot, Charles H. *Medicine in Medieval England*. New York: American Elsevier, 1967.

Talbot, Charles H. and E. A. Hammond. *The Medical Practitioners in Medieval England*. London: Wellcome Historical Medical Library, 1965.

Thompson, A. Hamilton. "William Bateman, Bishop of Norwich, 1344–1355." *Norfolk and Norwich Archaelogical Society Transactions* 25(1935), 102–37.

Thompson, James Westphal. *The Medieval Library*. New York: Hafner, 1967; first published, 1939.

Thornton, Gladys A. *A History of Clare, Suffolk*. Cambridge: W. Heffer and Sons, 1928.

———. "A Study in the History of Clare, Suffolk, with special reference to its development as a Borough." *TRHS*, 4th series, 11(1928), 83–115.

Tomkinson, A. "Retinues at the Tournament of Dunstaple, 1309." *EHR* 74(1959), 70–89.

Tomlinson, Edward M. *A History of the Minories, London.* London: Smith, Elder, 1907.

Tout, T. F. *Chapters in the Administrative History of Mediaeval England.* 6 vols. 1928. Reprint, Manchester: Manchester University Press, 1967.

———. *The Place of the Reign of Edward II in English History.* 2nd rev. ed., edited by Hilda Johnstone. 1936. Reprint, Westport, Conn.: Greenwood, 1976.

Tuck, Anthony. *Crown and Nobility, 1272–1461.* Totowa, N. J.: Barnes and Noble, 1985.

Underhill, Frances A. "Elizabeth de Burgh: Connoisseur and Patron." In *The Cultural Patronage of Medieval Women,* edited by June Hall McCash. Athens: University of Georgia Press, 1996.

Vale, Juliet. *Edward III and Chivalry: Chivalric Society and its Context, 1270–1350.* Woodbridge: Boydell Press, 1982.

Veale, Elspeth M. *The English Fur Trade in the Later Middle Ages.* Oxford: Clarendon Press, 1966.

Walker, David. "The Medieval Bishops of Llandaff." *Morgannwg* 6(1962), 5–32.

Walker, Sue Sheridan. "Proof of Age of Feudal Heirs in Medieval England." *Medieval Studies* 35(1973), 306–23.

———. "Feudal Constraint and Free Consent in the Making of Marriages in Medieval England: Widows in the King's Gift." Canadian Historical Association. *Historical Papers* (1979), 97–109.

Ward, Jennifer C. "Fashions in Monastic Endowment: The Foundations of the Clare Family, 1066–1314." *Journal of Ecclesiastical History* 32(1981), 427–51.

———. "Elizabeth de Burgh, Lady of Clare (d. 1360)." In *Medieval London Widows, 1300–1500,* edited by Caroline M. Barron and Anne F. Sutton. London: Hambledon Press, 1994.

Wardale, J. R. *Clare College.* University of Cambridge College Histories. London: F. E. Robinson, 1899.

Warren, Ann K. *Anchorites and their Patrons in Medieval England.* Berkeley: University of California Press, 1985.

Waugh, Scott L. "For King, Country and Patron: The Despensers and Local Administration, 1321–1322." *Journal of British Studies* 22(1983), 23–58.

———. *The Lordship of England: Royal Wardship and Marriages in English Society and Politics, 1217–1327.* Princeton: Princeton University Press, 1988.

Wilkinson, Bertie. *The Chancery under Edward III.* Manchester: Manchester University Press, 1929.

Wright, J. Robert. *The Church and the English Crown, 1305–1334.* Toronto: Pontifical Institute of Mediaeval Studies, 1980.

INDEX